RUSSIAN POLITICS

The Struggle for a New Order

R. J. ...on Mitchell

University of New Orleans

Allyn and Bacon

Boston • London • Toronto • Sydney • Tokyo • Singapore

Vice President, Social Sciences: Sean Wakely
Editorial Assistant: Susan Hutchinson
Marketing Manager: Quinn Perkson
Editorial Production Service: Elm Street Publishing Services, Inc.
Manufacturing Buyer: Megan Cochran
Cover Administrator: Suzanne Harbison

Copyright © 1997 by Allyn & Bacon
A Viacom Company
Needham Heights, MA 02194

Library of Congress Cataloging-in-Publication Data
Nogee, Joseph L.
   Russian Politics: the struggle for a new order / Joseph L. Nogee,
   R. Judson Mitchell
      p.   cm.
   Includes index.
   ISBN 0-02-388062-7
   1. Soviet Union—Politics and government—1985–1991. 2. Russia (Federation)—
Politics and government—1991–   I. Mitchell, R. Judson. II. Title.
DK288.N64   1996
320.947—dc20   96-14435
                                                      CIP

Printed in the United States of America
10 9 8 7 6 5 4 3 2 1   01 00 99 98 97 96

To our wives,
Carol and Jo

Contents

PREFACE

Russian Politics: The Struggle for a New Order is written for use in college courses on Russian government and politics. The overnight collapse of the Soviet Union in 1991 rendered obsolete many of the books written for classroom use on contemporary Russian politics. Therefore, new textbooks on the governments of Russia and the other republics that emerged from the former Soviet Union as independent states are needed.

When we began this book we had hoped that we might be able to describe the new institutions of government and identify the direction that post-Soviet politics in Russia might take. We hoped that the dust would settle sufficiently to reveal a clear pattern in Russian politics. It is evident that we were overly optimistic about the prospects for stability in Russia. The dust has not settled, and it appears that Russia is headed for years of transition from the Soviet system to what ultimately will succeed it.

However, a great deal has transpired amid the chaos of Russian politics. The country has been under the governance of two distinctly different constitutions; there have been two general elections for new parliaments; major strides have been made in transforming the economy from a command to a market economy; numerous political parties have been formed and have disintegrated. The country has yet to develop a party system, and society has experienced considerable social disorder—particularly crime and economic hardship—in large part as a result of its newer freedoms. Boris Yeltsin's efforts to transform the country are impeded by a steady decline in the nation's living standard since the Soviet collapse.

As an independent state, Russia was confronted with three fundamental political questions: (1) what would be the country's economic structure, (2) what type of a constitutional order to build, and (3) what kind of a relationship could be maintained with the West. It was clear that the Soviet answers to those questions—a command economy, the dictatorship of the Communist Party, and cold war—were neither desirable nor even possible. But it was not at all evident what the ultimate answers to those questions would be. Boris Yeltsin had already committed the Russian Republic to economic reform, but there was no certainty that a genuine market economy would be created. Constitutionally, there was no agreement in the country on whether the government should be presidential or parliamentary or what the respective powers of the branches of government should be. As to relations with the West, Mikhail Gorbachev had already ended the Cold War but Russia had yet to establish a working partnership with the major powers of the West.

Our purpose in writing this book was to examine how Russia has attempted to answer these questions, to describe the political institutions of Russia as an independent state, and to analyze the forces that will determine how those institutions develop. After four years the constitutional order of the post-Soviet state remains uncertain. We cannot be certain that a democratic system will be established in the country or even that the Russian Federation will not disintegrate. Any textbook on Russian government written after the first four years of Russian government must of necessity be tentative in its description of institutions and assessment of what changes to expect.

The Soviet system is dead (and, in our opinion, not likely to be revived whatever happens) but the fact that it preceded the current regime for about three quarters of a century means that it will be a long while before the impact of that system on the present has run its course. We thus begin this text with a description of the Soviet system. Chapter One provides an overview of the Soviet government. Chapter Two describes the beginnings of reform under Gorbachev, and Chapter Three analyzes the failure of that effort, which led to the Soviet collapse described in Chapter Four. The remaining four chapters cover the period of independent Russia up through the end of 1995. Chapter Five describes the political struggles of the Yeltsin administration. Chapter Six describes the development of the Commonwealth of Independent States which includes, besides Russia, eleven of the former Soviet Republics. This chapter reflects the fact that not only is the constitutional order of Russia not resolved, neither is the question of the relationship between Russia and the other newly independent republics. Chapter Seven examines Russia's foreign policy. Finally, in Chapter Eight we assess the prospects for democracy in Russia. With the passage of time we can assume that the Soviet period will occupy fewer and fewer pages in a book about Russian politics.

The authors would like to thank Robert H. Donaldson, Victor Mote, Harry Walsh, Michael Speckhard, Kent Tedin, and Robert Jordan who read parts of this manuscript, as well as the following reviewers: Terry D. Clark, Creighton University; Dale R. Herspring, Kansas State University; Roger E. Kanet, University of Illinois at Champaign-Urbana; and Daniel S. Papp, Georgia Tech. They are in no way responsible for whatever flaws of commission or omission are in the text. Only we are. We thank Mark Shephard, Brad McKay, and Dena Shipley for assistance in the tricky business of putting text on disc. We also thank Maria Hernandez for research assistance and Linda Buchanan Allen for excellent copyediting.

CHAPTER 1

The Soviet System

The rise to power by Russian Communists, the development of the Soviet Union into a superpower, and the ultimate rapid collapse of this powerful state are among the most significant political phenomena of the twentieth century. In this book, we attempt to detail and explain the development of this political system, the causes of its downfall, and the contours and nature of the successor regime in Russia. We examine the problems confronting the post-Soviet Russian Republic and discuss the prospects for a stable democratic political system. Both problems and potential are firmly grounded in the historical formation of Russian institutions and political culture. Thus, our first focus of attention is upon this question: How did Russia get to the crucial turning point of regime change in 1991?

In 1917, Russia was an undeveloped country politically, socially, and economically. In 1991, the Soviet Union was, in many respects, as undeveloped relative to the advanced Western democracies in most respects as Russia had been in 1917. Marxism-Leninism, which had projected a short cut to modernization, had failed to fulfill its promise. Questions of development and modernization, which had topped the Bolshevik agenda in 1917, appeared to be the most pressing concerns of the new Russian state in the last decade of the twentieth century.

Yet the seventy-four years of Communist rule in Russia cannot be viewed as simply a postponement or retardation of modernization processes. The U.S.S.R. was, above all, a new form of governance that involved an unprecedented degree of control over society and the creation of a state system so powerful that it appeared immune to all challenges. As late as 1985, Communist control of the U.S.S.R. appeared unassailable; but by the end of 1991, this colossus had imploded and disappeared. The Soviet system represented not only a flawed model of modernization; it was also an experiment in social and political organization characterized by inherent structural deficiencies or (to use the Marxist terminology) "contradictions."

History offers no other example of a powerful state system that collapsed in such a fashion without foreign invasion or internal revolution. This outcome can be explained fully only by considering: 1) the initial problems confronted by the Communists; 2) the inherent flaws in the Communist system of rule; and 3) the policies pursued by the Gorbachev leadership between 1985 and 1991. In this chapter, we deal with the first two factors; in the following three chapters, we treat Mikhail Gorbachev's failed attempt to preserve the Soviet system.

DEVELOPMENT AND TOTALITARIANISM

Russia's relatively undeveloped condition posed theoretical problems for the Bolsheviks. Claiming the mantle of Marxism as a basis for legitimacy, the Bolsheviks confronted the necessity of explaining their most obvious deviation from Marx. The Marxian developmental theory had postulated the inception of revolution in the most industrialized countries, which would have large or majoritarian working classes. In the 1870s, Marx had allowed for the possibility of a different sort of revolution in Russia, one in which the peasantry would play a central role—the Populist solution. Lenin had rejected this option, arguing for a proletarian revolution despite the fact that Russia's industrial working class was quite small, accounting for no more than 4 percent of the population as late as 1917.

In retrospect, it appears that Russia's backwardness was an essential precondition for the Bolshevik Revolution. In advanced democracies, the proletariat had been largely integrated into the general political system, losing its zeal for revolution. Only in the undeveloped countries, lacking in a regime-supportive infrastructure, have revolutions claiming to be Marxist actually succeeded. But the logic of actual developmental processes denied the primacy of a proletarian-based revolutionary party, Lenin's principal claim to Marxist orthodoxy.

The Bolshevik answer to this dilemma was the doctrine of "the weakest link of imperialism," propounded by V. I. Lenin, founder of the Bolshevik party and of the Soviet state. Capitalism had developed into a global system, so the argument ran, permitting the "buying off" of the proletariat in the advanced countries due to the profits of imperialism derived from the greater opportunities for exploitation in the dependent, undeveloped areas. This did not necessarily mean that revolution would occur first in the most exploited areas, as claimed by Eastern Communists in the Comintern (Communist International).* Rather, it would begin where the capitalist control structure was weakest. In 1917, Russia had been the "weakest link" of the imperialist system and this had created the opportunity for the Bolshevik Revolution.

More important than this strained theoretical justification were the practical consequences of Russia's earlier development. According to Henry Jacoby, it was no coincidence that, after the collapse of Czarism, power was ultimately acquired by the party "which most clearly embodied the Russian bureaucratic principle."[1] The "Oriental Despotism" that had long characterized Russia had left in its wake a political culture inured to rule by administrative fiat.[2] The interplay of political forces that in the West had promoted tolerance and bargaining processes had been almost totally absent in Russia. Institutions of self-government, when present, had been rudimentary in form and function. Behind the outer political structure lay a society poorly geared toward democratic development.

The small, middle class lacked cohesion and effective political organization. Its ranks included bourgeois intellectuals and former peasants, among other elements, the diversity promoting a fragmentation of its nascent political organizations. About three-fourths of the population was peasant, mostly illiterate. The new proletariat, concentrated in a few areas, was largely drawn from the peasant class. The peasant-turned-industrial-worker typically brought with him or her anachronistic attitudes characteristic of the old rural order.

The Bolsheviks, who from 1918 were restyled as Communists, moved in this social disarray to forge under Lenin the foundations of totalitarianism.[†] All opposition parties were eliminated; the secret police (*Cheka*) was established; the system of labor camps, primarily for political prisoners (the Gulag) was set up.[3] The organizational framework for a command-administrative economy was developed in the burgeoning governmental bureaucracy. The soviets (popularly elected councils), legislative bodies at the various levels of government, were reduced to the status of "transmission belts" for the conveying of orders and information, as were the trade unions. The governmental administration was headed by the Council of Ministers and there

---

* The international organization of Communist parties under Moscow's leadership, 1919-43.

† Totalitarianism: dictatorial control of all social structures by the central political authority.

were similar councils in all of the union-republics. (Union-republics were the major constituent elements of the union.) At each level of the system, the governmental units were subject to control by the Communist Party.

With the elimination of all social structures independent of the central leadership, completion of the totalitarian system was comparatively easy. This was the work of Josef Stalin, whose first step was to seize total dominance over the party. Elected general secretary of the party in 1922, Stalin proceeded to stack the apparatus with his own appointees, thereby gaining control of admission processes. The party quadrupled in size between 1923 and 1929, and the new members were recruited by Stalin's loyalists.

The characteristics of the new members proved to be crucial in the rapid escalation of totalitarianism. The party was flooded with opportunists, who saw party membership as the ticket to advancement in the society. The social origin of the fresh wave of communists was more important than their motivation. Preference was given to the new proletariat. These were people not far removed from peasant backgrounds, poorly educated, reflecting the anti-intellectualism pervasive among the *narod* (folk) who had traditionally distrusted the intelligentsia. This was highly suitable raw material for Stalin's drive to build a monolithic party and crush the middle-class intellectuals such as Leon Trotsky, Grigorii Zinoviev, and Lev Kamenev who had played prominent roles in the early years of the regime.[4]

Expansion of the party permitted substitution of regime loyalists for holdover specialists in economics and governmental administration. Training of cadres emphasized economic skills, particularly engineering, and communist ideology as interpreted by Stalin. Thus, the emerging political elite was mainly composed of narrowly educated technicians, organized on a paramilitary basis.

Doctrinally, the concept of "democratic centralism" supported development of a monolithic party. Lenin had summed up "democratic centralism" as "freedom of discussion, unity of action." Higher party bodies were to be elected by lower ones but, once a decision was taken by the highest organs, it was absolutely binding on the entire party.[5] In practice, co-option was combined with the fiction of elections to assure control from the center and there was no open discussion at Party congresses between 1925 and 1956. With the "democratic" element suppressed, what remained was "centralism" and the monolith.[6]

The cult of Lenin, originated by Stalin, provided further ideological support for this type of party. The term "Marxism-Leninism" dates from the early years of Stalin's leadership. As party leader, Stalin could claim to be Lenin's heir, and skillfully exploited the veneration of the regime's founder to legitimize his own policies.

STALIN'S DICTATORSHIP AND LEGACY

Using his control of the party apparatus and rank-and-file to pack Party congresses, Stalin had eliminated all prominent Old Bolsheviks from positions of influence by 1930 and had established a personal dictatorship. Already, under his leadership, the party had dismantled the New Economic Policy, which involved a partial return to capitalism, and had launched the drive for collectivization of agriculture. Theoretically, collectivization was dictated by the necessity to provide capital investment for urban industrial expansion. Politically, the purpose was elimination of a potential source of power among the rural small-holders. By the early 1930s, the central authorities had gained total control over both urban and rural sectors of the economy.

There were three political phases of the drive toward totalitarianism. The first, between 1924 and 1929, had been intraparty, a struggle between the new proletariat under Stalin and the old-line, middle-class intellectuals. The second phase, 1929 to 1934, coincided with the first Five-Year Plan and featured a war of the party against the peasantry. One result was a devastating famine in the Ukraine.

The third phase was that of the "terror," which affected the party, the army, and finally the general population. The terror was foreshadowed by the murder of the party's second most-powerful figure, Sergei Kirov, probably on Stalin's orders, in Leningrad in December of 1934.[7] In the aftermath of Kirov's murder, provision was made for the bypassing of formal judicial procedures to administer the death penalty and other punishments for "political" crimes, setting the stage for the massive purges of 1936–39.

In the purges of those years, three-fourths of the army officers ranking colonel or higher and 98 of the 139 members of the Central Committee elected at the XXVII Party Congress in 1934 were eliminated.[8] At its peak, the terror hit the general population on a purely random basis, especially in the Ukraine. Soviet historian Roy Medvedev has estimated the number of Stalin's victims under collectivization and terror to be 20 million.[9] Other students of the period place the total even higher.

By 1939, the party had been effectively displaced as the ruling force in society, replaced by the police state. The extent of the party's downgrading is indicated by the failure to hold a Party Congress between 1939 and 1952 and by the fact that only one meeting of the Central Committee was convened between 1945 and 1952. The secret police apparatus was kept subservient to Stalin's will by a variety of methods, with his personal Secretariat playing a major role in processes of control; two successive police chiefs perished in the purges.

If totalitarianism was made possible by the condition of undeveloped social and political infrastructure, its full development was also facilitated by modern technology. A totalitarian dictatorship would have been impossible in nineteenth-century Russia. Although Russia remained backward by Western standards throughout the first half of the twentieth century, its technological level was sufficient to give the new regime an edge toward total control that the czars never possessed. This was probably as important a factor in controlling of the outlying regions as in European Russia. In the former areas, control of subordinate nationalities was a primary concern.

Prior to the revolution, exploitation of the non-Russian nationalities had been a favorite theme of Bolshevik propaganda and "national self-determination" had been a key plank of Lenin's platform. After the tide turned in the Civil War, Lenin and his associates made strenuous efforts to recover those areas of the old Czarist empire which had been lost in 1917–18. While the reestablishment of an empire was essentially a result of military force, a fiction of voluntary union and "self-determination" was maintained by the creation of the Union of Soviet Socialist Republics in 1922. Union-republics and autonomous regions were organized to recognize the most populous ethnic groups in particular areas. Lenin's formula, "national in form, socialist in content," was put forward as the short-run solution to the nationalities problem. In the long run, given the Marxist belief in the primacy of economic determinants of behavior, it was assumed that economic development would lead to amalgamation into a single Soviet nationality. This assumption became so ingrained among Marxist-Leninists that even so perceptive and cosmopolitan a figure as Mikhail Gorbachev appeared to be strongly influenced by it in his approach to nationalities questions in the 1980s.

Stalin had been Lenin's principal advisor on nationalities matters before the revolution and after the seizure of power served as Commissar of Nationalities. A Georgian, Stalin fancied himself an expert on issues related to the more than one hundred national groups in the U.S.S.R.

There is considerable difference of opinion among students of the Soviet period as to whether the Communist regime, in practice, was a denial of Russian culture or a manifestation of Russian nationalism.[10] But there is no question that Stalin did exploit Russian nationalism for his own purposes and that precedence was given to Russians in governance of the outlying areas. Moreover, when nationalist discontent became evident, brutal suppression was the usual remedy.

The movement of Russians to the periphery of the empire, a migration that had begun in the late nineteenth century, proceeded apace under Stalin, providing an additional means of control as the Russian settlers, generally more highly skilled than the locals, received the most lucrative positions in the economy, assuring their loyalty to Moscow. This outflow of Russians, which was further promoted under Khrushchev in the 1950s, would have effects extending beyond the life of the Soviet state, leading to frictions in the 1990s among the newly independent states of the former U.S.S.R.

While the non-Russian nationalities were undoubtedly subject to exploitation and forced to submit to a degree of "Russification,"[11] the Soviet regime did also provide certain opportunities. The most backward areas did feel some effects of modernization as the comprehensive social-services system provided a degree of economic security previously unknown by most subjects of the Czar; illiteracy was virtually eliminated. And general living standards did rise between 1917 and 1953, in both European Russia and in other areas, although the Communist leadership always treated consumption as a secondary priority.

In the Stalinist model of economic development, the highest priority was creation of a heavy industrial base in order to increase the military power of the U.S.S.R. and thus enhance the chances of the socialist regime's survival. The secondary status of light industry (plus the disruption of the agricultural sector resulting from the collectivization drive) necessarily meant that consumption would be limited. All sectors of the economy were, of course, adversely affected by the devastation of World War II. Overall production and income did not regain 1928 levels until 1952.

Despite the suffering of the population in World War II, postwar policy continued to emphasize heavy industry, with special emphasis upon nuclear and other weapons production even before inception of the Cold War.[12] Following this economic strategy, Stalin did succeed in raising the U.S.S.R. to a position of world power matched or surpassed only by the United States. The defeat of Nazi Germany in World War II and the creation of a Soviet empire in Eastern Europe could be attributed plausibly to Stalin's policies on economic development.

The socialist experiment in Russia had from the start contained a basic contradiction between economic and political aims, a phenomenon accentuated by Stalin's imposition of totalitarianism. The Communists intended to achieve economic modernization while avoiding the political consequences that normally accompany it, for example, the pluralism involved in the articulation of political interests by groups engaged in processes of economic development. In this sense, the Soviet Union was a profoundly reactionary regime. This was most obvious in the agricultural sector, where collectivization really entailed the reimposition of serfdom under a new name. Further, in a state supposedly operated for the benefit of the proletariat, workers had no right to strike and were denied freedom of contract. The country's largest industry, by far, in the latter portion of Stalin's reign was the economic colossus directed by the secret police, the slave labor Gulag Archipelago.

Lopsided economic development did, however, yield a new "intelligentsia,"* the scientists, technicians, and other professionals whose expertise was required in an increasingly complex economy. As the Stalin era drew to

---

* The term "intelligentsia" was used in the nineteenth century to refer to educated radicals. Under the Communist regime, this term was applied to white-collar professionals.

a close, a major question concerning this social stratum confronted the leader's would-be successors. Could this economic elite function effectively in competition with the West without changes in the Stalinist system?

Any alteration of the system would be difficult. Entrenched political elites were unlikely to surrender their special privileges without resistance and the masses, thoroughly cowed by the terror, were unprepared to assume a more active role. The centralized-command economy, denied the discipline of the market, functioning on the basis of administrative fiat, could not be modified without threat to the elaborate structure of political control. Its self-imposed isolation assured the regime of fulfillment of the nightmares conjured up by its ideology. Moreover, Bolshevism's dynamism had always been geared to the identification of enemies. The specters of "capitalist encirclement" and "bourgeois restoration" provided justification for maintenance of the monolith.

Perhaps the most enduring legacy of Stalinism was the intensification of collectivism. A new social differentiation, warranted by the exigencies of rapid industrialization, had emerged in the Stalinist era. Nevertheless, the ideology and policies of the regime had encouraged a psychology of leveling. Before the revolution, the collectivism endemic to the traditional, predominantly peasant society had weakened in the first stirrings of modernization. The Stalinist dictatorship had ruthlessly stamped out all vestiges of individualism. Now every social activity was subject to a stringent rubric of collectivism, and individual initiative was suspect. The egalitarian aspects of the ideology were internalized among virtually all strata of the population under the pressures of a constrictive social structure and the monopolistic drumbeat of regime propaganda.

THE RISE AND FALL OF KHRUSHCHEV

Stalin's death in March 1953 set off an intense power struggle among the institutional components of the Soviet system, which had been kept in check by the leader's personal dictatorship. Nikita Khrushchev was the surprise winner in this competition. Named to head the Party Secretariat in March 1953, he was formally elected as first secretary in the following September. By the time of his election as first secretary, the first phase of the power struggle was over.

The phases of this systemic conflict bear some resemblance to Stalin's takeover in the 1920s and 1930s and suggest at least a partial emulation of his tactics. However, power relationships among the institutional components had been profoundly altered by Stalin's dictatorship, lending an immediate urgency to the question of succession. Lavrenti Beria had succeeded in reestablishing his control, curbed during the last years of Stalin's rule, over the entire police apparatus and threatened to introduce his own personal dictatorship. In the summer of 1953, all of the other members of the Politburo, assisted by the army, staged a palace coup, arresting Beria, who was subsequently executed. This was followed by the separation of the main police agencies to facilitate party control and the dismantling of most of the Gulag empire. Marshal Georgi Zhukov, who had lent the army's help in the overthrow of Beria, was rewarded with an alternate seat on the Politburo.

Khrushchev's collaborators on the Politburo, most notably Vyacheslav Molotov and Georgi Malenkov, had all been close associates of Stalin and were disdainful both of the new first secretary's leadership and of his early liberalizing reforms.

Most importantly, they resisted his criticism of Stalin's "cult of personality," which threatened their legitimacy as members of the successor leadership, and were highly critical of his moderate policies toward the East European satellites, policies that led to the Hungarian Revolution of October–November 1956. In the summer of 1957, they moved to oust Khrushchev, apparently winning a close vote in the Politburo. An emergency session of the Central Committee overruled the Politburo. Khrushchev's opponents were expelled from the leadership (but not subjected to physical violence, as under Stalin).[13] This outcome was made possible by Zhukov, who had Khrushchev's supporters flown to the capital for the "rump" session that sustained the first secretary. Zhukov was again rewarded, this time with full membership on the Politburo.

Zhukov's personal popularity and the twice-confirmed dependence on the army posed a vulnerability unacceptable to Khrushchev. While he was visiting Yugoslavia in the fall of 1957, the marshal was fired both from the Politburo and from his post as defense minister. With this last hurdle out of the way, Khrushchev was able to displace the bumbling Nikolai Bulganin as premier in early 1958, thus assuming command of state as well as party. For more than two years (until May 1960) Khrushchev's leadership was apparently unchallenged; this was the heyday of his personal power.

The key to Khrushchev's ascendancy was the party, as had been the case with Stalin in the 1920s. During Stalin's last years, the party had itself become a "transmission belt" but still possessed a huge organizational network. Khrushchev devoted prodigious efforts to reviving the party as a governing force. Given his role as first secretary, this was the only possible course for Khrushchev to pursue if he hoped to gain dominance over the entire system. Between 1955 and 1957, he used the process of co-option to pack the ranks of regional secretaries with his supporters. The regional secretaries served, in effect, as governors of their assigned areas. The organizational measures regarding the party paved the way for Khrushchev's victories in 1957 and 1958.

Khrushchev displayed an awareness, lacking in other holdover bigwigs from the Stalin era, of the changes in the U.S.S.R. wrought by technical modernization and the resulting new environment for political leadership. The motivations for Khrushchev's domestic policies were not unlike those of Gorbachev thirty years later and his liberalizing actions provided an example for the reformers of the later period. Gorbachev's principal supporters frequently would be referred to as "children of the Twentieth Congress." At that congress, held in February 1956, Khrushchev delivered his stunning "secret speech," denouncing some of the crimes of Stalin.

A limited campaign to rid society of both symbols and substantive aspects of the Stalin era followed.[14] A second "de-Stalinization" drive was launched at the XXII CPSU Congress in 1961. The most oppressive features of the police state were removed, although its structure was only partially dismantled, an erratic "thaw" in cultural matters was allowed, and popular participation in political processes was encouraged. Seeking to reenergize the regime's goal culture, Khrushchev emphasized the utopian core of the ideology. The Party Program, adopted at the XXII CPSU Congress in 1961, stressed the "withering away of the state" (although practical measures toward this end were purely superficial) and projected the economic surpassing of the United States by 1980, with rapid entry into an era of communism.

The economic projections did not seem unreasonable to many Western analysts in view of the fact that Soviet growth rates had far exceeded those of the United States during the 1950s. However, the U.S.S.R. was involved in a second "take-off" stage, concentrated upon extensive development. As the economy matured, growth rates would inevitably drop. Consumption by the populace did increase significantly, due to the expansion of the economy and a marked increase in the amount of cultivated land. However, the quality of light industrial goods remained far inferior to those produced in the West, as highest priority continued to be assigned to military production. In the second half of the 1950s, development of intercontinental missiles was pushed vigorously. When the Soviets launched a small satellite called Sputnik in October 1957, the reaction in the West was one of panic, especially in the United States, where unfounded fears of a "missile gap" in favor of the U.S.S.R. colored arguments about security policy into the early 1960s.

In general, Khrushchev could scarcely be called an economic liberalizer. His policies were designed to make the command administrative system more efficient, not to weaken it. His frequent reorganizations and tinkering with the economy led many among the managerial elite to conclude that, whatever his intentions, he was indeed weakening the structure.

In 1958, Khrushchev pushed through a scheme for decentralization of the economy. Regional economic councils (*sovnarkhozy*) were given control of basic decision making and were supposed to take account of local needs as the central bureaucracy could not. By the end of 1960, the scheme had been abandoned and centralization was reinstated. In 1962, the Supreme National Council of the Economy, headed by First Deputy Prime Minister Dimitri Ustinov, was set up to coordinate the activities of the various economic bureaucracies. This structure apparently had little impact and was scrapped shortly after Khrushchev's fall from power.

In agriculture, Khrushchev did act to remove the stultifying control of the Machine Tractor Stations* over the farms but, in a sense, he was an even more ardent proponent of collectivization than was Stalin. He preferred the state farms (*sovkhozy*), where the peasants were salaried employees of the state, over the collective farms (*kolkhozy*), which retained some vestiges of private ownership in tools and livestock and fostered some degree of individual initiative. Khrushchev's favorite mode of organization for the farms was the *agrogorod,* the "agricultural city," which grouped many farms in a huge complex.[15] This was in line with the first secretary's penchant for "gigantomania," the planning of big, splashy projects useful for propaganda purposes but usually poorly geared to economic rationality. The "gigantomania" syndrome continued under Khrushchev's successors, resulting in much waste of valuable resources.

In foreign affairs, Khrushchev was a tactical innovator while adhering to Stalin's aims of maximizing Soviet regional and world power. Tactical versatility was most evident in relations with modernizing and newly emergent countries. Alliances, support for revolutionary movements, and economic and military aid put the U.S.S.R. in competition with the United States and other Western democracies for influence in the Third World. A close relationship was forged with India, the most prominent new state, and Cuba was quickly brought into the Soviet orbit after Fidel Castro assumed power in 1959.

Khrushchev theorized that Third World countries would be naturally inclined toward cooperation with the U.S.S.R. due to their preference for socialist economic development and their opposition to imperialism. These countries, together with the members of the "socialist camp," constituted the "peace zone." The combined weight of the "third camp" and the Soviet bloc, coupled with the end of the American nuclear monopoly, meant, according to Khrushchev, that imperialism could no longer make gains via war. In the most common type of overt conflict in this era, wars of "national liberation," anti-imperialist forces were inexorably detaching areas from the "imperialist camp." Otherwise, conflict was largely reduced to economic competition. Here Khrushchev professed to believe that the inherent advantages of the socialist model of development would ultimately prove decisive.[16]

---

* Agencies in charge of all motorized equipment used on the collective farms.

With "peaceful coexistence" as the proclaimed Soviet policy, Khrushchev proved adept at launching "peace offensives" designed to take advantage of the Western fear of war and yearning for normalcy in international affairs. But his most characteristic tactic was the bluff. Recognizing the U.S.S.R.'s overall inferiority in what the Soviets called the "correlation of forces," Khrushchev sought to achieve his policy goals by brinkmanship and by exaggerated claims of Soviet strength. Examples of this approach included his threat to bomb the Acropolis during the Suez crisis of 1956; his encouragement of the "missile gap" idea; the claim, totally fabricated, about Soviet possession of a "two-way" missile that could avoid American defenses by flying over the South Pole; the on-again, off-again threats to sign a separate peace treaty with East Germany; and the explosion of a thermonuclear superbomb in 1961. But the bluffs were ultimately self-defeating, encouraging instead cohesion and military buildup in the NATO alliance.

The irrationality of bluff and bluster was finally demonstrated clearly to the world by the Soviet retreat in the Cuban missile crisis of October 1962.[17] Moreover, Khrushchev's success in conveying an image of recklessness undermined a general policy approach toward the West that was based upon rational calculation and prefigured the Soviet "two-track" policy of the 1970s. While vigorously pursuing Soviet interests diametrically opposed to those of the West outside Europe, Khrushchev pushed for detente (relaxation of tensions) with the United States and its allies, hoping to secure the East European bloc, reduce or eliminate American influence in central Europe, and lull the West into a relaxation of its defensive stance vis-a-vis the U.S.S.R.. A first round of detente, initiated with much fanfare at the Geneva summit of 1955, collapsed with the bloody suppression of the Hungarian Revolution in October–November 1956. A second attempt, in 1959–60, was terminated abruptly by the downing of an American U-2 spy plane over the Sverdlovsk region on May Day in 1960. A modest effort at a revival of detente followed the inauguration of John F. Kennedy as U.S. president in 1961. Erection of the Berlin Wall in August 1961 again dashed hopes for a relaxation of tensions.

The spectacular end of the second detente episode in May 1960 greatly weakened Khrushchev's position within the Soviet leadership, which was realigned in the aftermath of the U-2 affair. Subsequently, Khrushchev was under pressure to demonstrate firmness toward the West, and his critics within the Politburo gave an extra impetus to overt belligerence and risk taking. The Cuban missile crisis was precipitated, at least in part, by Khrushchev's domestic political difficulties at the top level. The Soviet humiliation in October 1962 provided additional ammunition for the leader's critics but was probably not decisive in his downfall. Relations with the bloc countries may have been of greater consequence.

Even Stalin had been unable to maintain the desired levels of bloc cohesion. Expulsion of Yugoslavia from the Cominform in 1948 had not led, as Stalin expected, to the downfall of Tito but rather to the inception of a Yugoslav "road to communism." Stalin had been forced to compromise with Mao in difficult negotiations in Moscow during the winter of 1949–50 over issues arising from the Communist conquest of the Chinese mainland. Khrushchev had welcomed Yugoslavia back into the fold, verbally accepting "many roads to communism." But he had attempted to enforce conformity among the East European satellites on domestic policies. The satellite leaders became enmeshed in the "scissors crisis" of 1954–56: pressured by Moscow to follow liberalizing policies, they could assure their continuation in power only by maintenance of Stalinist methods. The "scissors crisis" plus spillover effects from the legitimizing of Titoism led to the 1956 eruptions in Poland and Hungary, which almost cost Khrushchev his job.[18]

In the aftermath of these upheavals, it had been necessary to accept a separate Polish approach to socialism in exchange for Warsaw's support on bloc and world policies. Romania took advantage of Moscow's bloc difficulties to pursue an independent line on regional integration and other issues. Another full defection from the bloc followed in 1961. Albania, fearful of Yugoslav domination and leery of Khrushchev's continued wooing of Belgrade, lined up with China in the growing rift between Moscow and Beijing.

The Communist victory in China had been the single most important gain for the "socialist camp" in the world "correlation of forces." At the same time, it posed the most difficult problem for bloc cohesion. China's size, its potential, and Mao's seniority among world Communist leaders all worked against Chinese acceptance of Soviet domination. On the other hand, from Moscow's perspective, bloc unity could only be achieved via adherence to "proletarian internationalism," that is, deference to Soviet leadership. In these circumstances, tensions were inevitable.

In the late 1950s, Moscow and Beijing clashed over the Great Leap Forward (the People's Republic's drive for rapid industrialization and collectivization of agriculture during the late 1950s), China's conflicts with Taiwan and India, issues of economic aid, and the question of Soviet support for Chinese nuclear development. In 1961, at the XXII CPSU Congress, the growing split became overt, centering on the issue of de-Stalinization. In 1962–63, the conflict reached virulent levels, including a brief border war between the two countries.[19]

Beijing chose to leave the door ajar for reconciliation by blaming the split on Khrushchev and vowing that it would never negotiate with him. In October 1964, China became a nuclear power and Khrushchev was ousted, raising the stakes in the Sino-Soviet conflict. Notably, in his speech to the Central Committee when Khrushchev was voted out, the CPSU's *eminence grise* Mikhail Suslov reportedly strongly emphasized the failure of Khrushchev's China policy.

All of these misadventures in world affairs were certainly damaging to Khrushchev's leadership position but it now seems virtually certain that the most important considerations involved in his dismissal were related to the domestic distribution of political power.

Following his assumption of the premiership in 1958, Khrushchev had tended to concentrate upon the direction of the government, leaving much of the detailed work of running the party to his lieutenants in the Secretariat. This provided an excellent opportunity for Khrushchev's chief supporters in the party to strengthen their patronage networks ("organizational tails") as potential sources of independent power. Further, supposedly as a means for strengthening party control over the police, General Ivan Serov had been replaced as head of the KGB in 1958 by Aleksandr Shelepin, head of the Komsomol (Young Communist League). Shelepin proceeded to staff key KGB positions with former Komsomol officials and, when he moved to the Secretariat in 1962, left the secret police in the hands of a close associate. Finally, the generals had been alienated by the severe cuts in personnel initiated by Khrushchev in 1958. Thus, the main elements of the anti-Khrushchev coalition of 1964 were well positioned to coalesce and bring him down at the appropriate time.

Khrushchev had revived the party organization in the mid-1950s. Initially his only source of power, the party organization had been used by Khrushchev to crush his opponents. But his preferred leadership style was authoritarian populism, an appeal to the populace over the heads of all the bureaucracies. Given the absence of a legal opposition, this led inexorably to a new "cult of personality," despite the first secretary's continuing disavowal of such practices. Although this concentration upon a single person was resented by other members of the leadership group, "democratic centralism" was so firmly entrenched that Khrushchev was usually able to carry the Central Committee with him on controversial issues. Such an issue was the bifurcation of regional party organizations, pushed through by Khrushchev in 1962, ostensibly to promote economic efficiency. The regional organizations were divided into separate sectors for industry and agriculture, each part to have its own directing secretary.

The reorganization actually did not enhance efficiency; rather, it produced extreme confusion in the functioning of economy and society. But, more importantly for Khrushchev's fate, it undermined the power of the key, mid-level elites in the party organization. The regional secretaries had functioned as prefects or governors in their areas and constituted a vital link between party and society. Now, with no single party boss in each region, the influence of the regional party organizations vis-a-vis the center was diminished. The regional first secretaries who had been reduced to half-secretaries naturally resented their loss of power and prestige. And their interests happened to coincide with those of the most powerful members of the Politburo, those who were also members of the Secretariat. The power of these four men—-Mikhail Suslov, Leonid Brezhnev, Nikolai Podgorny, and Andrei Kirilenko—-was largely grounded in their continuing dominance of regions in which they had served as first secretaries. Bifurcation of the party organizations not only reduced the influence of the regions they controlled, it also muddled the direct linkage between the central party apparatus and the regional leaders, thus posing a threat to the hierarchs' "organizational tails." Over a period of several months, Suslov matured the planning of a coup and by October 1964 had added all of the major bureaucracies to an anti-Khrushchev coalition.

Not surprisingly, the first significant domestic action of the successor leadership was the reversal of the policy on bifurcation of regional party organizations. Khrushchev's most grievous offense had been to threaten the post-Stalin political settlement, which we next examine in some detail.

THE POST-STALIN POLITICAL SETTLEMENT

When Stalin died in March 1953, there had been uncertainty about who would rule the U.S.S.R. and, more importantly, about how the country would be ruled. Continuation of control of the society by a relatively narrow governing elite, the *nomenklatura*,* was not in question. Undetermined was the distribution of power among the institutional components of the governing system and the extent of their control over society as a whole. Over the following two years, these questions were answered definitively by the decisions worked out in the interplay of political forces. The resulting arrangements served to establish the framework and functions of the mature Soviet system. Although variations in the relative weights of the institutional components could be observed from time to time, these variations were contained within clearly understood parameters and the general outlines of the settlement were maintained well into the Gorbachev era.

Curbing of the police colossus was the first step in realignment of the system. Next followed a clarification of the role of the governmental bureaucracy in the system. The vast expansion of the functions performed by the various layers of this bureaucracy under Stalin and the debilitation of party mechanisms had evoked doubts about the division of decision-making power between party and government. Georgi Malenkov used the premiership as a platform for a challenge to Khrushchev and sought to rally the

---

* The term *nomenklatura* officially referred to lists of offices and of personnel qualified to hold these offices. In popular usage, the term was used to denote the "class" of office holders.

masses to his standard by championing consumer interests and relaxation of international tensions. But the only institutional components that figured to gain by such policies were light industry and the agricultural bureaucracy; real power lay elsewhere. Khrushchev countered by attacking Malenkov's recommendations, appealing for the support of the "military-industrial complex." After the defeat of Malenkov, Khrushchev adopted, at least rhetorically, Malenkov's policy positions. Malenkov's dismissal from the premiership in early 1955 confirmed the essential subordination of government to party that would continue throughout the remaining years of the Soviet regime.

Reassertion of party dominance over the political system was evident by the XX CPSU Congress in 1956. Khrushchev's denunciation of Stalin at that conclave was not idiosyncratic, for it touched the fundamental concern in the realignment of the system, protection of political elites against the unlimited exercise of arbitrary power. It was clear that the Soviet system depended upon the coercive instrumentalities for its survival. The party was the only institution capable of controlling those agencies. Such control ultimately hinged upon the prevention of combination for united action by the coercive instrumentalities.[20] Linkage between the military establishment and the KGB was unlikely, since the memory of police repression of the army in the Great Purge was still fresh. But, in conditions of unsettled relationships among the institutional components, the army was potentially a powerful political force, as the events of summer 1953 had demonstrated. The new role of Marshal Zhukov evoked for some political elites the specter of Bonapartism, thus rendering control of the army a concern second only to the reining in of the secret police.

Party organizations in the coercive agencies served as one means of control. Police and army were subject to political supervision by the Department of Administrative Organs in the Central Committee which investigated all important appointments in those organizations. The work of the Department of Administrative Organs was overseen by a member of the Secretariat,* usually a full Politburo member. More significant, perhaps, was the reemphasis on the party's central role, particularly in the realm of ideology. As the supposed repository of historical truth, the party was the only legitimizing agent in the system. Legitimacy of other structures was based upon their relationships to the party. Constrained to act in the name of the party, other systemic elements necessarily accorded it at least formal deference.

While the party's political supremacy was acknowledged, it was understood that party officials would recognize the professional expertise of specialists in other systemic structures. *Podmena*, interference in the day-to-day

---

* Secretariat: the party secretaries, usually eleven or twelve in number, who supervised the work of the Central Committee bureaucracy.

functioning of other organizations by party officials, was to be avoided. In the case of government agencies, this principle was often honored only in the breach, particularly in the regions. Moreover, dependence upon decision making by the party permitted some avoidance of onerous responsibility by bureaucrats in the governmental administration. Nevertheless, in the "mature" socialist system, there was an unavoidable diffusion of functional power.

This diffusion of functional power yielded the party's most important role in the realigned system, which was now characterized by the interaction of massive complex bureaucracies. The most important questions now revolved around the competition among these bureaucratic components concerning the distribution of resources and influence.[21] Bargaining processes resolved these conflicts. Only the party was in a position to serve as an arbitrator among these competing interests. In accord with democratic centralism, the bargaining process channeled ultimate decision-making power toward the party hierarchy at the center. However, the bargaining mode was operative down to the lowest levels, thus providing at the same time a functional basis for diffusion of power within the party.

Cohesion of the entire system rested heavily upon the continued utilization of co-option and selection procedures for the *nomenklatura*.[22] At each level, the highest party official had his own segment of the *nomenklatura* framework, with control over appointment of certain designated officials. Technically, the party first (after 1966, general) secretary had no formal *nomenklatura* appointive power, except in regard to his own staff; his degree of dominance over the party depended upon his ability to influence those with formal appointive power. In practice, this influence was extensive.

The first or general secretary served as head of the Secretariat which, in the absence of a separate Russian party, supervised directly the regional organizations in the Russian Federation. In the other union-republics, "second" secretaries were responsible for party organization and these officials were selected by the CPSU Central Committee Secretariat. In the predominantly non-Slavic republics, the "second" secretaries were invariably Russians or Ukrainians, usually Russians.[23] The union-republic first secretaries were selected at the highest levels of the CPSU.

Theoretically, the highest party organ was the Congress, which, under the party rules, was convened at least once every four or (after 1971) five years. The Party Congress, numbering about five thousand delegates, was also subject to the typical procedures of formal election and informal cooption. It served as a propaganda rally for the Five-Year Plans that set goals for the economy and as a platform for policy pronouncements by party leaders[24]. Its principal function was election of the Central Committee, which involved unanimous ratification of a list prepared by the Secretariat. Most Central Committee memberships were held by virtue of positions filled elsewhere; for example, the first secretaries of the most important regions were automatically entitled to full membership on the Central Committee. The Central Committee elected the Politburo and Secretariat, but the composition of these organs was determined by the Politburo. Essentially, the Politburo operated like a private club, deciding its own membership, but due account had to be taken by its members of the balance of political forces in the system as a whole.

Despite democratic centralism, there was an element of power sharing in these arrangements. The Politburo filled the role of the Cabinet in Western parliamentary systems although it was more powerful than the Western organizations. Ostensibly, the Politburo was committed to the principle of collective leadership—but some members were "more equal" than others. The inner core of the Politburo, which usually consisted of those members who also served as party secretaries and the first or general secretary (who presided), ordinarily had the greatest influence. Several key Politburo members also served on the Defense Council, which had general responsibility for security policy.

In general, the Politburo functioned as an aggregator of interests among the system's bureaucracies and Western Sovietologists could to some extent gauge the relative weights of these components by the composition of the Politburo. One of these interests was the governmental bureaucracy, primarily concerned with the economy, which was always represented on the Politburo by the chairman of the Council of Ministers (premier). However, the premier did not oversee a united, monolithic administrative apparatus. There was considerable ambiguity in the relationship between the council, usually numbering around 110 members, and the party leadership.

For one thing, there was some interchange of party and governmental elites, with officials moving back and forth between party and governmental assignments. More importantly, each ministry or state committee was subject to general supervision by a department of the Central Committee. Finally, three governmental agencies—the foreign ministry, the KGB (Committee for State Security), and the ministry of defense—had special relationships with the party that rendered them largely immune to direction by the premier (unless he happened to be also head of the party, as was the case between 1958 and 1964).

Ambassadors to the bloc countries reported directly to the Central Committee department responsible for relations with the socialist states and were usually drawn from the ranks of the party apparat.* The KGB's independence from the overall governmental structure was emphasized by a change in its formal legal designation in 1978. The Defense Ministry necessarily maintained close functional ties with the several ministries responsible for armaments. This "military-industrial complex" formed a distinct, separate

---

* Apparat: Officials of the CPSU bureaucracy.

interest often at odds with the premier and the council's Presidium. Another agency developed a marked degree of independence vis-a-vis both party and governmental leaderships because of its essential functional role and expertise. The State Planning Commission (Gosplan) was the central cog in the command-administrative system, since it formulated both the Five-Year Plans and the annual plans for the economy. Its longtime head, Nikolai Baibakov, was able to defy party leader Yuri Andropov publicly in August 1983 on the issue of decentralization of the economy. But even Gosplan could not stand in the way of a clearly dominant general secretary: Gorbachev fired Baibakov two years later.

Nominal legislative and judicial structures assisted the party and governmental apparatuses in controlling the country. The Supreme Soviet, formally organized as a bicameral legislature with joint sessions, assembled twice a year to rubber stamp legislation initiated by party or government. The "legislative" soviets at various levels continued to serve as "transmission belts" and membership was honorary, conveying no actual power. Only at the lowest levels, where the soviet executive committees constituted the local governmental administration, did the soviets have real influence and even here tended to be overshadowed by parallel party organs. The courts were thoroughly politicized, with no tradition or practice of an independent judiciary. At most levels, trials were conducted by a judge and two lay assessors, without juries. Judges and prosecutors were on the same "team," both being subject to the Procuracy administration and to the Department of Administrative Organs of the Central Committee.

The "mature" socialist system was thus characterized by massive and overlapping bureaucratic structures; by strictly formalized hierarchy with lines of authority somewhat blurred by the overlapping of structures; and by a real diffusion of power generated by functional complexity. In contrast to the Stalinist era, the system was now more rule-governed and the exercise of authority was less arbitrary.

While the distribution of power among the various bureaucracies was a paramount consideration, the masses were also included in the post-Stalin settlement. The citizenry, subject to wholesale terror, mass deportations, and exceptional sacrifices under Stalin, were now encouraged to expect more normal relations with the political authorities and improvement in the material conditions of life. Employment was guaranteed; social services were expanded; the cost of living was kept artificially low by price controls and subsidies of food, housing, and transportation. In exchange for this economic security, the Soviet citizen was expected to accede to the political supremacy of party and state; the nature of this "social contract" was clearly understood. Official propaganda emphasized the alleged voluntary nature of these arrangements. Consumption levels were far below those of the West but the people were said to prefer the "Soviet way of life," which was claimed to be spiritually superior to the frenzied consumerism of the capitalist world. The "new Soviet man," an individual committed to the general welfare of society and disdainful of narrow self-interest, was depicted as the foundation for a cohesive, purposeful society. The actual tensions and hardships of everyday life were glossed over or concealed by processes of mobilization and indoctrination.

To sum up, the major features of the post-Stalin settlement were as follows:

1. Assurance against random terror affecting either the general population or the *nomenklatura;*
2. A "social contract" between state and society, guaranteeing economic security for the individual in exchange for unquestioning allegiance to the existing political system;
3. Recognition of a distribution of power and functional responsibilities among the bureaucratic elements of the political system;
4. Acceptance of the party's role as the central structure of the system and the ultimate arbiter of conflicts among the bureaucracies;
5. Reassertion of collective leadership within party and government while maintaining "democratic centralism," which was interpreted less stringently to allow greater flexibility in decision making at lower levels of the system.

Two more explicit provisions were added to the terms of settlement following Leonid Brezhnev's election as first secretary in 1964. The Central Committee adopted a resolution declaring that the offices of premier and first secretary should not be held by the same person. Brezhnev reportedly attempted unsuccessfully to overturn this resolution and assume the premiership in 1970. The second provision guaranteed lifetime tenure in the *nomenklatura* for Central Committee members subject to good behavior. These moves were designed to protect the post-Stalin sharing of power among systemic elements that had been allegedly threatened by Khrushchev and to prevent a reversion to autocracy.

The fundamental structure of the Soviet system was only slightly modified by the reordering described above but there was nevertheless a qualitative change in its functioning. Western scholars were slow to detect this decisive turn away from Stalinism and further developed the "totalitarian model." Friedrich and Brzezinski's classic formulation of the model was published in 1956.[25] For nearly a decade after Stalin's death, the totalitarian model was largely unchallenged as a theoretical construct for study of the Soviet system.

Most Western scholars gradually concluded that the model was in many, if not most respects, empirically untenable under the new conditions prevailing in the U.S.S.R. Soviet studies were dramatically affected by the ascendancy of behavioralism in American political science. Committed to the measurement of actual behavior in the Soviet system, a new generation of scholars drew upon available alternative theoretical sources, all of which were based upon Western experience. Interest group, organization, development, and coalition theories, among others, were applied in the attempt to integrate Soviet studies into the rapidly emerging general field of comparative politics.

Gabriel Almond's application of structural-functionalism strongly influenced all of the new approaches. According to Almond, the same requisite functions were performed in all political systems. Comparative politics primarily involved examination of the structures that performed the requisite functions.[26] While the new Sovietology produced many valuable empirical studies and did enhance knowledge of relationships among component elements of the Soviet system, its Almondesque origins were reflected in a tendency to regard the U.S.S.R. as a polity differing only in degree from Western systems, particularly in studies of interest groups and bureaucracies. In the conception of "institutional pluralism," this tendency was carried further, with indications of a "convergence" between the Communist Party states and the Western democracies. Indeed, much of the literature on Soviet development in the 1970s contained the implicit assumption of such a "convergence."

The new Sovietology generally overlooked the continuing presence of totalitarian structures in the U.S.S.R., the fact that the Soviet system's maintenance required performance of requisite functions absent in democratic polities, and the central role of ideology. The inherent flaws of the Soviet system—the conflict between politics and economic rationality, the inefficiencies inherent in overcentralization, the absence of normalized procedures for conflict resolution—receded into the background of most analyses. In retrospect, it appears that the new Sovietology was largely unprepared for the collapse of the Soviet system.[27] The surprise was all the greater because the first three years of the Gorbachev leadership lent superficial credence to the thesis of "convergence." However, it should be noted that the totalitarian model offered perhaps even less theoretical guidance for the breakdown period. Most practitioners who disdained the new Sovietology were strongly convinced of the staying power of the Soviet system.[28]

Only a handful of Soviet dissidents, Western scholars, and public figures accurately predicted the imminent collapse of the Soviet system. Failure to foresee the fall of the U.S.S.R. was traumatic for Sovietologists. More important was the fact that the subject of their studies had disappeared. Postmortems sought reasons for the presumed failures of the subfield scholars while erstwhile Sovietologists searched for a new appropriate name for their multidisciplinary field.

Most Slavicists concluded that there was much worth salvaging in the old Sovietology but that future studies of the replacement political system should concentrate on that which is distinctively Russian in its makeup.[29]

Further, it was generally agreed after the fact that the "mature" socialist system had been highly vulnerable due to structural flaws or "contradictions" that had rendered it a transitional form rather than an enduring one, as had been commonly assumed.

While most Western scholars had difficulty addressing these problems, the practical confrontation of the "contradictions" by the Soviet leadership was even more lackluster. As we shall see, the leadership of Leonid Brezhnev approached the problems with an attitude of denial. After an interregnum to resolve the succession, the Gorbachev leadership attacked some of the underlying problems. Yet, even under Gorbachev, an attitude of denial persisted, a belief that the framework of socialism was basically sound.

STAGNATION UNDER BREZHNEV

The tenure of Leonid Brezhnev as CPSU General (to 1966, First) Secretary was marked by the U.S.S.R.'s attainment of recognition as superpower on the same level as the United States. Central to this elevated status was the achievement of parity, at least, in intercontinental ballistic missiles. The SALT I agreement, signed in Moscow in 1972, confirmed the Soviets' gains in the nuclear arms race and was hailed by Moscow as a belated acknowledgment by the "imperialists" of the U.S.S.R.'s role as a global superpower. Further, the Helsinki accords of 1975, which confirmed existing European borders, appeared to legitimize the Soviet bloc in Eastern Europe. Subsequently, the Soviets claimed that the Helsinki accords incorporated "socialist internationalism" (the relationships among socialist states) into general international law. Helsinki's Basket Three, which concerned fundamental human rights, was flagrantly ignored by the U.S.S.R. but not entirely with impunity. The agreement led to the creation of dissident "watch" groups in the U.S.S.R. and some of the satellites, and provided the legal justification for the U.S. President Jimmy Carter's human rights campaign directed against the Soviet bloc.

In September 1975, Soviet foreign minister Andrei Gromyko declared that "the present marked preponderance of the forces of peace and progress give them the opportunity of laying down the direction of international politics."[30] Successes by Soviet proxies in Third World "liberation" struggles seemed to confirm the general trend favorable to the "socialist camp" and the installation of SS-20 missiles in Eastern Europe, which began in 1977, promised an overwhelming strategic advantage over NATO. To the end of the decade, the Soviets confidently projected the "restructuring of international relations," an irreversible alteration in the world "correlation of forces" in their favor.

Rank as a global superpower unquestionably enhanced the prestige of the regime and system leaders were not shy about claiming credit for the achievement. While the U.S.S.R.'s military muscle was kept strong at the expense of the average Soviet citizen's material welfare, it was also true that world power could not have been sustained without domestic stability, general consensual acceptance of the regime, and at least minimal satisfaction of social needs. In the unsettled conditions of the 1990s, many Russians would look back nostalgically upon the Brezhnev era as a time when order was maintained and the "shops were full," albeit with low quality goods. However, the Brezhnev era was a time of "stagnation," the term later applied to the period by Gorbachev. The "stagnation" was apparent in the four major aspects of systemic activity—political, economic, social, and ideological.

Politically, the regime lost vigor due to the exaggerated application of the post-Stalin settlement, the organizational approach that was referred to as "stability of cadres" policy. At each level of the party, office holders tended to remain in place until retirement or death. When regional first secretaries retired, they were usually replaced by their subordinates.[31] There was little mobility, either vertical or horizontal, within the party and this effect was also observable, although less prominent, in other systemic structures. The virtual guarantee of lifetime tenure was the primary reason for Brezhnev's popularity within the party and made his position as general secretary almost unassailable, since any replacement would threaten the existing arrangements. At the same time, the policy prevented the full consolidation of power over the party by Brezhnev.

Two negative by-products of "stability of cadres" were fragmentation of the party and a marked increase in corruption. The high level of security rendered lower-level officials more independent of the center and made for a real functional decentralization, despite the apparent subservience to top party leaders.

Regional party leaders usually found it more expedient to collaborate with local economic interests in dealings with the central authorities rather than to serve simply as Moscow's representatives in the provinces. This common practice did have its positive side, in the articulation of local interests, but it tended to blur and diminish the party's overall role in the society. Further, regional secretaries, generally denied the possibility of advancement, were tempted to maximize gains from their secure fiefdoms and often enriched themselves through illicit activities, especially in areas of the Russian Federation distant from Moscow. Widespread corruption was even more blatant in some of the other Union-republics, notably Uzbekistan, Azaerbaijan, and Georgia.

In these circumstances, there was little incentive for policy innovation; indeed, any fundamental change in policy would upset the accepted relationships among the various levels of the system. "Stability of cadres" inhibited the flow of new blood into leadership circles; a generation of party administrators was confined to relatively low positions. When replacements were necessary at the center, they were invariably drawn from proteges and close associates of party hierarchs and subsequent to their elevations were kept under close watch.

At the top, the principal actors were beneficiaries of the purges of the 1930s who had survived the Stalin and Khrushchev eras and now jealously guarded their positions against all comers. Between 1973 and 1978, six of the sixteen Politburo members elected at the XXIV CPSU Congress in 1971 were dismissed, superficially indicating extreme instability. However, replacements were either proteges of the troika of party hierarchs—Brezhnev, Suslov, and Andrei Kirilenko—or were representatives of major bureaucracies and were, on average, several years older than the members displaced. By 1980, the aging of the leadership was quite pronounced, with septuagenarians filling most of the highest positions. In 1981, for the first time in almost sixty years, a Party Congress reelected the sitting Politburo and Secretariat without a single change.[32]

Economically, the system confronted slow growth rates, to some extent a natural phenomenon associated with passage beyond the hectic "take-off" stage. Most alarming to the leadership was the glacial rise in productivity. This was partially due to lack of incentives for workers and also could be attributed to inefficient management and coordination of supply of raw materials. But the most important factor was technological adaptation. With the dawning of the computer age, the country's shortcomings in this area became more evident and each year the technological gap between the U.S.S.R. and the industrialized democracies widened further.

Near the end of the 1970s, regime leaders faced a serious conflict between their objectives and available resources, requiring difficult decisions on allocations among armaments, consumption, and investment. Unwilling to sacrifice military strength and wary of the political consequences of a cut in consumption, they opted for cuts in investment, a decision that would adversely affect all areas of the economy in the 1980s.[33] The railroads, the country's primary transportation arm, were especially hard hit. It was assumed that existing tracks and rolling stock could handle an expected increase in traffic over the following decade. This projection proved to be wildly optimistic and by 1983 the railroads were overburdened to a point approaching gridlock.

Socially, the contrast between egalitarian pretensions and actual conditions became more apparent. Officially, the regime recognized two "nonantagonistic" classes, the proletariat and the peasantry, and one "stratum," the "toiling intelligentsia." These social sectors, as well as the various nationalities, were said to be drawing together in a process of "homogenization."

Actually, the U.S.S.R. was becoming more of a class society, with distinctions of rank and special privileges counting more than nominal incomes, which did show some tendency toward equalization. Generational transfer of class advantages was evident, as children of elites generally enjoyed special opportunities for higher education and professional careers. Even within the industrial proletariat, social stratification was becoming more pronounced.[34] And the citizenry increasingly measured their standard of living against the outside world, rather than against their previous condition. There was an acute awareness that living standards were higher even in most bloc countries, as evidenced by demand for goods from Eastern Europe, considered superior to anything produced in the U.S.S.R..

Ideologically, the lack of interest by the masses in Marxism-Leninism was repeatedly acknowledged by regime spokesmen. The utopian Party Program adopted in 1961, clearly out of sync with Soviet reality, was not repealed but was quietly shelved to avoid embarrassment. Nevertheless, progress toward communism was claimed. The concept of *razvitie* (developed) socialism, rather ambiguous in specific content, was put forward to assert the achievement of an unprecedented level of social development.[35]

In practice, the U.S.S.R. had become a very conservative society, directed by a political elite mainly concerned with maintaining its privileged status. But the Soviet system was legitimized by a revolutionary ideology that projected the disappearance of social classes, the "withering away of the state," and the abolition of political power. How then to explain and justify the continuing and intensifying elitism in the U.S.S.R.?

This problem was dealt with by two theoretical approaches that involved a double rejection of Marx and showed clearly the ideological bankruptcy of the regime. First, communism was redefined in a campaign spearheaded by Anatolii Egorov, director of the Institute for Marxism-Leninism.[36] The most basic tenet of original Marxism, abolition of the division of labor, was turned upside down. It was maintained that functional specialization would not only continue into the stage of communism; it would necessarily accelerate under communism. Among other things, the agencies of state power would continue in the stage of communism. The Marxian structural criteria for identification of communism were totally missing. Presumably, communism would be defined solely in terms of the amassing of sufficient material resources to overcome general scarcity and want, which for Marx had been only a precondition for communism.

The second ideological thrust pertained to international affairs, relations between the two competing "camps." It was argued that only Soviet weight in the world "correlation of forces" made possible gains by the "national liberation" movements in the Third World, which was now the main arena of conflict.[37] The organization of the Soviet system was ultimately responsible for detachments from the "imperialist" camp by revolutionary forces that were usually peasant-based but never founded upon an urban proletariat. Thus, the revolutionary legitimacy of the conservative Soviet system was derived from forces disdained generally by both Marx and Lenin.

Gorbachev and his associates were thus correct in identifying the Brezhnev era as a time of "stagnation." But what Gorbachev either failed to see or refused to acknowledge was that this "stagnation" was not purely subjective, not simply a matter of wrong decisions by the people in power. Many policy errors were made but attribution of all the ills of the system to individual decisions was both un-Marxist and nonempirical. Stagnation was the essential characteristic of the mature Soviet system.

THE ANDROPOV AND CHERNENKO INTERLUDES

The election of Yuri Andropov to the general secretary's post, following the death of Brezhnev in November 1982, was a direct consequence of "stability of cadres" policy. The troika of Brezhnev, Suslov, and Kirilenko had protected their positions by suppressing or controlling the mobility of younger officials with leadership potential. In the late 1970s, Kirilenko, who although three months older than Brezhnev, appeared to be the most likely successor, fell out of favor with Brezhnev and other key members of the Politburo and was gradually stripped of his responsibilities as main overseer of the economy. All three of the titans departed in the course of 1982; Suslov died in January and Kirilenko was formally dropped from the Politburo in November.

Brezhnev's chosen heir apparent, Party Secretary Konstantin Chernenko, a longtime administrative aide to the general secretary, had gained full Politburo rank in 1978. He was a poor candidate for the leadership, widely held in contempt as a "paper shuffler" and Brezhnev lackey. Another party secretary who had been elected to full Politburo membership in 1980, Mikhail Gorbachev, was too young and untested to be considered seriously for party leadership. Brezhnev had avoided Khrushchev's mistake of building up lieutenants who might unseat him but had left a void of experienced party officials in the central leadership who might be viable candidates for the succession.

Yuri Andropov, who had been head of the KGB since 1967 and a full Politburo member since 1973, took advantage of the disarray in the central party leadership to position himself as a potential successor. Brezhnev's physical debility, the fading of other longtime hierarchs, and the party fragmentation associated with "stability of cadres" all contributed to a situation in which leaders of nonparty structures obtained unusual influence. A firm coalition of Andropov, minister of defense Dimitri Ustinov, and foreign minister Andrei Gromyko proved to be crucial in the succession, which was effectively decided in May 1982 when Andropov was named to succeed Suslov as the unofficial "second" secretary.

Following his election as general secretary, Andropov expressed a far more realistic view of the U.S.S.R.'s problems than had his predecessor. He pointed out that systemic activities were too often characterized by "trial and error," an approach hardly suitable for a party supposedly possessing certain knowledge of historical truth, and asserted that the U.S.S.R.'s development was much less advanced than had been claimed by Brezhnev. The U.S.S.R., Andropov said, was only at the beginning of the period of "developed socialism."[38] Academicians were encouraged to study the actual conditions of Soviet life. One result of this initiative was the 1983 Novosibirsk Report, prepared by specialists of the Siberian Academy of Sciences, notably the sociologist Tatyana Zaslavskaya, which was circulated among elite officials and sharply criticized the operation of the Soviet system.

A campaign against corruption, which Andropov had set in motion even before his election as general secretary, was given highest priority. Two related campaigns, against alcoholism and absenteeism, aroused widespread resentment and were quietly shelved after a few months. A general attack on the problems of the economy, which the new leader indicated would involve decentralization of structure, remained in embryo; Andropov was not strong enough politically or physically to carry out a reorganization. Afflicted with heart and kidney ailments, Andropov was, in fact a dying man, and was not seen in public after August 1983.

One positive development of Andropov's final months was the effective scuttling of "stability of cadres" policy. When regular party elections were held in December 1983–January 1984, numerous regional secretaries were replaced in a "purge" directed by Gorbachev, who had become Andropov's chief lieutenant. This infusion of Andropov appointees prepared the way for the ultimate resolution of the long-running succession crisis and was to prove crucial in Gorbachev's rise to power. However, the turnover was not sufficient to enable Andropov's closest associates to grasp fully the reins of power when he died in February 1984.

Meanwhile, the U.S.S.R.'s international isolation had become acute. The invasion of Afghanistan had alienated most of the Moslem sector of the world. Afghanistan and the SS-20 gambit had thoroughly soured relations with the West. The policies of the Reagan administration threatened a technological escalation of the arms race that would impose possibly unbearable strains upon the Soviet economy. The shooting down of an unarmed, Korean civilian airliner by the Soviets on September 1, 1983 horrified the world and seemed to confirm U. S. President Reagan's rhetoric about the "evil empire." When the installation of Pershing-2 and Cruise missiles by NATO finally began in November–December 1983 in response to the SS-20 challenge, it was clear that Moscow's European policy had failed completely. The "restructuring of international relations" had come unraveled and the world "correlation of forces" appeared to be turning decisively against the U.S.S.R..

Confronted with major challenges at home and abroad, the Soviet political machine was stalled in neutral. There was no consensus within the leadership on how to proceed and the so-called "reformers" associated with Andropov constituted a definite minority of the Politburo. The "purge" of the provinces had pushed two old-line collaborators of Andropov back into the "Brezhnevite" camp and potential kingmakers Gromyko and Ustinov were determined to maintain their independent positions, which would be threatened by a strong, presumably long-term general secretary. Following Andropov's death in February 1984, the Politburo met in nearly round-the-clock session for two days and hammered out a compromise makeshift distribution of power.

The seventy-three-year-old *apparatchik* Chernenko was named as general secretary, obviously consigned to an interim and almost nominal leadership. Gorbachev became the unofficial "second" secretary, with general responsibility for party organization, ideology, and the economy. The other surviving member of the Secretariat with full Politburo rank, Grigorii Romanov, was made party supervisor of the police and military; the latter function was rendered somewhat pro forma by the confirmed continuing dominance of the armed forces by defense minister Ustinov. Foreign minister Gromyko was accorded a virtual monopoly over foreign policy and candidate Politburo member Vladimir Dolgikh was to direct industry, subject to the general supervision of Gorbachev. Brezhnev crony Nikolai Tikhonov, seventy-eight years old, remained as premier, in charge of those governmental functions not parceled out to other Politburo members.

These arrangements were a recipe for inertia and no major policy initiatives were forthcoming during the thirteen months of Chernenko's tenure. Ill with emphysema, Chernenko was the third successive general secretary in failing health; expectations of another succession dominated the political scene for the remainder of 1984. The two major contenders were Gorbachev and Romanov.

During Chernenko's frequent absences, Gorbachev presided over the Politburo and further strengthened his position with the few party appointments that were allowed during the period. The hopes of Romanov, who lacked an extensive "organizational tail" in the party, hinged upon the forging of a coalition combining Brezhnevites, police and military. Romanov was unable to rally the Brezhnev holdovers to his standard and the KGB stood firmly behind Gorbachev. Although the army generals were mostly opposed to Gorbachev, the dismissal of Chief of Staff Nikolai Ogarkov in September 1984 and the death of Ustinov in December eliminated the army as a major factor in the succession sweepstakes. When the Politburo met to select a successor to Chernenko following the general secretary's death in March, Gorbachev won, reportedly by the narrowest of margins,[39] and the choice was confirmed by the Central Committee.

After years of decline and uncertainty at the top, the U.S.S.R. at last had a young, vigorous leader with prospects of a lengthy tenure. It remained for him to consolidate his hold on power, to set a new course, and to rally support for it.

ENDNOTES

1. Jacoby, Henry. *The Bureaucratization of the World.* Berkeley: University of California Press, 1973, p. 127.

2. See Wittfogel, Karl A. *Oriental Despotism.* New Haven: Yale University Press, 1959, especially chapter 1.

3. For a detailed account of the development of labor camps under Lenin, see Solzhenitsen, Aleksandr I. *The Gulag Archipelago.* New York: Harper and Row, 1973, chapter 2.

4. See Shapiro, Leonard. *The Communist Party of the Soviet Union.* New York: Harper and Row, 1973, chapter 2.

5. Moore, Jr., Barrington. *Soviet Politics: The Dilemma of Power.* Cambridge: Harvard University Press, 1951, pp. 138–139.

6. Hunt, R. N. Carew. *The Theory and Practice of Communism.* New York: MacMillan, 1952, p. 151.

7. Ulam, Adam B. *Stalin.* New York: Viking, 1973, pp. 370–384.

8. Bullock, Alan. *Hitler and Stalin: Parallel Lives.* New York: Alfred A. Knopf, 1992, p.77.

9. *Argumenti I Fakti,* February 3–10, 1989, p. 4.

10. See Krasnov, Vladislav. *Russia Beyond Communism.* Boulder: Westview Press, 1991, pp. 1–22 and 233–237.

11. See Belinsky, Yaroslav. "Education of the Non-Russian Peoples in the U.S.S.R., 1917–1967: An Essay," *Slavic Review,* Vol. XXVII, no. 3, September 1968, pp. 411–437.

12. Baradat, Leon P. *Soviet Political Society.* New York: Prentice-Hall, 1989, pp 83–86.

13. Deutscher, Isaac. "New Lineup in the Kremlin," in Sidney I. Ploss, ed., *The Soviet Political Process.* Waltham, Mass: Ginn and Co., 1971, pp. 213–219.

14. See Ulam, Adam B. *The Communists: The Story of Power and Lost Illusions, 1948–1991.* New York: Charles Scribner's Sons, 1992, pp. 125–131.

15. For a detailed discussion of agriculture under Khrushchev, see Medvedev, Roy. *Khrushchev.* New York: Anchor Press/Doubleday, 1983, chapter 15.

16. Khrushchev, Nikita S. "Dlva novii pobedi u mirovoi kommunisticheskii dvizhenia" [For new victories in the world communist movement], *Kommunist,* 1961, no. 1 (January). pp. 31-38.

17. See Abel, Elie. *The Missile Crisis.* New York: Bantam, 1966. See also Ulam, Adam B. *Expansion and Coexistence: Soviet Foreign Policy, 1917–73.* New York: Praeger, pp. 668–677.

18. Brzezinski, Zbigniew K. *The Soviet Bloc: Unity and Conflict.* New York: Praeger, 1960, chapters 9–11.

19. Mehnert, Klaus. *Peking and Moscow.* New York: G. P. Putnam's Sons, 1963, pp. 354–448.

20. For a former "insider's" view of the balancing process involved in party control over army and politics, see Suvorov, Viktor. *Inside the Soviet Army.* New York: MacMillan, 1982, pp. 22–25.

21. Brzezinski, Zbigniew K. "The Soviet Political System: Transformation or Degeneration?", in Brzezinski, ed., *Dilemmas of Change in Soviet Politics.* New York: Columbia University Press, 1969, pp. 1–34.

22. The classic study of the *nomenklatura* is Voslensky, Michael. *Nomenklatura: The Soviet Ruling Class.* Garden City, N.Y.: Doubleday, 1984. See also, Lane, David. *The Socialist Industrial State.* London: George Allen and Unwin, 1986, pp. 56–59.

23. Carriere d'Encausse, Helene. *Decline of an Empire: The Soviet Socialist Republics in Revolt.* New York: Newsweek Books, 1979, pp. 142–155.

24. See Hill, Ronald J. and Peter Frank. *The Soviet Communist Party,* 3rd ed. Boston: Allen and Unwin, 1986, pp. 56–49.

25. Friedrich, Carl J. and Zbigniew K. Brzezinski. *Totalitarian Dictatorship and Autocracy.* New York: Praeger, 1956, revised edition, 1965.

26. See the introduction to Almond, Gabriel A. and James S. Coleman, eds. *The Politics of the Developing Areas.* Princeton: Princeton University Press, 1960.

27. For a penetrating critique of the new Sovietology, see Malia, Martin, "From Under the Rubble, What?", *Problems of Communism,* vol. 41., no. 1-2 (January-April 1992), pp. 89–105.

28. See Kirkpatrick, Jeane J. *The Withering Away of the Totalitarian State. . .and Other Surprises.* Washington D.C.: The AEI Press, 1990, pp. 1–5.

29. See Gross Solomon, Susan. *Beyond Sovietology: Essays in History and Politics.* Armonk, N.Y.: M. E. Sharpe, 1993, pp. 1–7.

30. Gromyko, Andrei A. "Programma mira v deistvii" [The peace program action], *Kommunist,* no. 14 (September), 1975, p. 5.

31. Willerton, John P. Jr., "Clientelism in the Soviet Union: An Initial Examination, *Studies in Comparative Communism,* vol. 30, no. 3 (May-June 1981), p. 17.

32. *Pravda,* March 4, 1981, pp. 1–2.

33. See Ploss, Sidney I., "Signs of Struggle," *Problems of Communism,* vol. 31, no. 5 (September-October) 1982, p. 48.

34. Meissner, Boris, "The 26th Party Congress and Soviet Domestic Politics," *Problems of Communism,* vol. 30, no. 3 (May-June), 1981, pp. 17, 35.

35. See Evans, Alfred B. Jr., "Developed Socialism in Soviet Ideology," *Soviet Studies,* vol. XXIX, 1977, pp. 409-428. Shabanov, Yu. V. *Problemy Sovetskoi Sotsialisticheskoi Democratii i Period Stroitel'stva Kommunizma* [Problems of Soviet socialist democracy in the period of building communism]. Minsk: Nauka i tekhnika, 1969.

36. Egorov, Anatolii G., "Partii Nauchnogo Kommunizma" [The party of scientific communism], *Kommunist,* 1973, no. 2 (February), pp. 48–49, 53–54, and "Kommunisticheskaya Partiia v Usloviyakh Razvitogo Sotzializma" [The communist party in conditions of developed socialism], *Kommunist,* 1976, no. 15, (October), pp. 55–70.

37. See statements by Central Committee secretary Boris Ponomarev in *Pravda*, February 13, 1979. p. 2 and in "Xeopolimost Osvoboditelnogo Dvizheniya Invincibility of the revolutionary movement], *Kommunist*, 1980, no. 1 (January), p. 23.

38. Andropov, Yuri V.,"Uchenie Karla Marksa i Nekotorie Voprosy Sotsialisticheskogo Stroitelstva v U.S.S.R." [The teaching of Karl Marx and certain aspects of the building of socialism in the U.S.S.R.], *Kommunist*, 1983, no. 2 (February), pp. 9–23.

39. Evans, Rowland and Robert Novak, "Gorbachev's Mandate," *Washington Post*, November 1, 1985, p. A 25.

CHAPTER 2

The Beginning of Reform

When Mikhail Gorbachev assumed leadership, the U.S.S.R. was enmeshed in what he would soon describe as "precrisis" conditions. As Soviet society became more open in the late 1980s, Gorbachev's early appraisal appeared to understate considerably the situation. Nevertheless, the new leader was clearly aware that a rejuvenation of the Soviet system was imperative; he later dated the inception of reform from December 1984. Walking on the beach at Pitsunda, Gorbachev and Eduard Shevardnadze (leader of the Georgian republic, who would soon become the U.S.S.R.'s foreign minister), agreed that "things cannot go on this way."[1] In the same month, in a speech on ideological questions, Gorbachev used the terms "acceleration" and "intensification,"* which would become the early hallmarks of the reform process.[2]

In 1988, Egor Ligachev, then the second-ranking figure in the party, would depict the reform initiative as a more cooperative decision by tracing

---

* These terms related to the upgrading of productivity and "intensive" as opposed to "extensive" development of industry.

its origins to the April 1985 plenum of the Central Committee.[3] Actually, neither man was entirely correct. Recognition of the need for basic changes in the system's operation had been growing for years within a sector of the *nomenklatura,* as was demonstrated by the limited intraparty debates allowed during the brief Andropov period. But activation of reform elements did require a decisive impetus from the top.

In the spring of 1985, the most immediate problem appeared to be psychological. To both political elites and populace, the society seemed to be adrift and rudderless. Years of infirm leaders and their unwillingness or inability to disturb the status quo had generated a profound, general pessimism about the country's future.[4] Gorbachev's first task, therefore, was to reverse this defeatist mentality and restore confidence in the political system. His early activism seemed to be just the right prescription for this deadening social malaise.

A common assessment of the U.S.S.R. by Western analysts was that it was First World in military power and Third World in everything else; thoughtful Soviet observers privately agreed. The average Soviet citizen was now becoming more aware of the disparity between East and West in living standards; but more important was the downturn in expectations. Soviet leadership had always pointed to the future and, since the time of Stalin, had provided gradual improvements in material well-being. Now the average Soviet citizen expected material conditions to get worse rather than better. Moreover, the general boredom and conformity of Soviet life left a spiritual vacuum that the frayed ideology of Marxism-Leninism could not begin to fill. Individual initiative was largely confined to the daily routine of seemingly endless lines outside of shops and to dealings *na levo** (with the underground economy) in search of the necessities of life. One of the few amenities offered as an antidote to the prevailing apathy was an ever-increasing supply of Soviet-made television sets. Unfortunately, these frequently exploded, killing or injuring viewers.

Mikhail Gorbachev may have been genuinely concerned with the welfare of the Soviet people. On the other hand, he clearly enjoyed the perks of his privileged position (a few years later, he would spend $9,000 on clothing in one shopping foray in Italy). At the same time, his consistent rhetoric provided a self-portrait of a dedicated Communist and he continued to maintain his allegiance to communism even after the failed coup of August 1991.

Gorbachev's wife, Raisa Maksimovna, was reputed to be even more given to high living than was her husband. She was also said to be a committed Communist; she had been a lecturer in Marxism-Leninism at Moscow State University. Perhaps neither of them saw any contradiction between the personal interests of leaders and the goals of communism. The Soviet elite

---

* *Na levo* (on the left): technically illegal business activities such as bartering or dealing with the "black market."

had always lived well while extolling the glories of the coming classless society; Lenin himself had a custom-made Rolls Royce. But "social justice," like all the other issues, lay sputtering just below the surface. When Boris Yeltsin brought the issue of elite privilege into the open at the XXVII CPSU Congress,[5] he created a sensation, opening a fissure in the body politic that would continue to widen.

It is tempting to regard Gorbachev as a typical product of the Soviet system, a party *apparatchik** with limited horizons. He had touched all the bases on his rise to the top, playing by the rules, never alienating the powerful. He had appeared to be a consummate team player and his coaches and teammates had included such worthies as Mikhail Suslov, Yuri Andropov, and the leading officials of the KGB. In retrospect, it can be argued that it was the narrow horizons of the *apparatchik* that doomed Gorbachev to failure, that rendered him oblivious to the difficulties inherent in the herculean task he had set for the system. However, it must be conceded that from the outset, Gorbachev had a very broad vision of political change.

That vision contained two interrelated levels of analysis. The first pertained to the domestic scene, to the internal operation of the Soviet system. The system must be reinvigorated and made more efficient. This, Gorbachev apparently thought, could be done by working with the existing system, by fine tuning and adjusting it, by breaking the stranglehold of the stability of cadres, and by enhancing the morale and commitment of the masses. An overall blueprint for change was certainly lacking, particularly in regard to the economy. At the outset, Gorbachev's preferred approach to restructuring in all areas was mainly recentralization, rather than the decentralization favored by most would-be reformers.

While Gorbachev's view of domestic requirements was hazy, his conception of the world scene was somewhat clearer and his aims in regard to the former were apparently dictated by the latter. On a number of occasions, Gorbachev stressed that, without reform of the system, the U.S.S.R. could not continue into the twenty-first century as a great power. His use of the term "great power" rather than "superpower" (a status the U.S.S.R. had attained at enormous cost) was not rhetorical or accidental. Gorbachev appears to have had, sooner than any other major world leader, an understanding of the developing diffusion of power in the international arena. The era of the superpowers was fading; neither the United States nor the U.S.S.R. could sustain much longer the burdens of a basically bipolar struggle.

The two superpowers had guaranteed for nearly forty years an uneasy general peace based on the reality of assured mutual destruction and adherence to the principle of inviolability of base blocs (states most

---

* *Apparatchik:* A member of the "apparatus," i.e., a party or government official.

closely associated with each of the superpowers). Now both superpowers were fraying at the edges but the decline of the U.S.S.R. was proceeding at a faster pace than was the case with the United States. Unwilling to state unambiguously the facts of the new situation, leading Soviet spokesmen had already implicitly acknowledged that the world "correlation of forces," the favorable trends of which had been trumpeted so loudly in the 1970s, was turning inexorably against the U.S.S.R.[6]

While military strength had been the foundation of the U.S.S.R.'s superpower ranking, the methodology of warfare was changing. This would not be demonstrated in the field until the Gulf War of 1991, but was already apparent to some Soviet military planners. In a controversial exposition of the problem in May 1984, Chief of Staff Marshal Nikolai Ogarkov had warned that the U.S.S.R. was lagging badly in the development of new military technology and had issued a peremptory warning that Soviet forces "must" be provided with the necessary tools of war.[7] The political leadership had turned thumbs down on Ogarkov's demand and in September 1984 he was dismissed from his post. The U.S.S.R. simply could not afford to engage in a new arms race while its economy was barely able to meet the country's other pressing requirements.

There was also a growing recognition that military power was either counterproductive or irrelevant in the evolving world order. The developing diffusion of power was partly a function of the waning influence of the superpowers, caused largely by the long-term drain upon their economies by stupendous military expenditures. The beneficiaries of the Soviet-American standoff had been the emerging centers of power based solely on industrial strength and efficiency in the exploitation of natural economic advantages. These included Germany, Japan, the European Economic Community, the oil-rich states of the Middle East, even the small, rising Third-World dynamos of the Pacific Rim, Taiwan and South Korea. If the U.S.S.R.'s status as a military superpower was dubious owing to the technological lag, its position as even a great power would be threatened as world power was increasingly tied to purely economic factors.

On the other hand, the U.S.S.R. was still the repository of the world's greatest hoard of natural resources and there was no visible threat to the maintenance of the domestic political system. A way must be found to maximize the U.S.S.R.'s advantages and continue in the game within a context of changing rules. This was Gorbachev's task; the logic of *perestroika* was founded upon the exigencies of national power. From this starting point, a program for systemic revival slowly took shape. But an agenda for reform would be worthless without the leader's ability to harness the system to his plans. Realizing this, Gorbachev started amassing personal power immediately upon assuming office as general secretary.

TURNOVER OF POLITICAL ELITES

Appointment of new personnel had been the tried-and-true weapon of incoming leaders for gaining control of the Soviet system from the time of Stalin. Typically, a new leader would concentrate first on placing reliable figures in key party positions. This was dictated by the party's central role in the system and by the fact that the general secretary's initial power base lay in the party (Andropov was the one exception). Then, with a clear foothold in the party, the new leader would employ the leverage thus gained to expand his influence outwardly to the governmental apparatus and the coercive instrumentalities.

Of course, some leaders were more successful than others and, after Stalin, there were always limits on the extent of power consolidation. However, these limits were undefined. Each new leader was compelled to push toward those limits because election as general secretary did not automatically convey the necessary clout for system domination; a power structure had to be built. Slippage in the process, indicating weakness of the leader, could result in his dismissal. Gorbachev understood the required strategy and the reality underlying it very well, as he was to demonstrate dramatically over the following three and one-half years.

This process of power consolidation was not merely a matter of the leader's personal political ambitions; it also served important systemic purposes. Given the milieu of democratic centralism, the system was geared to something like "one-man rule." Indeed, it seemed to function best when there was a leader with relatively unchallenged authority. Moreover, under conditions of lengthy leadership, the system tended to run down because the leader eventually acquired the appearance of "lame duck" status, with diminished authority; and the beneficiaries of earlier elite turnover tended to entrench themselves in office, inhibiting the rise of new blood in leadership circles. In view of Gorbachev's reform aims, personal and systemic considerations were especially interconnected in the early days of his leadership.

Gorbachev held several significant advantages in the process of elite turnover. First, the "stability of cadres" policy had resulted in aging elites at all levels. A substantial proportion of party officials was due, or overdue, for retirement. Second, the scarcity of powerful figures at the party's highest levels left Gorbachev relatively free to dominate the process of selection. Third, as Andropov's lieutenant and as Chernenko's unofficial "second secretary," he had moved skillfully to place his loyalists in key positions of the central apparatus, assuring needed support behind the scenes.

On the downside, Gorbachev had no protegés at either level of the Politburo or in the Secretariat. Andropov appointees clearly were in a position to assume that Gorbachev owed much more to them than they did to him. Also, Gorbachev's restricted position in the agricultural sector until late in the succession sweepstakes meant that his "organizational tail" was quite limited. Perhaps most important was the fact that two decades of low mobility by the elite had yielded a shortage of highly qualified young administrators to fill the posts of those forced out of office.

Despite these disadvantages, Gorbachev proceeded to carry out what appeared to be the fastest power consolidation by any leader in Soviet history. The first moves came at the April 1985 plenum of the Central Committee. KGB head Viktor Chebrikov was promoted from candidate to full member of the Politburo, obviously a reward for support in the succession decision. Nikolai Ryzhkov, party secretary for the economy, and Egor Ligachev, secretary for party organization, were elected as full Politburo members without having passed through candidate status. Viktor Nikonov, a specialist in the farm sector, was named as Gorbachev's successor in the party secretaryship for agriculture.[8] Following the plenum, Leningrad party chief Lev Zaikov was brought to Moscow to become party supervisor of the defense industry and Sverdlovsk first secretary Boris Yeltsin was named head of the CC Construction Department.

The next meeting of the Central Committee, at the beginning of July, brought more impressive changes. Grigorii Romanov, Gorbachev's principal opponent in the Secretariat, was summarily fired from the Politburo and retired "for reasons of health." Georgia's party boss Eduard Shevardnadze, closely associated with the new General Secretary, was promoted to full Politburo member, after more than six years in candidate status. Zaikov and Yeltsin were named as party secretaries.[9] On the day following the CC plenum, the Supreme Soviet met and Gorbachev executed what an admiring Western diplomat called an "elegant solution" to a ticklish problem.[10] Andrei Gromyko, foreign minister for twenty-eight years, had gained near-total control of the foreign policy establishment, a fact unprecedented in Soviet history; his stature and independence stood in the way of Gorbachev's consolidation of power. The solution involved kicking Gromyko upstairs to the ceremonial presidency and installing Shevardnadze as foreign minister. The move was generally assumed to mean that Gorbachev intended to be, in effect, his own foreign minister; in any case, he was taking direct control of foreign policy. The long-term result turned out to be quite surprising: Shevardnadze exerted a greater impact on Soviet foreign policy than had Gromyko.

In the fall of 1985, the turnover continued. The eighty-year-old prime minister, Nikolai Tikhonov, a Brezhnev protege, retired and was replaced by Ryzhkov, a technocrat who had made his reputation as director of the giant Uralmash factory in Sverdlovsk.[11] Another technocrat, reportedly close to Gorbachev, Nikolai Talyzin, was named first deputy prime minister and head of the state planning agency, Gosplan.[12] Gorbachev's earliest patron in the party, Vsevolod Murakhovsky, who had been the former's hand-picked successor as first secretary in Stavropol, was also appointed as first deputy prime minister. Moreover, five governmental departments were combined in a new structure, Gosagropom, the Agro-Industrial Complex; Murakhovsky was placed in charge of the agency.[13]

In the last week of 1985, Viktor Grishin, who had reportedly spearheaded the last-ditch effort to block Gorbachev's accession to power, was fired as Moscow party chief and replaced by Yeltsin.[14] Grishin was forced to endure the humiliation of listening abjectly at the meeting that sealed his fate as Yeltsin denounced the corruption and inefficiency of the Moscow party organization under Grishin's direction. Meanwhile, regular party elections resulted in a substantial purge of regional secretaries, in preparation for the XXVII CPSU Congress.

When the Congress met in February–March 1986, the Central Committee was reconstituted, with approximately 40 percent new members. Only one new full member, Zaikov, was added to the Politburo. Two new candidate members were elected (Yeltsin had already attained this rank at a pre-Congress meeting of the CC). Five new party secretaries were named, the most important of whom were Aleksandr Yakovlev, Gorbachev's closest associate in the party apparatus and the prime architect of *glasnost,* and Anatolii Dobrynin, longtime U.S.S.R. ambassador to the United States.

Some shortcomings in this selection of officials would later bedevil Gorbachev, but these were not yet apparent. In his first year in office, control of personnel turnover was the leader's principal weapon in gaining dominance of the system and moving it forward. Gorbachev appeared to wield that weapon expertly, conveying the impression that he was fully in control.[15] And Gorbachev's deft handling of the levers of command contributed greatly to rising expectations that the Soviet Union really could be reformed.

PERESTROIKA AND GLASNOST

Under the Soviet regime, each new general secretary was obliged to present a new agenda, promising positive changes without altering the fundamental nature of the system. Periodic sluggishness was inherent in a political order that encouraged concentration of power and long-term leadership, with consequent declines in vigor, policy initiatives, and overall efficiency. Given the modernization goals of the regime, the primary criterion for measuring success was economic performance. Each new general secretary promised improvement and these promises were contained in the leader's agenda, which inevitably involved some discrediting of his predecessor. In Gorbachev's case, Brezhnev was identified as the real predecessor; the latter's period of rule was soon characterized as the "era of stagnation."[16] Since system performance was manifestly unsatisfactory in the wake of this "era of stagnation," Gorbachev faced the task of constructing an agenda that offered not just modest changes but a clear alternative to previous policies. This requirement posed several serious problems.

First, the tendency toward personalizing the criticism of predecessors had always contained a threat to system legitimacy. If the construction of socialism was dependent upon broad underlying historical forces, how could the regime's failures be attributed to the flawed decisions of particular individuals? The alternative seemed to be an admission that the system was defective and that Marxism-Leninism did not, after all, possess the ultimate truth about historical development. This continuing ideological contradiction could be dealt with only by limiting criticism of previous leaders and by maintaining a firm monopoly of communications to inhibit discussion of the basic contradiction. If these conditions were absent, the threat to systemic legitimacy could become very real and immediate.

Second, there was the question of the flexibility and durability of Soviet institutions. Entrenched patterns of control and systemic functioning had the quality of established norms. How much change in behavioral practices was compatible with the overriding goal of systemic survival? Moreover, dissatisfaction with system performance could, under conditions of liberalization, bring to the fore an endemic problem of the Communist party-state, that of unresolved conflict. In other words, the essential question was this: Could the Soviet system reform itself? To judge by his public pronouncements, Gorbachev was confident of an affirmative answer. Further, he professed to believe that such a reform must be carried out.

If it could be assumed that reform of the system was feasible, then a third question had to be confronted: What kind of reform? The issue of reform was initially couched in economic terms and several models were available for consideration from the existing practices of other political systems.

Hungary's new economic model, which involved partial introduction of a free market, had shown encouraging results. China's economic reform was yielding remarkable growth rates; the PRC's plan allowed capitalist enterprise in certain border zones and some production for profit in the farm sector. Both of these models were carefully studied by Soviet economic specialists. Hungary's plan was generally considered suitable for a small country but too risky for a huge, diverse economy such as that of the U.S.S.R. There was a degree of ideological resistance to copying of China's approach; adoption of the Chinese model would mean implicit acknowledgement of the PRC as the "leading" socialist country. There was also awareness of the strains that were beginning to appear in China's economy associated with extremely rapid growth.[17]

Japan's rise to economic superpower status was acknowledged as demonstrating the growing importance of economic factors in the "correlation of forces," but Japan's political system and culture differed so greatly from Soviet experience that it could offer no practicable model for the U.S.S.R.. Late in the game of economic reform, the emerging small economic powers of East Asia, which combined political authoritarianism with the free market, attracted much attention but, by that time, consideration of such an alternative could be only academic.

There was also a model available from Soviet experience and this was the one most favored by Gorbachev's closest advisors on the economy. Within just seven years, Lenin's NEP (New Economic Policy), introduced in 1921, had brought an economy that was devastated by the Civil War back up to its 1914 level. NEP had the advantages of identification with the U.S.S.R.'s revolutionary past and of having been sanctioned by Lenin. However, it had involved a partial reintroduction of capitalism in both urban and rural areas, and any "return to NEP" would meet stubborn resistance from the bureaucrats who were the heirs of Stalin's command-administrative system.

Eventually, the leadership would opt for an approach closely resembling NEP, but arrival at that point would require nearly three years of experimentation and controversy. Meanwhile, some structural change had occurred that was incompatible with an NEP-like approach. Tentative moves toward marketization had helped to spur the development of a determined, intra-party opposition to change and questions of economic reform had become enmeshed in the ideological controversies of the period. Was the Lenin of the NEP experiment the "true Lenin?" Could an NEP-type economic reform be carried out without the political rehabilitation of Nikolai Bukharin, the "old Bolshevik" most closely identified with the policy and whose retrieval from the ranks of "nonpersons" would become a touchstone for party "liberals?" And any reversal of the command-administrative system would necessarily stir the explosive issue of Stalinism.

In retrospect, one of the fascinating "what ifs" of the Gorbachev era concerns this issue. If an NEP-type policy had been instituted right at the start of Gorbachev's leadership, might not economic progress have been achieved without collapse of the political system? Only highly speculative answers can be given to this question but we can be fairly certain about some conditions with a bearing upon it. First, Gorbachev lacked the political strength to initiate such a program prior to the maturation of his power consolidation drive. Second, Gorbachev was uncertain how to proceed and was bombarded with conflicting advice from his economic "experts."

Many Western economists have argued that the place to begin economic reform was the agricultural sector, in order to provide a sufficiency of food products as a buffer against the inevitable disaffections that would come with the restructuring of industry and the comprehensive welfare state. Given the dismal state of Soviet agriculture, prospects for success via this route may not have been very promising. But assuming that it was the most rational course, there was at least one roadblock to its implementation. Gorbachev was a child of the collectivized countryside. His career had been largely built on the structures of collectivization and he appeared to have a strong ideological resistance to the restoration of capitalism among the peasantry.

At the outset, there was general agreement on two points: the necessity for shifting from extensive to intensive economic development and the urgent requirement for upgrading productivity. There was also strong support for, but no general consensus on, the need to introduce market elements, in order to provide incentives and reasonable measurement of real costs of production. The system was slow off the mark on marketization. It was not until December 1986 that the first hesitant authorization was given for cooperatives, which had been a standard feature of Soviet economic life prior to the imposition of Stalin's dictatorship.

Gorbachev chose to concentrate initially upon intensive development and the upgrading of productivity; this approach was promoted under the general rubric of "acceleration." Wasteful investments and incomplete projects had been sore spots for the economy; now emphasis was placed upon maximal usage of existing facilities instead. The problem of technological advance was also addressed, but this mainly concerned long-range goals. Theft of Western technology had become one of the principal functions of the KGB. But however many industrial secrets the KGB stole, the pilfering could not have real effects on the economy unless technological adaptation was mastered. The vital problems concerned management and the work force. Modification of behavior seemed to promise the biggest payoff in economic revitalization and, like Andropov, Gorbachev concluded that this was the place to start. An initial stress upon workers' performance had the additional advantage of postponing confrontation with the structural interests that would be affected adversely by any massive reorganization of the economy; this was important in the early stages of power consolidation.

Absenteeism in the work force was clearly a major factor in low productivity, and alcoholism was acknowledged to be the principal culprit. Andropov's 1983 drive against alcoholism had been short-lived. Gorbachev was determined to make a more lasting impression. Setting an example from the top, the new leader decreed that nothing stronger than fruit juice would be served in the Kremlin, overturning at a stroke the long-standing practice of imbibing vodka at official functions.

Production of vodka and other alcoholic beverages was curtailed sharply, as were the hours when alcoholic products could be dispensed in stores and restaurants. One result was a massive increase in the production of *samogen*, Soviet "moonshine," and sugar shortages in some areas. Another effect was a substantial reduction in state revenues, complicating a budget problem that would not be openly admitted until the middle years of the Gorbachev era. The antialcohol drive and other measures to upgrade work performance did yield some improvement in overall productivity, but this was overshadowed by the negative reaction of workers. There was no perceptible improvement in living standards and "more work for less vodka" became a common complaint.[18]

Despite working-class grumbling, hopes remained high among the population in general, particularly in the ranks of the intelligentsia. Gorbachev's enthusiasm was infectious and his vigorous leadership was refreshing. For nearly two years, reform remained largely rhetorical. Gorbachev's set speeches tended to be long winded and boring in the great Soviet tradition, but he was a master at the introduction of catch phrases and slogans that defined the aims of his leadership. While "acceleration" continued to be much discussed, by the end of 1985 the buzzwords of reform had become *perestroika* and *glasnost.*

Perestroika (restructuring) and *glasnost* (openness or publicity) were not terms invented by Gorbachev. They bore a venerable lineage, having been employed by various political leaders all the way back to nineteenth-century czars. The purpose had always been essentially the same: to manipulate elements at the lower levels of the social order in order to control the middle (the bureaucracy), and preserve and strengthen the power of the supreme ruler at the top. A more extreme version of this "authoritarian populism" had been the centerpiece of Mao's Great Proletarian Cultural Revolution in China. Adopting this time-honored approach, Gorbachev adapted it to the specific problems that had to be dealt with in his revitalization program.

A freer flow of information was deemed necessary for economic development. The prevailing patterns of vertical communication and the system's obsessive secrecy inhibited the exchange of information, particularly on technological innovations, that was essential for economic modernization. The relatively closed information channels also had dysfunctional political effects. This approach bred suspicion of the regime and skepticism about official pronouncements, rendering the "rumor factory" a parallel and uncontrolled counterchannel of communication. Enhanced trust of the regime and a sense of meaningful participation among the masses were required for popular commitment to the goal of general improvement in economic performance. With elaborate control structures remaining in place, it was apparently assumed that the more liberal dissemination of information could be calibrated carefully from above. And so it was, in the early stages. But the effect of a small dose of freedom upon the habitually passive citizenry was not as calculable as anticipated and *glasnost* would eventually acquire a momentum of its own.

Perestroika was a broader concept, although rather rudimentary in outline during Gorbachev's early months in power. Much emphasized in articles and speeches was a "new style" of work eschewing "bureaucratization" and demanding broader and more direct contact with the "masses." In short, an effort was made to change the "boss" mentality endemic to the command-administrative system. Some structural reorganization was also carried out to promote greater efficiency. In general, it was intended to foster more freedom of action by lower-level administrators, curb the ministries that were seen as roadblocks to effective action, and concentrate overall decision-making power in the center. This approach also applied to the party, which had tended to fragment into regional fiefdoms under Brezhnev's "stability of cadres" policy. *Podmena* (interference by party officials in the day-to-day functioning of the economic administration) was discouraged. Although much of this remained in the realm of slogans, the net effect was to reduce the authority of mid-level elites in both party and state, which was much resented. This backlash was to be a major factor in the push for political reform beginning in January 1987.

The most effective structural reorganization of this early period was that of the Foreign Ministry, carried out in the summer of 1986 under the direction of Foreign Minister Shevardnadze and new Central Commitee International Affairs Secretary Dobrynin. The aim here was to realign the ministry's structure along more rational functional lines, an aim that appears to have been largely realized. Other reorganizations had less fortunate outcomes. The concept of "superministries" in industry and agriculture, reflected in the aggregations of power around Gosplan (the State Planning Commission) and Gosagropom (the Agro-Industrial Complex), was a total flop. These experiments demonstrably encouraged the very bureaucratic ills they were designed to eliminate and were shelved without fanfare during the middle years of the Gorbachev leadership.

In retrospect, the most impressive feature of this early period is how little was done, or even attempted, to reorder the rickety Soviet system, at a time when Gorbachev commanded the public's attention and general disillusionment had not yet set in. Nevertheless, some gains were reported on the economic front. The Central Statistical Administration reported rises of 5.7 percent in national income, 5.6 percent in industrial output, and productivity gains of 5.2 percent in industry, 4.9 percent in construction, and 8.9 percent in railroad transportation for the first half of 1986.[19] Foreign observers generally agreed that Gorbachev's initiatives had yielded some economic gains, particularly in regard to absenteeism, and the harvest of 1986 was reportedly the best in years. But the fundamental problems of the economy had not yet been confronted when one of the greatest disasters in Soviet history brought into question both *perestroika* and *glasnost*.

The explosion at the Chernobyl nuclear plant in the Ukraine in April 1986 led to severe setbacks in both industry and agriculture, produced short- and long-range adverse medical effects on thousands of Soviet citizens, left parts of the northern Ukraine and Byelorussia a radioactive wasteland, and exposed to the outside world the serious dangers inherent in

Soviet inefficiency. Despite the disaster, Soviet leaders, short on options, reaffirmed their commitment to nuclear power. Meanwhile, *glasnost* had failed to pass its first major test.

Moscow remained silent about Chernobyl as reports circulated around the world about an unprecedented catastrophe in the Ukraine. The first official statement confirming the incident came from Boris Yeltsin on a visit to Western Europe in early May[20]; given Yeltsin's subsequent record, there may be some doubt as to whether his response to Western reporters was officially authorized. Gorbachev did not speak out publicly until two and one-half weeks after the explosion. When he finally appeared on television to discuss Chernobyl, Gorbachev seemed subdued and was not very forthcoming on the facts.

As increased levels of radioactivity were reported in Northern Europe and then in North America and Western Europe, the Soviet media reported in some detail the heroic, even suicidal, efforts to contain the fire at the Chernobyl nuclear reactor. It was also necessary to accept Western medical assistance for treatment of the casualties, further publicizing the matter and accentuating Soviet backwardness. Alongside the monumental human tragedy, Chernobyl was clearly a public-relations fiasco. However, for the long run, Chernobyl gave an impetus to *glasnost*. Sobered by the negative publicity, the leadership promoted greater openness and subsequent disasters, such as the sinking of a cruise ship in the Black Sea in August 1986, were reported in detail.

Gorbachev was only temporarily deflated by the Chernobyl disaster. By mid-summer, he was back in form—cajoling, prodding, using the general secretaryship as a "bully pulpit" to press the urgency of reform. In late July, he set out on a grand tour of the Soviet Far East, campaigning for both domestic and foreign consumption. At Vladivostok, he enunciated a new East Asian policy of cooperation with countries of the region, designed primarily to neutralize Chinese hostility, but also aimed at allaying general fears about Soviet "hegemonism" (a term used as shorthand for alleged attempts by the U.S.S.R. to dominate the Far East; a term incorporated in the 1978 PRC-Japan treaty). At Khabarovsk, Gorbachev delivered a much-publicized speech on reform in which he said that "I would equate *perestroika* with revolution."[21]

One and one-half years into Gorbachev's leadership, *perestroika* did not look very revolutionary; the structure of the Soviet system was essentially unchanged. But the Khabarovsk declaration did contain two portentous implications. First, there was the implication that the U.S.S.R. was not really revolutionary, a position fully supported by the "stagnation" rhetoric of the early Gorbachev years. Second, it appeared to be a signal that Gorbachev intended to go much further in reordering the system. The general outlines of that reordering remained ambiguous, perhaps purposely so.

Other than the few weeks following Chernobyl, during this early period Gorbachev consistently conveyed the impression of supreme confidence that the momentum of socialist development could be restored, that the Soviet system could be reformed to render it an efficient vehicle of progress. But these assumptions were easier to maintain at a time when real reform had not been attempted, when the powerful forces behind "real, existing" socialism had not been challenged directly.

Gorbachev's confidence was also buoyed by his early successes in foreign policy. He had quickly seized the initiative for a bold new direction in international affairs and his popularity and political standing abroad had repercussions on the domestic scene. In view of the exposed, isolated position of the U.S.S.R. in the world, so clearly revealed in the first half of the decade, Gorbachev's demonstrated skill in the diplomatic arena seemed to make him an indispensable figure as Soviet leader. But power in external relations ultimately depends upon domestic sources of strength. During Gorbachev's first three years in office, the U.S.S.R. was still recognized explicitly as a Superpower and domestic stability seemed largely assured. When both the U.S.S.R.'s superpower status and its domestic stability were brought into question, the Gorbachev mystique, the "Gorbymania" popularized by the Western media, tended to fade rather quickly.

THE NEW POLITICAL THINKING

Gorbachev's achievements in foreign policy were spectacular and undeniable. In some quarters, he was hailed around 1987 as the Bismarck of the late twentieth century. His foreign policy paved the way for the end of the Cold War and thus decisively altered the context of international politics.

For the long run, a sober retrospective assessment must necessarily be more mixed. Gorbachev's policies contributed significantly to the collapse of the Soviet bloc, the dissolution of the U.S.S.R., and the new global instabilities that followed the end of bipolarity. But these long-range effects were not anticipated on either side of the Iron Curtain while Gorbachev stood at the pinnacle of his international prestige and dominated diplomacy among the powers with his initiatives.

The new course in foreign policy was based initially upon a rational assessment of the world "correlation of forces." The United States and the U.S.S.R. were both declining relative to other powers. Under the circumstances, the superpowers could not maintain the status quo centering on the division of Europe that had provided the basis for an uneasy general peace for forty years; other arrangements were deemed necessary. The faster pace of the U.S.S.R.'s relative decline put special pressure upon decision makers in Moscow.

Two particular problems lent urgency to the reevaluation of policy: the growing technological lag vis-a-vis the industrialized democracies that now adversely affected the U.S.S.R.'s position in military hardware and the U.S.S.R.'s dramatic diplomatic isolation. These developments had not gone unnoticed in the last years prior to Gorbachev's accession. There had been at least three striking indications of an ongoing debate within the leadership:

1. The 1983 and 1984 Bolshevik anniversary speeches by Romanov and Gromyko, both of which contained implicit admissions concerning the U.S.S.R.'s declining position in the world "correlation of forces;"
2. Ogarkov's startling May 1984 interview on the military-technological lag, discussed above;
3. The "diplomatist" versus "unilateralist" debate of 1983–84. The "unilateralists," whose principal spokesman was Marshal Ogarkov, argued that the U.S.S.R.'s position in the world depended upon its own resources, especially the maximization of its military power. The "diplomacists," led by Gromyko, contended that the U.S.S.R.'s major gains in the world "correlation of forces" had been associated with diplomatic successes and that diplomacy remained a primary weapon in the Soviet arsenal.[22]

While there appeared to be general consensus within the leadership on the need for a foreign policy overhaul, there was disagreement about priorities. Aleksandr Yakovlev, Gorbachev's closest confidant in the party (who became successively head of the Propaganda Department, party secretary, candidate Politburo member, and full Politburo member between 1985 and 1987), supported a "borderlands" strategy, concentrating on removal of the hostility of countries close to the U.S.S.R. In Yakovlev's view, too much emphasis had been placed upon the superpower relationship

Yakovlev's position sounded very much like traditional "correlation of forces" analysis. Any expansion of Soviet influence on the Eurasian land mass would mean a subtraction of the other superpower's weight in the world "correlation". Indeed, Gorbachev's early emphasis upon the "common European home"—a posited community bound by economic, cultural, and other interests extending from the Atlantic to the Urals—was widely interpreted as a ploy designed to get the United States out of Europe. Appealing to the yearning for a reassertion of Eurocentrism in world politics, the "common European home" theme struck a resonant chord in Western Europe.

But Gorbachev was evidently not thinking in such zero-sum terms. His public statements indicated the assumption of a game of mixed gains and losses related to the ongoing diffusion of power in the world, a game in which the U.S.S.R. could overcome some of its disadvantages through effective diplomacy. In any case, the Cold War could not be terminated solely through pursuit of the "borderlands" strategy.

In late spring 1986 Anatolii Dobrynin, respected in the West as the U.S.S.R.'s most competent diplomat, returned to Moscow after twenty-five years as ambassador to the United States to assume his new posts as party secretary and head of the CC International Department. He lent support to another foreign policy thrust, one already tentatively explored at the November 1985 Geneva summit with U. S. President Reagan. In Dobrynin's view, the great issues—the nuclear balance, confrontation between the United States and the U.S.S.R.—could be settled only by direct negotiations between Washington and Moscow. The superpower connection retained its crucial importance.

Gorbachev proceeded to combine the Yakovlev and Dobrynin approaches, seizing the initiative on virtually all major international issues. Over a period of three years, assisted by the unexpected virtuosity of Shevardnadze, he executed a diplomatic tour de force, seemingly making Moscow the center of international politics. Gorbachev's performance did definitely end the U.S.S.R.'s isolation, reduced the pressure on his country's overburdened resources, and established the international environment needed for domestic reform. But this was achieved by yielding, after hard bargaining, to Western demands or even going beyond what the U.S.S.R.'s erstwhile opponents requested. At the December 1987 Washington summit, Gorbachev accepted the "zero option," elimination of modernized NAT0 missiles in Western Europe in exchange for removal of SS-20s from Eastern Europe, a proposal that had been advanced by Reagan in 1981, generally assumed at that time to be a bargaining ploy or public relations gesture by the American administration. A year after the Washington summit, in a speech to the United Nations General Assembly, Gorbachev promised massive unilateral cuts in Soviet manpower and armaments on the European continent.

A strong rationale had to be advanced for such a radical departure from previous policies. The theoretical formulation supporting the change, under the rubric "new political thinking," had the following main points:

1. Military power per se was declining as a factor in the world "correlation of forces." Excessive reliance on military strength by the U.S.S.R. and accompanying aggressiveness in foreign policy had been counterproductive, resulting in a net decrease in Soviet security. This trend could be reversed only by political means, by negotiated settlements rather than by threat or use of force.
2. The principal factor in world-power relationships was now economic strength. The U.S.S.R.'s major problems were domestic and economic. Solving of these problems required a peaceful international environment

and possibly economic assistance from the advanced industrialized democracies.

3. The main area of confrontation between the blocs in recent years had been the Third World. The economic and technological advantages of the capitalist countries were so great that even if the U.S.S.R. won in all the "national liberation" struggles—in which it was generally losing—this would be insufficient to reverse unfavorable trends in the world "correlation of forces." If the U.S.S.R. was the center of the "world revolutionary movement," then the analysis implied that it was a very hollow center.

4. Quantum leaps in communications and technology were creating conditions of growing interdependence among nations. The great problems—security, the economy, and the environment—swept across national borders and required international cooperation; the nature of the problems, which affected all humankind, transcended national and class boundaries.

5. These changed circumstances dictated a commitment to "universal human values," rather than the traditional class approach of Marxism.[23]

Aleksandr Yakovlev even attempted to prove that there was no conflict inherent in the last point. In his long-range public debate with Egor Ligachev in the summer of 1988, Yakovlev claimed that "universal human values" had been an inherent element of original Marxism.[24] A week earlier, Ligachev had asserted that the class approach was absolutely essential to Marxism.[25]

Anatolii Dobrynin added his great prestige to the drive for theoretical revision, arguing in a spring 1988 speech in Prague that capitalism's staying power had been seriously underestimated, implying that the socialist system would have to live indefinitely with capitalist expansionism.[26]

Some of Gorbachev's advisors, most notably foreign minister Shevardnadze, concluded that the East European satellites cost the U.S.S.R. more than it gained from them and that Moscow would be in a better position if it could rid itself of the bloc. Gorbachev himself did not share this view. While recognizing that new security arrangements were necessary for Europe, he apparently believed until late in the game that socialism and the alliance system could be maintained in Eastern Europe.

All of this was bound to raise the hackles of powerful interest groups in Moscow and create problems of domestic political cohesion for Gorbachev. That adversely affected interests were cool or frigid toward the new approach was evident, although efforts were made to conceal the disagreements. What was not generally recognized, especially in the West, was that the "new political thinking" was basically the obverse of the "restructuring of international relations" stance of the 1970s.

The "restructuring of international relations" had posited an unstoppable decline of the capitalist portion of the world. The "diplomatic struggle of the two worlds," conducted primarily through processes of detente, provided the vehicle for the "imperialists'" graceful acceptance of decline vis-a-vis the socialist camp while minimizing short-term losses. "The new political thinking" dealt with a situation in which the roles were reversed. It was not merely a formula for dealing with relative Soviet decline; it was a prescription for acceptance of "imperialist" domination.

On a deeper level, "new political thinking" posed an even more serious theoretical threat. The Soviet system, grounded in coercion and ideology, had always relied upon identification of an "enemy." "New political thinking" banished the concept of "enemy" from the U.S.S.R.'s theoretical armory. If there was no external threat, what was the justification for maintaining the control mechanisms of the Soviet state? Why should not the Soviet system give way to some other sort of system, ending the oppressiveness of structures geared to a siege mentality? The point was not lost on the "democratic" opposition that gradually developed with the expansion of *glasnost* and on the non-Russian subject peoples of the empire.

"New political thinking" was thus central to Gorbachev's basic dilemma. His power depended on his control of existing Soviet institutions; the more extensive the reform, the less power those institutions would have. "New political thinking" undercut the legitimacy of those institutions upon which Gorbachev's power ultimately rested. Moreover, it brought into question the *raison d'etre* of the entire system. Thus, the stage was set for the later counterattack from the Right, spurred by the alleged dismantling of Soviet power. That drama would be played out in 1990–91, culminating in the dissolution of the U.S.S.R.

THREE TURNING POINTS

On December 19, 1986, Gorbachev called Andrei Sakharov in Gorky, inviting him to return to his former work.[27] Carted off to Gorky in January 1980 after the invasion of Afghanistan, the U.S.S.R.'s leading human-rights activist had spent nearly seven years in internal exile, kept away from Western reporters in the "closed" industrial city northeast of Moscow. Gorbachev could not have chosen a more powerful symbol for the policy of *glasnost*.

Returning to Moscow in something akin to a triumph, Sakharov was again free to give interviews to the Western media. The outside world was impressed and it appeared that Gorbachev had scored another of his public-relations successes, which by now had become somewhat commonplace. But a certain skepticism remained. For several months prior to the sensational move, Moscow had been following a relatively "hard" line on dissent and human rights.

A signal that a threshold had indeed been crossed was not long in coming. Three weeks later, KGB head Chebrikov announced in a front-page *Pravda* article the firing of a subordinate for the illegal arrest of a journalist in the Ukraine.[28] This mea culpa by the head of the security agency was unprecedented in Soviet history and convinced audiences both at home and abroad that Gorbachev was serious about *glasnost*. Many foreign observers thought that Gorbachev had brought the KGB to heel and was rounding out his power consolidation by gaining domination over the secret police but this speculation proved to be premature.

After his return to Moscow, Sakharov became an enthusiastic supporter of *perestroika* and usually endorsed Gorbachev's proposals. The General Secretary's apparent co-option of Sakharov bound the dissident intelligentsia closely to the regime leader, muffled talk of the "Evil Empire" abroad, and gave an impulse to the rising "Gorbymania" in the West. But this coup had its downside. Gorbachev was setting up the leadership of a "democratic" opposition that would later challenge him, once political reform afforded it the opportunity for an official voice.

Three days before the freeing of Sakharov, Dinmukhamed Kunaev had been replaced as first secretary of Kazakhstan's CP. This was not unexpected; Kunaev had reportedly joined the last-ditch effort to block Gorbachev's election as general secretary. But his successor was a surprise. Ignoring the long-standing practice of appointing a member of the largest indigenous ethnic group as first secretary in union-republic CPs, Gorbachev installed Gennadi Kolbin, an ethnic Russian with no experience in Kazakhstan. Almost immediately, rioting by Kazakh students erupted in downtown Alma Ata. The violence mounted over a period of several days and Party Control Committee Chairman Mikhail Solomentsev was dispatched to Kazakhstan's capital to direct operations. Order was restored by the end of the year and Gorbachev did not back down on the selection of Kolbin. However, an ethnic Kazakh, Sagidulla Kubashev, first secretary of Semipalatinsk *obkom*, was named to the post of second secretary, in charge of party organizational affairs.[29] This position had been reserved in the past for an ethnic Russian, usually an outsider.

As a superficial calm was imposed upon Kazakhstan, Gorbachev turned to other, apparently more pressing matters. But another threshold had been crossed, with Gorbachev displaying no recognition of the epochal nature of the December uprising. Nationalism, so long suppressed and denied, was now out in the open and it would subsequently be impossible to force the genie back into the bottle. Under the triple impact of *glasnost*, *perestroika*, and political reform, the contagion would spread until finally it became the most tangible manifestation of the disintegration of the empire.

A third major development was the beginning of political reform. *Demokratizatsiya* really dates from the January 1987 plenum of the Central Committee. By that time, Gorbachev had concluded that resistance to reform was so deep-seated in both industrial and party bureaucracies that it could be overcome only by introducing institutional arrangements that would give the rank-and-file some measure of direct control over their organizational superiors. Prior to the plenum, Gorbachev had proposed secret-ballot, multiple-candidate elections for party posts. The plenum resolution gave only a vague approval to the concept of intraparty democracy but, in his keynote speech, Gorbachev made it clear that he was going to pursue his earlier proposal. He also asserted that such changes would not violate the fundamental principle of democratic centralism, according to which decisions of higher bodies, including those on personnel, were absolutely binding on lower ones.[30]

The plenum also approved in principle a plan for industry that was formally announced a week later as the Draft Law on State Enterprises. All supervisory personnel up to the level of enterprise director were to be elected by the labor collective; however, party organizations were to direct the activities of the collective and its self-management bodies.[31]

Another reform proposal approved at the January plenum was to have more of an impact, both immediate and long range. The first multicandidate elections for deputies to district, city, and regional soviets were held on June 21 and produced the first electoral shock of the Gorbachev era: 57 percent of newly elected deputies in the Russian Republic were reported to be nonparty members.[32] Not only were these elections the most impressive proof to date of a commitment to democratization, they paved the way for the creation of a parliamentary system two years later.

Even as political reform appeared as a beacon cutting through the darkness of totalitarianism, an ominous warning signal was also apparent. "Democratic centralism" and democratization were incompatible, yet Gorbachev insisted upon promoting both and would continue to do so in the following years. Convinced that democratization was necessary to move the various bureaucracies, Gorbachev was unwilling to sacrifice the system's fundamental principle of governance, upon which his own power ultimately depended, and was apparently confident that he could control both processes of democratization and the party apparatus. Yet the more democratization was institutionalized, the more superfluous would the party structures become.

Thus as Gorbachev moved from one political triumph to another, both at home and abroad, he was undermining in practice as well as theory the essential foundations of the Soviet regime. Superbly versed in the mechanics of the system, he failed to understand its intractable nature. Behind Gorbachev's dazzling legerdemain, a few perceptive critics observed not the visage of a system redeemer but rather the face of Aleksandr Kerensky.*

ENDNOTES

1. Shevardnadze, Eduard. *The Future Belongs to Freedom.* New York: The Free Press, 1991, p. 23, 37.

2. *Izvestiia,* December 11, 1984, p. 1. Cf. Medvedev, Zhores A. Gorbachev. New York: W. W. Norton and Co., 1986, pp. 158–159.

3. *Pravda,* July 1, 1988, p. 3.

4. Bialer, Seweryn. *The Soviet Paradox.* New York: Alfred A. Knopf, 1986, p. 109.

5. *Pravda,* February 27, 1986, p. 4.

6. See Grigorii Romanov's Bolshevik Anniversary speech, *Pravda,* November 6, 1983, p. 2, and Andrei Gromyko's Bolshevik Anniversary speech, *Pravda,* November 7, 1984, p. 3.

7. *Krasniia Zvezda,* May 9, 1984, p. 1.

8. Mydans, Seth, "Soviet Chief, Sharing New Rule, Promotes Three to the Politburo," *The New York Times,* April 24, 1985, p. 4.

9. *Pravda,* July 2, 1985, p. 1.

10. Schmemann, Serge, "Gromyko Named Soviet President; Shevardnadze Is Foreign Minister," *International Herald Tribune,* July 3, 1985, p. 1.

11. *Izvestiia,* September 28, 1985, p. l.

12. Ibid, October 16, 1985, p. 2.

13. *Pravda,* November 2, 1985, p. 2.

14. Ibid, December 25, 1985, p. 1.

15. See Sakwa, Richard. *Gorbachev and His Reforms.* New York: Prentice Hall, 1990, pp. 11–14.

16. Ibid, p. 87.

17. See Bogomolov, Oleg, "Menyayushchiisya Oblik Sotsializma" [The changing Image of Socialism], *Kommunist,* no. 11 (July) 1989, pp. 33–42.

18. *BBC Caris Report,* January 24, 1986.

19. *Pravda,* July 20, 1986, pp. 1-2.

20. *BBC Caris Report,* May 6, 1986.

21. *Pravda,* August 2, 1986, p. 2.

22. Strode, Dan L. and Rebecca, "Diplomacy and Defense in Soviet National Security Policy," *International Security,* vol. 8, no. 2 (Fall 1983), pp. 91–116.

23. See Gorbachev, Mikhail. *Perestroika: New Thinking for Our Country and the World.* New York: Harper and Row, 1988, p. 129.

---

* Leader of the Provisional Government, May-October 1917, whose insistence upon continuing the war opened the way for the Bolshevik seizure of power.

24. Moscow Central Television. August 12, 1988. In his book, *The Fate of Marxism in Russia* (New Haven: Yale University Press, 1993), Yakovlev flatly rejects Marxism and dates his conversion from 1987. This raises questions about the sincerity of his views expressed in 1988 which, in any case, involved a bizarre interpretation of Marxism.

25. *Sovietskaia Rossiia*, August 6, 1988, p. 1.

26. *Tass*, April 12, 1988.

27. *The New York Times*, December 20, 1986, p. 1.

28. *Pravda*, January 8, 1987, p. 1.

29. Alma Ata Domestic Service, January 10, 1987, *FBIS*, January 13, 1987.

30. *Pravda*, January 28, 1987, p.1; Bohlen, Celestine, "Gorbachev Presses for Secret Ballot," *Washington Post*, January 28, 1987, pp. Al, A17.

31. *Pravda*, February 8, 1987, pp. 1–2.

32. *Tass*, June 28, 1987.

CHAPTER 3

Perestroika on Trial

In the first six months of 1987, Gorbachev's power consolidation gained momentum. In January, Aleksandr Yakovlev was elected to candidate membership on the Politburo and Anatolii Lukyanov, a former schoolmate of Gorbachev at Moscow State University Law School, was added to the Secretariat and given the responsibility of supervising the security organs. When a young German named Matthias Rust flew a small, single-engine plane across Western Russia and landed in Red Square on Border Guards Day in late May, Gorbachev took advantage of the embarrassing lapse in security to have Marshal Sergei Sokolov fired as defense minister. Sokolov was replaced by General Dimitri Yazov, a supposed supporter of *perestroika* in the military who had been brought to Moscow by Gorbachev in January from the Soviet Far East. It appeared that Gorbachev had taken two giant steps toward gaining control over the coercive instrumentalities. In retrospect, the appointments are more clearly indicative of Gorbachev's poor judgment of men.

When the Central Committee met in June, industrial overseer Nickolai Slyunkov, Nikonov, and Yakovlev were elected as full members of the Politburo. Yazov replaced Marshal Sokolov as a candidate member of the Politburo. The Gorbachev steamroller seemed unstoppable and the leader was confident enough to take an extended vacation in the South, where he worked on the manuscript of his book, *Perestroika,* apparently unperturbed by public rumblings of dissent from Ligachev, Chebrikov, and Ukraine's party leader Vladimir Shcherbitsky. There were indications that Ligachev was emerging as the leader of a conservative opposition but he seemed a less-than-vociferous voice crying in the wilderness. Moreover, at this point his carping served a useful purpose. Neatly positioning himself between Ligachev and the radical Yeltsin, Gorbachev could present himself as a moderate, a proponent of a reasonable approach to reform.

While Gorbachev's continuing power consolidation attracted much attention, far more important were the portents of systemic change. In that relatively uneventful summer, it was becoming clear that the future of Gorbachev and the U.S.S.R. itself were dependent upon four policy thrusts and their interrelationships: economic restructuring, *glasnost,* political reform, and the foreign policy grounded in "new political thinking." A misstep in any of the four could affect all of the others; conversely, a success in one of the areas could have spillover effects in other areas. But economic reform retained its central position. Without economic progress, *glasnost* and political reform could lead to internal turmoil and the U.S.S.R.'s influence in the world political arena would be diminished sharply.

ECONOMIC REFORM

In the years 1987–88, five major measures of economic reform were introduced:

1. In January 1987, quality-control inspectors were assigned to 1,500 enterprises under twenty-eight different ministries.[1] This was an adaptation of the approach used so successfully in the defense industry and was designed to correct the general shoddiness of Soviet goods, which was attributed in large measure to the emphasis on quantity of production.
2. In February 1987, a new wage policy was introduced, aimed at eliminating the prevailing disincentives for individual worker achievement. Differentials up to 24 percent for quality work and 12 percent for productivity were provided. Formerly, when a firm overran its production quota and bonus money was available, it was distributed among all workers regardless of their performance; this practice was now abolished.[2]
3. About 60 percent of industrial enterprises were forced to adopt *khozra-chet* (self-financing) as of January 1, 1988.[3] Individual firms were not

only required to arrange their own finances, they were expected to show a profit. Unprofitable firms could be closed down.

4. A law authorizing limited private enterprise took effect on May 1, 1988, finally making the organization of cooperatives practicable, after nearly eighteen months of dawdling over this aspect of reform.[4]

5. In August 1988, a new policy on agriculture was announced. Individual farmers would be permitted to lease land for up to fifty years and to buy tractors and trucks from the state.[5]

Each of these measures could be justified separately on grounds of economic rationality. Moreover, their measured introduction avoided the dangers inherent in an "all at once" approach to economic reform and left intact general governmental control over the economy, without which political control over the country by the Communist Party would be imperiled. But collectively, these measures had little positive impact upon the economy and serious problems appeared in the implementation of each.

The imposition of quality control led to a slowdown of growth rates without producing any appreciable upgrade of products. The new wage policy produced widespread disaffection among workers already somewhat dubious about *perestroika*. *Khozrachet* was undermined by the simultaneous introduction of the *gossakazy* (state order) system. State orders, requested by the ministries and Gosplan, were expected to account for 50 to 70 per cent of production, with the remainder consisting of direct sales by the firms. By mid-1988, these orders accounted for some 80 percent of production by the affected firms and, in some cases, the state orders exceeded 100 per cent of production.[6] Managers were more comfortable with the certainties of state orders and tended to eschew the responsibility for finding their own consumers. In October, steps were taken to limit the state orders but considerable damage had been done.

The cooperatives initially made headway only in the service sector of the economy, where the impact was substantial; by the beginning of 1989, about 48,000 private businesses had begun operation. But in the state-controlled economy, private enterprise remained an anomaly. When the cooperatives needed credit, they were at the mercy of state banks. For equipment and supplies, they depended upon state agencies or resorted to the "black" or "gray" markets (however, restauranteurs generally preferred the free market for supplies). The difficulties of supply drove prices up well beyond those prevailing in the state sector. There were also inflationary pressures on the demand side. Consumers had amassed enormous savings as they disdained the shoddy offerings of the Soviet marketplace. Now their rubles flooded the economy, chasing scarce and higher quality goods and services.

Soviet consumers wanted the offerings of the free market but they also expected the artificially low prices to which they were accustomed; charges of price gouging arose everywhere. The egalitarian culture had also bred a deep-seated hostility against profit making. Envy and resentment colored perceptions of the cooperative movement, yielding widespread suspicions about anything that smacked of capitalism. Old-line regional leaders opposed to economic reform capitalized upon this consumer backlash, donning the mantle of protectors against exploitation. In January 1989, the government responded to this backlash, imposing regulations providing for the withholding of state credit and supplies for enterprises that did not follow official guidelines on prices and permitting local authorities to impose price controls.[7] Some local officials declared war on the cooperatives and the fledgling free enterprise movement was dealt a severe blow.

Success of the leasing scheme in rural areas was inhibited by demographics and historically induced attitudes. Young people tended to flee the farms for the cities at the first opportunity. The collectives were now disproportionally populated by children and the elderly, unlikely candidates for entrepreneurship. Further, decades of collectivization had bred attitudes of dependency; a steady income from the state was generally preferred to the risks of independent operation. In addition, memories of Stalin's drive against private ownership in rural areas were still alive in the villages, and there was an understandable wariness concerning promises by the Soviet state.

Some economists thought that price reform was the key to economic progress. To the more radical economists, this meant a total freeing of prices, allowing markets to find their own levels. But there was some question as to just how free the markets could be when most of the economy was controlled by the state; few understood that the expression, "Soviet free market," was an oxymoron. Most high state officials conceived price reform as simply the raising of prices by government fiat. However it was to be done, there was clearly a need to address the problem of the disparity between prices and real costs of production. In 1988–89, top officials, including Gorbachev, indicated that price reform would come "soon." But the leadership was unwilling to make this big jump, ostensibly because it would lead to an increase in the budget deficit, a problem now openly admitted. A more important reason was the leadership's fear of the political consequences that might ensue from abolition or reduction of the subsidies for food, housing, and other goods and services.

Thus the economy staggered on, with the *nomenklatura* stoutly resisting radical change. It is quite possible that, through trial-and-error methods, the leadership eventually could have found measures that would produce real, although surely not spectacular, gains for the economy. But the controllers of the Soviet economy did not have the luxury of a lengthy waiting period for the achievement of results. However, the temporizing and half-measures of the Gorbachev administration did not produce the breakdown of the economy, which figured so heavily in the downfall of the Soviet state. That outcome must be attributed to the peculiar structure of the command economy and to the spillover effects of political reform.

The natural phenomena of climate and the geographical distribution of resources conditioned the Soviet economy's operation. Thus, most of the country's wheat was produced in the black-soil region of the Russian Republic, the Ukraine, and Kazakhstan; petroleum extraction was concentrated in the Tyumen region of Siberia and around Baku. The "socialist division of labor," geared to the alleged efficiency of concentrated and specialized production, added to this factor. This principle was often carried to the extreme, with a single supplier of a product for the entire country; for example, certain optical goods were produced only in Armenia, some heavy machinery was manufactured only at the Uralmash complex in Sverdlovsk. Finally, under the command economy, supply, production, and distribution were all determined centrally and linkage networks among system components revolved around the certainties of control from the top. By the end of 1989, *khozrachet* and the cooperative movement had made only a slight dent in the overall centralized system but the attempt to transfer functions from party to state left some doubt among managers about who was really in charge.

The carefully constructed organization of the economy really depended upon centralized political control. As subordinate political units claimed and obtained unprecedented autonomy, possibilities for economic blackmail by regions and by suppliers arose at a time of sluggish production and expected price increases. Consumers naturally reacted to this situation by hoarding, driving prices up on the black market. In late 1989 and in 1990, the distribution system collapsed and the economy went into freefall; the political authorities at the center no longer possessed the power to stop the plunge to disaster.

THE YELTSIN AFFAIR AND THE ISSUE OF STALINISM

The Central Committee meeting of October 1987 was expected to be a routine affair. The retirement of Geidar Aliev, "for reasons of health," was the one major item of business. Aliev, like Gorbachev a protege of Yuri Andropov, had apparently been a supporter of the present leader in March 1985 but had reportedly become an increasingly vocal critic of *perestroika* behind the scenes. But Aliev was in a vulnerable position. Upon his appointment as first deputy prime minister in November 1982 he had been charged with the reorganization of the railway system. Now, in the fall of 1987, the overburdened railways were as close to gridlock as they had been in 1982, making Aliev an easy target. His departure was scarcely mourned by anyone, not even by Ligachev, who had publicly criticized the sectors of the economy for which Aliev was responsible.

Aliev's ouster further strengthened Gorbachev's position within the Politburo, but this was overshadowed by a dramatic scene at the plenum. Central Committee sessions were still closed. The public was provided only with the information the leadership decided to release after the event, and this was especially the case with this meeting. But word of a controversy spread through the Moscow grapevine and party officials were forced to acknowledge it, without immediately giving details.

Apparently, Boris Yeltsin was not scheduled to speak, but had demanded the floor to raise an issue that, according to Gorbachev's later statement, he had agreed to defer until after the seventieth-anniversary celebration of the Bolshevik Revolution. Yeltsin told the Central Committee that he had become very frustrated in his work as head of the Moscow party organization, that he was hindered in carrying out *perestroika* by members of the leadership, especially Ligachev, and asked to be relieved of his duties as Moscow *gorkom* first secretary. Speaker after speaker rose to denounce Yeltsin, with Ligachev leading the pack. Yeltsin's case was put on hold until the anniversary celebration could be completed. After denying the most extreme rumors circulating in Moscow, Yeltsin entered the Kremlin Clinic, reportedly for a heart condition.

Three weeks after the plenum, Yeltsin was forced to leave his hospital bed and attend a meeting of the Moscow city party committee, which relieved him of his post. In contrast to the October 21 Central Committee plenum, the meeting was fully reported in the press. Gorbachev personally led the charge, denouncing Yeltsin for "political adventurism," for "splitting the Politburo," and for promoting a "big boss syndrome." Further, Gorbachev said that "Comrade Yeltsin has put personal ambition above the interests of the party."[8]

Ironically the scene was something of a repeat of the treatment accorded Grishin by Yeltsin less than two years earlier. But Yeltsin's humiliation exceeded that of his predecessor; he was also compelled to confirm publicly everything Gorbachev had said, to perform an act of penance by confessing that his vaulting ambition was responsible for his errors. For reformers, the episode not only made a mockery of *glasnost,* it was eerily reminiscent of the Moscow show trials of the 1930s and cast a pall over the democratic forces.

Although disgraced, Yeltsin was not ousted from the *nomenklatura.* He was given a job as deputy minister for construction, perhaps to send a signal to Ligachev that the victory over his archenemy was not complete. There was much speculation as to why Gorbachev acted as he did. One motivation was probably anger over Yeltsin's breaking party discipline and embarrassing him on the eve of the big anniversary fete. The political effects were more certain. Gorbachev had personally demolished the foil on the left that had allowed him to pose so artfully as a centrist. He would now be subject to increased pressure from the right.

The proof was already evident. Reformists had looked forward to Gorbachev's anniversary speech, hoping that he would make a decisive break with the past. Much to the disappointment of liberal opinion at home and abroad, the speech rendered an ambiguous verdict on Stalinism.

Gorbachev did declare that Stalin had committed "enormous and unforgivable crimes" and promised to continue rehabilitation of his victims. However, he numbered Stalin's victims in the thousands, rather than the millions who actually perished in the terror. Reformers had hoped for a rehabilitation of Bukharin, the champion of NEP, but Gorbachev criticized him and also denounced Trotsky. The party leader also defended Stalin's collectivization of agriculture and endorsed the 1939 Nazi-Soviet pact.[9]

The drive for the accurate rewriting of Soviet history, sparked by liberal historians, was dealt a damaging blow and it was to be a long, cold winter for reformers in general. The censorship agency, Glavlit, was still operating, but censorship was now largely voluntary, with media workers, scholars, and officials taking their cues from the top as to how far they could go safely. Following the events of October and November, the tone of public discourse was considerably subdued; there was widespread fear of a return to the totalitarian past.

At the January 1988 plenum of the Central Committee, Gorbachev proposed multicandidate elections for party posts at the local and regional levels and left open the possibility of such elections at higher levels. Gorbachev clearly indicated his belief that entrenched partocrats constituted a major stumbling block to reform. At the same time, he reaffirmed the contention that his program was in accord with pristine Leninism.[10] Gorbachev's election proposal was indeed compatible with the original conception of "democratic centralism," a principle put forward by Lenin, although not in line with its practice over the decades.

Perhaps alarmed by Gorbachev's January proposals or, perhaps emboldened by the setbacks for democratization in fall and winter 1987, hard-line elements in the party made a daring counterattack. Ligachev was again the central figure and, in the great Kremlin tradition of intrigue, he made his move when the leader was out of town. *Sovetskaia Rossia,* a newspaper noted for a "Rightist" editorial viewpoint, on March 13 published a letter (later more accurately described by Ligachev as an "article") purportedly written by Nina Andreeva, a Leningrad chemistry teacher, just as Gorbachev was leaving on a trip to Yugoslavia.

The letter defended Stalin's leadership and sharply attacked the critical reexamination of Soviet history, which was depicted as undermining respect for the party, the country, and communism. More interesting than the viewpoint on Soviet history was the letter's own history. Reportedly rejected by three publications the previous autumn, the letter apparently had been edited before publication, with only five of the eighteen pages being the work of Andreeva.[11] According to reports circulating in the capital, Ligachev had supervised the entire operation. Following publication in *Sovetskaia Rossia,* Ligachev, now in charge in Gorbachev's absence, lauded the letter and it was reprinted widely over the next two weeks.

Upon his return from Yugoslavia, Gorbachev launched a counterattack. The Politburo reportedly censured Ligachev and the editor of the newspaper but anxious reformers had to wait another three weeks before the Andreeva letter was denounced in an editorial as "an attempt at revising party decisions on the sly."[12] *Sovetskaia Rossia* reprinted the letter on the following day without comment and on April 15 published a full-scale recantation.[13] Subsequently, Ligachev reportedly was relieved temporarily of his duties, with his ideology portfolio being assumed by Yakovlev. Nevertheless, Ligachev took his usual place at the Lenin anniversary celebration on April 22, where new Politburo candidate member Georgii Razumovsky delivered a speech strongly supporting the reform program.[14]

Events in the following month tempered enthusiasm for the apparent victory of *glasnost* in April. More than two dozen members of a fledgling "opposition" party, the Democratic Union, were arrested (the CPSU was still the only legal political party in the U.S.S.R.). Sergei Grigoryants, editor of the unofficial magazine *Glasnost,* was also arrested and his journal was closed down. Meanwhile, several thousand previously banned works by early Soviet authors were cleared by the censors but there was no general approval of forbidden literature.

While proponents of *glasnost* tried to push further the boundaries of what was permissible, there was usually an acerbic response from opponents. For example, in December the liberal journal *Novii mir* had published several poems by the Nobel prize-winning dissident Yosif Brodsky. In March 1988, the conservative newspaper of the Young Communist League published several articles containing harsh personal attacks upon Brodsky, with anti-Semitic undertones.[15] Moreover, Gorbachev himself reminded editors and writers from time to time that there were limits to *glasnost* and made it clear that those limits would be determined at the top. Nevertheless, *glasnost* gained momentum during the year.

Several leading victims of Stalin's terror were rehabilitated; these included Bukharin, Rykov, Zinoviev, and Kamenev.[16] Although not rehabilitated, Trotsky left the ranks of nonpersons. During the summer, even the sacrosanct Lenin was subject to criticism in the "liberal" press for his use of terror, and the text of the Nazi-Soviet pact was published.

Perhaps more important than the growing toleration of expression was the proliferation of unofficial organizations. Most of these were organized for nonpolitical purposes but, whatever their aims, the existence of groups outside the direct control of party and government had a dramatic impact upon the political culture. Some were avowedly political, some organized to support *perestroika,* more formed to promote nationality or other interests. A new kind of politicization was giving reality to *demokratizatsiya*. The unofficial organizations would provide the foundations for the development of political parties in 1989–90.

Amid these changes in the political landscape, the manifestation of *glasnost* that most attracted the public's attention was the XIX CPSU Conference.

THE XIX CPSU CONFERENCE AND ITS AFTERMATH

Apparently, Gorbachev had been highly successful in his power consolidation within the party. He had proceeded steadily with cadre renewal, had broken up the usually corrupt regional aggregations of power, and had obtained clear majorities on both the Politburo and Secretariat. Nevertheless, the party now appeared as the principal obstacle to his reform program. Gorbachev's solution was a revival of the Party Conference as a device for both getting around and reconstituting the Central Committee. The most recent Conference had been held in 1941 and the once-common practice of convening such meetings between party congresses had now become merely a footnote in Soviet history.

In the old days, the Party Conference had had the right to renew up to 20 percent of the Central Committee's membership and to change the party rules. Unable to gain approval for either of these at the May Central Committee meeting, Gorbachev took a different tack. The Conference approved term limits for lower and middle-rank party officials but the limitations did not apply to incumbents. More important was the shifting of functions to local and regional soviets and the creation of a real all-union legislature headed by the president. Two-thirds of the 2,250 members of the Congress of People's Deputies were to be chosen by popular vote in multicandidate elections. The remaining one-third were to be elected by official organizations, including one hundred elected by the CPSU Central Committee. The Congress would meet twice a year to set general policy guidelines and would elect a Supreme Soviet from its ranks. The Supreme Soviet, about one-fourth the size of the Congress, would function as a continuing legislature. Among other powers, the Congress could confirm or reject government ministers appointed by the president, would control budgets, and would elect the president. Union-republic legislatures would have similar powers vis-a-vis executives. The Conference also approved a reorganization plan for the Central Committee that envisaged the establishment of six commissions to oversee its work.

Gorbachev's immediate problem was the "dead souls" on the Central Committee. By the summer of 1988, about fifty members (around one-sixth of the total full membership) had lost their primary positions but could not be dropped from the Central Committee until the next Party Congress. About 40 percent of the Central Committee members elected at the XXVII Congress in 1986 had been new, a substantial change reflecting the rapid turnover of elites in 1985, but Gorbachev had never been able to obtain a secure majority.

Moreover, many of the newly appointed regional secretaries not yet members of the Central Committee tended to rally around Ligachev, perceived as the champion of their institutional interests.

In a crunch, Gorbachev was usually able to get most of what he wanted from Central Committee plenums but the party organization remained a stumbling block for him; hence, the need to devise a way to get around the party resisters. The new legislative framework seemed an ingenious means for accomplishing this purpose.

The complicated two-tier structure appeared likely to enhance presidential domination of the system. Further, local and regional party chiefs were allowed to serve as heads of the soviet executives in their areas. It is not clear whether this was Gorbachev's proposal or a concession to the *nomenklatura* but, in any case, this double duty for mid-level party elites permitted a combination of pressures from above and below upon them. Many observers, including some prominent reformers, concluded that the whole scheme was merely a device for increasing Gorbachev's personal power.

The political reform initiated in the summer of 1988 turned out to be the most important structural change of the Gorbachev era. It provided the legal basis for the articulation of local and national interests and created relatively autonomous structures that would ultimately serve as platforms for the dissolution of the U.S.S.R.. Analysts in both the U.S.S.R. and the West recognized the reform as pivotal but it was generally considered as a major step in democratization of the political system compatible with the continuing single-party monopoly of the CPSU, in line with Gorbahcev's plans. For the average person, there was a more important focus of attention.

The Conference debates were televised and Muscovites were astounded to hear apparently open political discussion for the first time since around 1925. However, other than Yeltsin's speech asking for rehabilitation and Ligachev's harsh reply, key moments of confrontation at the Conference gave the distinct impression of being staged. Presiding, Gorbachev ran the show like a skilled ringmaster and the conclave contributed greatly to the "cult of personality" that he disdained. Supremely confident that he could control the pace of his "guided democracy," Gorbachev evidently was unaware that he was chipping away at the foundations of the system that he headed. The leader's ego was becoming a factor in the increasing fragmentation of the U.S.S.R..

Having yielded a great deal, party conservatives initiated a rearguard action following the Conference. In a speech in Gorky on August 5, while Gorbachev was on vacation, Ligachev rejected movement toward a market economy and insisted upon the "class character" of international relations.[17] Yakovlev replied, defending the market economy in Riga on August 10 and rejecting a "two camps" approach to international relations in Vilnius on August 12.[18] Conflict within the leadership was now quite public and

Ligachev was identified generally as leader of the anti-Gorbachev "opposition." In September, while Ligachev was away from Moscow, Gorbachev struck back suddenly, summoning both the Central Committee and the Supreme Soviet on three days' notice.

The September Central Committee plenum initiated the new commission system. Ligachev and Chebrikov were "kicked upstairs" to become commissioners for agriculture and legal affairs, respectively. Other commissioners were Yakovlev (foreign affairs), Vadim Medvedev (ideology), Nikolai Slyunkov (economy), and Georgii Razumovskii (party organization). Gromyko and Mikhail Solomentsev "retired," as did Central Committee Secretary Dobrynin. Among other changes, Vladimir Dolgikh, a holdover from the Brezhnev era who reportedly had opposed Gorbachev's election in 1985, was dropped as candidate member of the Politburo and party secretary.[19]

Gorbachev succeeded Gromyko in the presidency and it was assumed correctly that he would be elected to the strengthened presidency under the reforms due to be implemented the following year. Anatolii Lukyanov was named vice-president. Boris Pugo, party chief of Latvia and former KGB head in that republic, succeeded Solomentsev as chairman of the Party Control Committee. Vladimir Kruichkov became head of the KGB. Vitalii Vorotnikov was moved a few days after the Supreme Soviet session to the presidency of the Russian Federation. Until the new constitutional arrangements took effect, this would be an empty office; Vorotnikov's former position, premier of the RSFSR, passed to Aleksandr Vlasov, a close associate of Gorbachev.

The party leader's victory was not complete. Ligachev and Chebrikov remained on the Politburo, with much less power but still able to serve as cheerleaders for the "opposition." On the other hand, Gorbachev had won the newly valuable prize of the presidency and perhaps of equal importance had eliminated or neutralized most of the "independents" who had secured his election in 1985 and who owed no obligations to the party leader.

In all the commentaries on the most extensive intraparty coup since Khrushchev's defeat of the "antiparty" group in 1957, there was no indication that Gorbachev had reached certain significant limits. The two meetings in September and October 1988 marked the high point of Gorbachev's personal power. There would be later occasions when the leader seemed to reach new heights through deft maneuvering, application of democratic centralism, or invocation of presidential powers. But all such apparent accretions of power were illusory. While Gorbachev continued to add layers of formal authority, his actions became increasingly irrelevant to the underlying forces that were altering the political system. There were four basic reasons for this diminution of power that coincided with an enhanced institutional role for the leader.

First, in order to rally mass support for restructuring under his direction, Gorbachev needed either to show improvement in the economy or to hold out a credible promise that present sacrifices would lead to future gains. Gorbachev could do neither of these. The average citizen could detect no improvement in his or her standard of living and there were indications that it was getting worse. By the end of 1989, the economy was enmeshed in severe crisis and in 1990 the general standard of living was definitely lower than it had been in 1985.

Second, *glasnost* had set loose forces that Gorbachev was unable to control. The filling in of the "blank pages" of Soviet history, which proceeded apace during 1988, particularly emphasizing the crimes of Stalin, completed the ideological undermining of the regime that had begun with Gorbachev's criticisms of previous leaderships. Further, the proliferation of nonofficial organizations spurred a politicization of the citizenry that could not be directed from above and led quickly to the formation of nationalist and other dissident groups and, eventually, to the rise of political parties.

Third, Gorbachev's foreign policy no doubt contributed to Soviet security but it removed the concept of the "enemy" as a galvanizing force for the political system. U.S. President Ronald Reagan's May 1988 visit to Moscow marked the symbolic end of the Cold War, and Gorbachev's December 1988 meeting with Reagan and President-elect Bush in New York, combined with his UN speech in which he promised massive unilateral arms reductions, appeared to write *finis* to a confrontational Soviet foreign policy.[20] Also, by the end of 1988, it was clear that the Sino-Soviet conflict that had extended over thirty years was essentially resolved. While conducting a diplomacy that was designed to end the U.S.S.R.'s acute isolation, Gorbachev had appeared an an indispensable figure, given his standing in the West. Now that the U.S.S.R.'s basic foreign-policy problem had been solved, Gorbachev's presence was no longer essential. Further, as the Soviets' satellites fell away in 1989 and 1990 and the U.S.S.R. became more dependent upon the United States and the Federal Republic of Germany, foreign policy became a liability for Gorbachev and a source of incohesion for the Soviet system.

Fourth, Gorbachev's political strategy for controlling the system and directing change became increasingly untenable as *perestroika* proceeded. Gorbachev sought to lead both government and opposition, traditionalists and democrats, and maintain something akin to a coalition of the whole. For a time, this seemed to work but, as politicization broadened and new structures for participation began operation, the system became more and more unmanageable. The leader did not meet the expansion of the political system with an innovative strategy. Instead, Gorbachev continued to try to hold all the strands of power in his own hands, a physical impossibility, and to position himself as the indispensable moderate between extremes. Both traditionalists and democrats became disenchanted with this approach and

Gorbachev, faced with the double problem of holding the system together and pushing reform, was unable to come down firmly on either side.

GLASNOST AND THE NATIONALITIES

In his drive for reform, Gorbachev needed all the support reserves that he could muster, in view of the opposition from entrenched vested interests. Here one of his greatest miscalculations concerned the nationalities. Gorbachev assumed that the non-Russian nationalities would be among the strongest supporters of *perestroika,* since the reforms would give them more control over their own affairs. This assumption could have validity only if another assumption proved to be correct. The second assumption, which Gorbachev gave every indication of holding, was that the Soviet-nationalities policy had succeeded to the extent that the non-Russian ethnic groups gave voluntary adherence to the Soviet regime. But the non-Russian nationalities turned out to be far more anti-Soviet than pro-*perestroika.*

Some Western students of Soviet politics have suggested that an early, full-scale program to provide greater autonomy for the non-Russian nationalities might have preserved the regime by providing breathing space for dealing with other problems. The intensity of anti-Russian feelings revealed as *perestroika* unraveled may argue against this possibility, but it seems in retrospect to have been a logical place to start. Instead, nationalities issues were not put on the systemic agenda until the summer of 1989 and then only under the compelling pressure of events. By that time, it was too late to stop the avalanche as the forces of disintegration were moving forward inexorably.

Gorbachev did not take to heart the lesson of the December 1986 riots in Alma Ata, choosing to treat the outbreak as the work of hoodlums. As things simmered down in Kazakhstan and no spillover to other republics was immediately evident, the leader turned to other matters. When eruptions occurred in other republics in 1988 and 1989, Gorbachev treated them on a case-by-case basis, alternating conciliation with threats and vituperation, finally alienating virtually every dissident ethnic group. He did not seem to realize that, failing to recognize the seriousness of the problem until late in the game, he had created the conditions and structures that would maximize its impact.

Glasnost had opened up the nationalities question by the factual revision of Soviet history and by the legitimation of unofficial groups. These unofficial groups were often organized along ethnic lines. Protection of the environment was a common theme[21]; in all of the outlying republics, official recognition of non-Russian languages was an issue. Much of this could have been dealt with in the early phases of *perestroika.* As the nonthreatening complaints went unaddressed, alienation from Moscow grew, setting the stage for escalation of demands. Of course, anti-Russian nationalism was not the sole impetus. Much disaffection was regional, uniting diverse ethnic groups, and tensions between non-Russian groups were frequently fiercer than those between Russians and non-Russians. But political reform provided a platform for the dominant indigenous nationality in each republic to challenge Moscow. The independent executives and legislatures in the union-republics would ultimately provide the legal and structural basis for declarations of sovereignty and independence from the U.S.S.R.

Political reform was, however, only at the gestation stage when the country was rocked by a violent nationality conflict in the South, one that originally had no connection with anti-Russian feelings. The Armenians were among the first to take advantage of *glasnost* and press nationalist demands. Their primary concern was Nagorno-Karabakh, an enclave in Azerbaijan inhabited mostly by Armenians. In January 1988, massive demonstrations were held in Erevan, Armenia's capital, demanding that Nagorno-Karabakh be transferred from Azerbaijan to control by the Republic of Armenia. The enclave quickly became a battleground and, in February, the town of Sumgait, in Azerbaijan, was the site of a massacre of Armenians. Authorities estimated the number killed at thirty-one; an Armenian group put the number at more than five hundred.[22] Fighting continued in Nagorno-Karabakh along with further disorders in Azerbaijan; the Moscow leadership responded by dismissing party chiefs in both Azerbaijan and Armenia.[23] Later in the year, Azeri transport workers blockaded Armenia by stopping all rail shipments into that republic. Gorbachev sided with Azerbaijan in the territorial dispute and, at the XIX Party Conference, a sharp exhange with Armenian delegates left a residue of bitterness. Following a major earthquake in Armenia in December, Gorbachev completed the alienation of the Armenians by charging the republic's Popular Front with provocations. Azerbaijan's Popular Front soon also felt Gorbachev's wrath.

Nearly all of the outlying union-republics organized their own popular fronts, which became the prototypes for noncommunist political parties, something Gorbachev doggedly insisted should not exist. The most active fronts were those in the Baltic states. Baltic nationalism, already revived in 1987, was further inflamed by the disclosure in the summer of 1988 of the secret protocol of the 1939 Molotov-Ribbentrop pact, which had given Stalin the green light to seize the Baltic states. Subsequently, the three union-republics made demands for autonomy on economic, language, and other matters and sought to limit voting rights for recent Russian arrivals which, of course, included all Russian troops stationed in the area. Moscow replied that discrimination against Russians in the republics was a human-rights issue under provisions of the 1975 Helsinki Treaty. Undeterred, the popular fronts closely coordinated their activities and in August 1989 arranged a stunning human chain of protestors stretching across the three republics on the fiftieth anniversary of the Molotov-Ribbentrop pact.

Nationalist disturbances also occurred in the Central Asian republics and in Moldavia during 1988–89. The most violent confrontations in 1989 struck Georgia where, in May, police fired toxic gas into a crowd of demonstrators in Tbilisi. Efforts were made to distance Gorbachev from the police violence, as would be the case with later instances of excessive force; an "official" investigation cleared the party leader of involvement. Shevardnadze, the former Georgia party boss, had been dispatched southward to restore calm.[24] It was later revealed that he was so appalled by the Tbilisi incident that he threatened to resign as foreign minister.

Ukraine was surprisingly late in taking up the dissident banner but in September 1989 the Rukh nationalist organization held its first conference in Kiev. Within a year, Rukh would become the most powerful political force in the republic.

Most ominous was the rise of anti-Soviet nationalism in the RSFSR. Early on, outside observers saw this as a malevolent, reactionary phenomenon because of the publicity accorded to *Pamyat* (Memory), a virulently anti-Semitic organization. *Pamyat* was taken seriously enough that in 1987, while still Moscow party chief, Boris Yeltsin had met the leaders of one of its demonstrations in Red Square. But *Pamyat* was only the radical fringe. Anti-Soviet Russian nationalism was a rather amorphous, many-sided movement represented by numerous unofficial organizations that emphasized Russia's cultural heritage, protection of historical monuments, and environmental issues.[25] This wide-ranging, resurgent Russian nationalism, not democratic aspirations, would become the driving force behind Boris Yeltsin's rise to power.

The upsurge of multiple nationalisms within the U.S.S.R. was given added weight through its relationship to foreign policy. Moscow's treatment of the Baltic republics was subject to certain restraints due to the adverse effect any use of force would have upon relations with West Europe and the United States. The Baltic states constituted a special case because of the 1940 occupation; such Western interest and pressure was lacking elsewhere. But more important were the connections between the U.S.S.R. and the East European socialist countries that influenced political outcomes throughout the bloc.

Engaged in a reform program at home, Gorbachev could hardly pursue an antireform course in the satellites. Indeed, he seems to have assumed that the bloc countries would follow the Soviet lead, albeit at a slower pace, carry out *perestroika,* and remain loyal members of the bloc. However, overt pressure, one way or the other, was incompatible with "new political thinking." The "new political thinking" implied renunciation of the Brezhnev Doctrine,*

---

* Brezhnev Doctrine: The position of the U.S.S.R. enunciated in 1968 that all members of the "Soviet bloc" were responsible for the maintenance of socialism throughout the bloc. In practice, that meant that the U.S.S.R. would not allow the overthrow of Communist control in any bloc country.

which was, in effect, scrapped publicly in early 1988.[26] Gorbachev did quietly encourage reform in East Europe but mostly he acted as an interested observer; he had been disarmed ideologically by his domestic and foreign policy programs.

The nationalist outbreaks in the U.S.S.R. and the dwindling power of the Moscow center greatly encouraged those in East Europe who sought not reformed socialism but an end to communist rule. Whatever might have been his reaction in other cirsumstances, when the critical time came in the last four months of 1989 and Communist regimes fell in domino fashion in East Europe, Gorbachev was helpless. With major upheavals in Georgia and the Baltic republics and lesser crises elsewhere, the U.S.S.R. could not possibly intervene in East Europe. The success of the revolutions in East Europe, mostly bloodless except in Romania, greatly encouraged the supporters of independence movements within the U.S.S.R. and helped trigger the sovereignty declarations of 1990. The collapse of the bloc also produced an angry backlash from the Right, spurred on by the question "Who lost East Europe?" And just at this point leading democrats also jumped ship, convinced that Gorbachev could not or would not lead a real democratic revolution. With his support fading rapidly, Gorbachev looked around desperately for backers and could find them only in the ranks of his enemies.

THE CONGRESS OF PEOPLE'S DEPUTIES

When elections for the new Congress of People's Deputies were held in the spring of 1989, it marked the first time the citizenry had voted freely since the winter of 1917. In view of the novelty of the polling, the elections brought surprisingly little friction, but there were some hitches. Voters in some areas complained that local party bosses manipulated the selection of candidates and the election machinery. In the elections by official organizations, one controversy arose when Andrei Sakharov was left off the Academy of Science slate. This was resolved when a place was found for Sakharov on the Academy's list of nominees.

After a culling process, the Central Committee selected the one hundred representatives of the CPSU. A list prepared by the Secretariat was approved without opposition. Among those named was Gorbachev, who to the very end of the regime never deigned to submit himself to a popular vote. This contrasted starkly with the behavior of Boris Yeltsin, who staged a political comeback by winning election in a Moscow district. Yeltsin gained a stunning 90 percent of the vote in the country's largest constituency.

Other dramatic victories were scored by the democratic forces in large cities, especially Moscow, Leningrad, and Kiev. Several prominent Communists were defeated, including Leningrad party chief Yuri Solovyev, who lost despite running unopposed (under the Soviet system, election required a majority of the votes cast; it was possible to vote against an unopposed candidate by turning in a blank ballot). Gorbachev chose to interpret the elections as a victory for *perestroika* but it was clear that the party had sustained a devastating defeat. The party leader took advantage of this to solve his "dead souls" problem.

At the April plenum of the Central Committee, 110 full and candidate members and members of the Central Auditing Commission "retired,"[27] obviously under enormous pressure from Gorbachev and his close associates in the central party apparatus. Gorbachev now appeared to have attained supremacy over the party. And, despite the spectacular urban wins by the democrats, it seemed unlikely that any faction or combination of groups or even the CPSU would dominate the legislatures, thus enhancing prospects for Gorbachev's control over these new structures.

When the Congress met in May, Gorbachev received a rude shock. He was elected to the presidency with only token opposition but had to endure scathing criticism from the floor during the debate. Strong resistance to Anatolii Lukyanov for the vice-presidency forced Gorbachev to work out a behind-the-scenes deal to secure a Supreme Soviet seat for Boris Yeltsin, who had been left off the Moscow slate, in order to get Lukyanov elected. Gorbachev presided over the early sessions of the Congress in his usual imperious fashion but further challenges from delegates considerably eroded his image as a powerful leader.

The smaller Supreme Soviet proved to be somewhat more amenable than the parent Congress but neither body fulfilled the expectation that it would become an organizational arm subservient to Gorbachev. The government was compelled to compromise on budgetary matters and Gorbachev was forced to admit that military appropriations had been egregiously understated. The problem of the budget deficit, previously denied, was brought to light. And several ministers-designate were denied confirmation by the Supreme Soviet, requiring the leadership to search for suitable replacements.

Meanwhile, Ligachev, despite his diminished power, had returned to the public attack against Gorbachev's policies while widespread miners' strikes—a new phenomenon for the U.S.S.R.—hit Siberia and the Ukraine. When the Central Committee met in July, several Politburo members spoke out strongly against the growing anarchy in the country and the declining influence of the party; a particular complaint concerned the role of the Congress. Gorbachev, angered, promised a purge and it came at the September plenum.

Gorbachev had already sacked the disgraced Solovyev. Now he carried out a major turnover of the Politburo, dumping Shcherbitskii and Chebrikov, two of his severest critics, and Viktor Nikonov, and adding Kriuchkov and First Deputy Prime Minister Yuri Masliukov and four regional secretaries.

This demonstration that Gorbachev could still enforce his will at the top of the party had little effect on the political system as a whole due to the decline in the party's power. Within the legislatures, democratic forces had organized the Inter-Regional Group of Deputies, the first formal opposition in nearly 60 years, co-chaired by Sakharov, Yeltsin, and the historian Yuri Afanasyev. In December, the democrats proposed a debate on repeal of Article Six of the 1978 constitution, which guaranteed the CPSU's position as the only legal political party in the country. Gorbachev engaged in sharp debate with Andrei Sakharov on the issue two days before the latter's death. The proposal was defeated by a vote of 1,139 to 839, but less than half of the Congress members had voted to keep the proposal off the agenda. The rudder of Gorbachev's "guided democracy" was becoming uncontrollable.

THE COERCIVE INSTRUMENTALITIES

In all of the excitement over *perestroika* in the economy and the more visible institutions of government, the absence of *perestroika* in the coercive instrumentalities went largely unnoticed until late in the Gorbachev era. The KGB had played a key role in Gorbachev's rise to power. Moreover, the security organization was well informed about the actual condition of the country and was a major force pushing for *perestroika* at the outset. *Glasnost* and political reform were different matters, however, and KGB head Chebrikov became one of Gorbachev's more vocal critics. But Gorbachev needed the KGB as a last line of defense and was never willing to tackle the secret police head on. While the KGB undertook a major public-relations campaign designed to upgrade its image, it appeared that no restructuring at all of the organization took place prior to the summer of 1990 and any change thereafter was superficial. Gorbachev apparently relied heavily upon Kriuchkov, appointed to head the KGB in September 1988, considering him a loyalist with an open mind toward reform. But Kriuchkov was actually an old-line KGB professional and was to play a leading role in the attempted coup of August 1991.

The armed forces had been cool to Gorbachev's selection in March 1985 and relations did not improve much during Gorbachev's tenure. The party leader had high hopes for Yazov, appointed defense minister in May 1987, who seemed to be an ardent supporter of reform. But Yazov's commitment to *perestroika* turned out be largely rhetorical, and his conservative leanings became evident even before his participation in the August 1991 action. In any case, Marshal Sergei Akhromeyev, the chief of staff, appeared to have more influence with the officer corps. In the summer of 1988, Akhromeyev emerged as the principal public opponent of cuts in the military. When

Gorbachev announced large, unilateral reductions in troops and armaments at the United Nations in December, Akhromeyev resigned on the same day.[28]

Political reform did have some important effects on the coercive instrumentalities. A number of military officers jumped into electoral politics, including Col. Gen. Boris Gromov, the last Soviet commander in Afghanistan, and Col. Viktor Alksnis, soon to be notorious for his role in the sharp rightward turn by the Kremlin in late 1990. In their public political activities, these officers were not controlled by the Defense Ministry in Frunze Street. Further, after Boris Yeltsin became president of the RSFSR, he established close ties with some of the generals, a tactic that would pay off handsomely in August 1991.

The KGB also lost some of its monolithic character. It is instructive that Boris Yeltsin, as acknowledged leader of the Democrats, never called for abolition of the security organ. He wanted his own KGB and got it. It was not immediately clear whether the RSFSR KGB would actually be subordinate to the republic government. In the event, the RSFSR KGB supported Yeltsin rather than the Lubyanka in August 1991.

The MVD (Ministry of Internal Affairs) was one agency subject to Gorbachev-style *perestroika*. After Vadim Bakatin became Minister of the Interior in 1989, he carried out extensive reforms, particularly insisting upon the militia's adherence to legal norms. Unfortunately, his reforms coincided with an alarming increase in lawlessness. Accused of being "soft on crime," Bakatin was dismissed in December 1991, the first victim of the Rightist resurgence that preceded the collapse of the Soviet system.

ENDNOTES

1. *Pravda*, December 31, 1986, p. 2.
2. Ibid, February 17, 1987, p. 1.
3. Ibid, December 29, 1987, p. 1.
4. *Izvestiia*, May 2, 1988, pp. 1–2.
5. *Tass*, August 26, 1988.
6. *Pravda*, June 30, 1988, p. 2.
7. *Tass*, January 5, 1989.
8. *Pravda*, November 12, 1987, p. 1.
9. Ibid, November 7, 1987, p. 1.
10. Ibid, January 28, 1988, p. 1.
11. *L'Unita*, May 23, 1988, pp. 2-3.
12. *Pravda*, April 5, 1988, p. 1.
13. *Sovetskaia Rossia*, April 15, 1988, p. 1.
14. *Pravda*, April 23, 1988, pp. 1–2.
15. *Komsomolskaia Pravda*, March 15, 1988, pp. 3–4.
16. *Pravda*, February 6, 1988, p. l; June 8, 1988, p.1; June 14, 1988, p. 1; August 19, 1988, p. 2.
17. *Sovetskaia Rossia*, August 8, 1988, p. 1.

18. *Pravda*, August 11, 1988, p. 1; Moscow Central Television, August 12, 1988.

19. Quinn-Judge, Paul, "Gorbachev's Stronger Hand," *Christian Science Monitor*, October 3, 1988, pp. 1, 32.

20. Gordon, Michael B., "Western Officials Term Soviet Cuts Significant," *The New York Times*, December 8, 1988, pp. 1, 7.

21. See Dawson, Jane I. "Intellectuals and Anti-Nuclear Protest in the U.S.S.R." in Susan Gross Solomon, ed. *Beyond Sovietology*. New York: M.E. Sharpe, 1993, pp. 116–117.

22. Agence France-Presse, June 24, 1988.

23. Keller, Bill, "Soviet Dismisses Two Party Chiefs in Tense Republics," *The New York Times*, May 22, 1988, pp. 1, 10.

24. Shevardnadze, Eduard. *The Future Belongs to Freedom*. New York: The Free Press, 1991, pp. 193–195.

25. For a detailed account of the rise of anti-Soviet Russian nationalism, see Krasnov, Vladislav. *Russia Beyond Communism*. Boulder: Westview Press, 1991.

26. *Pravda*, March 19, 1988, p. 1.

27. Ibid, April 26, 1989, pp. 1–2.

28. Trainor, Bernard E., "Soviet Split Seen on Military Cuts," *The New York Times*, December 8, 1988. p, 8.

CHAPTER 4

Dissolution of the U.S.S.R.

Pressures on the Moscow center accelerated following the December 1989 meeting of the Congress of People's Deputies. Nationalist agitation mounted, particularly in the Baltic republics and in Azerbaijan. When Gorbachev visited Lithuania on January 10, he was greeted by a crowd of 100,000 demonstrators in Vilnius. Seeking to conciliate the Lithuanians, Gorbachev only inflamed nationalist passions. A tug of war ensued between the party leader and the Baltic republics that was to last, in one form or another, until August 1991.

In the South, the situation early in the year was even more alarming. Fighting continued on the border between Azerbaijan and Armenia and thousands of demonstrators camped out along the Iranian border, demanding incorporation of the border region of Nakhichevan into Iran. Major demonstrations hit Baku, spurred by the republic's Popular Front. One thousand army and police troops were sent in, arriving just as Nakhichevan declared independence. More than a hundred people were killed in Nakhichevan and

Baku and eighty Popular Front activists were arrested. As in Georgia in 1989, an attempt was made to distance Gorbachev from the violence.

Meanwhile, economic conditions were worsening, law and order were breaking down, and there was a strong negative reaction to the Congress vote on Article Six in December. Weakening under pressure, Gorbachev had said during his visit to Lithuania that he would not necessarily oppose multipartyism. The political temperature rose on the eve of a Central Committee meeting in early February when a crowd of 100,000, addressed by Boris Yeltsin, demonstrated in Red Square for repeal of Article Six. On February 6, the Central Committee voted to endorse the repeal of Article Six; Yeltsin cast the only dissenting vote, declaring that the measure did not go far enough.[1] This was perhaps the most impressive manifestation ever of democratic centralism in action, as the Communist Party agreed to surrender the exclusive power it had held for seventy-two years.

Events appeared to be in the saddle and riding Gorbachev. However, there were indications that the leader, confronted with an implacable opposition, had quickly devised an alternate strategy to serve his own interests. At the Central Committee meeting, Gorbachev also gained approval for a strengthened presidency. When the Congress met in March, both of these measures were approved and Gorbachev was elected to the upgraded presidency.[2]

Gorbachev was assisted in his new role by the Presidential Council, a group of advisors evidently scheduled to assume many of the functions formerly performed by the Defense Council, Politburo, and Secretariat. The Presidential Council counted among its members such luminaries as Yakovlev, Ryzhkov, Shevardnadze, Kriuchkov, and Yazov, but also included some appointees not previously connected with the leadership, such as the Russian environmentalist Valentin Rasputin.

From March 1990 onward, Gorbachev would be more an independent executive than party leader. He was restructuring his power base into oblivion, without building a compensating foundation of support elsewhere. Indeed, given the divisions in the democratic forces and their organizational weakness, it was unlikely that his leadership could be sustained by proreform elements.

In late winter and spring of 1990, Gorbachev was preoccupied with nationalities problems and the rebelliousness of the republics. In addition to the continuing impasse with the Baltic republics, there was trouble in Moldavia and violent inter-ethnic conflicts in Uzbekistan and Kirghizia. More serious was the "war of laws" between the center and the republics. By the end of the year, all of the republics had issued some form of "sovereignty" declaration. Most worrisome were the declarations by the Slavic republics.

Closely following the election of Boris Yeltsin as RSFSR president in May, the republic's Congress of People's Deputies on June 8 approved a draft declaration on the primacy of RSFSR laws over those of the union.[3]

Five days later, the parliament gave final approval to the draft. Many Western observers see this action as the crucial move toward the dissolution of the U.S.S.R. If Russia, the heart of the Union, could not be counted upon, what future did the Soviet system have?

On July 16, the Ukrainian parliament asserted its control over the republic's natural resources, demanded reparation for the Chernobyl disaster, and claimed the right to withdraw from military alliances.[4] Eleven day later, Belorussia's parliment approved a similar declaration.

However, it was not immediately clear where these republican claims would lead. Even the Baltic leaders at this point probably did not anticipate the achievement of independence. There are strong indications that the republican leaders were mainly jockeying for position in anticipation of a constitutional revision of the Soviet federal system, looking toward as much autonomy as possible. In any case, Gorbachev's center was shrinking markedly, a development compounded by the rise of Yeltsin as principal spokesman for the country's largest republic.

Yeltsin took the lead in organizing the Democratic Platform, a grouping of radical reformers within the party. Other prominent figures in the movement included Sergei Stankevich, the economist Stanislav Shatalin, and the newly elected reform mayors of Moscow and Leningrad, Gavril Popov and Anatolii Sobchak. While the Democratic Platform sought to push Gorbachev further to the left on restructuring and democratization, it was not useful for him politically. His old balancing act no longer played well for the audience.

This intraparty organization of reformers was, of course, a blatant violation of party rules against factionalism. Ligachev routinely denounced it and Gorbachev would not, and could not, support it. Neither party hierarch influenced the reformers for whom the party was now only a way-station toward overt opposition.

Party fragmentation was also evident elsewhere, always related to the effects of political reform. The republican parties acted more and more independently, forced to compete in electoral politics against the popular fronts and other nascent political parties. This effect was most dramatically demonstrated in the RSFSR. There had been no separate party organization for Russia since 1925; direct control of the RSFSR provincial organizations from the Central Committee building in Moscow's Old Square was a keystone of Soviet rule.

The organizing conference of the Russian Communist Party was held in June. Speeches at the conference were so scathingly critical of Gorbachev that he threatened to resign as party leader. He failed miserably in an attempt to get control of the breakaway organization, which selected as its first secretary Ivan Polozkov, one of the more outspoken opponents of reform in the party.[5] Polozkov, party first secretary in Krasnodar *krai,* once a bastion of

Gorbachev supporters, had personally supervised the demolition of the cooperative movement in that southern territory, closing down a thousand of the ventures. He had been able to do this because Gorbachev, responding to consumer backlash, had given local authorities wide powers to regulate the cooperatives.

The Russian party conference sent shock waves through the CPSU and there was talk of postponing the XXVIII CPSU Congress scheduled for July. However, the Congress did proceed as planned. A postponement would have magnified the image of a party in disarray and Gorbachev had another schedule to meet. He needed to get the Congress behind him before meeting German Chancellor Helmut Kohl on the status of Germany in the post-Cold War world.

Meanwhile, the economy slipped further into crisis. In May, the government proposed an increase in prices, asking for a tripling of the price of bread on July 1 and doubling of prices on other basics as of January 1, 1991.[6] The Supreme Soviet refused to go along and Gorbachev called for a popular referendum on the matter. Price "reform" was thus sidetracked for the moment, but the government announcement had set off a furious spree of panic buying. Moscow, usually the best-stocked city in the country, was especially affected because non-Muscovites shopped in the capital, searching for scarce goods. The city authorities instituted rationing of items in short supply and announced a requirement for shoppers to show IDs, with out-of-towners prohibited from shopping in Moscow. By the end of the summer, the capital would face a severe shortage of bread, evoking ominous memories of 1917.

The XXVIII CPSU Congress

Delegates assembled in Moscow on July 2, 1990 for what was destined to be the CPSU's last Congress. The meeting opened in an atmosphere of gloom and uneasiness, a product of the party's rapidly diminishing role in the society.[7] As expected, there were attacks from both Left and Right upon Gorbachev's leadership but the fireworks were more restrained than anticipated, due in part to an awareness on the right that a full-scale assault could lead to a breakup of the party. Conservatives were somewhat appeased when Yakovlev and Shevardnadze, two lightning rods attracting blasts from the right, announced that they would not be candidates for reelection to the Politburo. The radical reformers held most of their fire until the final stages of the Congress.

An indication that the leadership was losing control over the lower levels of the party organization came on July 4. Gorbachev met with city and district party secretaries, who demanded that he renounce *perestroika* and "put things in order." Gorbachev summarily rejected the demand. On the same day, his position was strengthened when Leningrad party leader Boris Gidaspov, considered a leading conservative, strongly endorsed the transition to presidential rule.

On July 6, Boris Yeltsin challenged the Congress to change the party's name to the Party of Democratic Socialism and compete openly with other parties. He also proposed a reorganization of the party along federative lines and advocated elimination of party cells in the armed forces, police, and KGB.[8] Yeltsin's proposals were not adopted, but his speech apparently had a sobering effect on the party's right.

Gorbachev's conservative opposition did, however, make two attempts to influence the future of the party. A proposal that delegates to any party conference should be chosen from those attending the XXVIII Congress was defeated by a vote of 2,582 to 1,357.[9] Ligachev ran for the new post of deputy general secretary of the party and was defeated soundly by Gorbachev's nominee, former Ukrainian party leader Vladimir Ivashko.

Yeltsin provided the greatest excitement of the Congress when he announced on July 12 that he was leaving the party. He was followed by Vyacheslav Shostakovskii, rector of the Moscow party school, and, a few days after the Congress, by Moscow and Leningrad mayors Popov and Sobchak.

The Congress approved a commission to draft new party rules and concluded by electing a new Central Committee of 412 members, with no candidate members, and a Politburo of 24 members, 15 of whom were leaders of union-republic party organizations. This new Politburo was designed to be virtually powerless and was reminiscent of Stalin's last Politburo, handpicked by the dictator at the XIX Congress in 1952. Unwieldy because of its size, the new Politburo was also handicapped by the fact that most of its members worked outside Moscow. Its power already eroded prior to the Congress, the Politburo was now for all practical purposes displaced by the Presidential Council and rarely met during the second half of 1990.

Following the Congress, Ligachev retired to Siberia, ostensibly to write his memoirs. With Yeltsin and his reformist friends going or gone, there was also no longer a party opposition on the Left. These developments did augur a smoother ride for Gorbachev within the party but this made little difference; conflicts shifted to another arena.

Ordinary Russians tended to ignore the Congress on grounds that the party no longer had any real effect on their daily lives. This perception was essentially correct, but the Congress did have an effect upon the structure of the political system. It brought to completion processes of subordination and fragmentation of the party that were dramatically altering the shape of the Soviet system.

Gorbachev had undercut the party's legitimacy with his ideological revisions; had transferred party functions to the state; had forced the party to surrender its legal monopoly of power; and had turned Politburo membership into a sinecure. The leader had reformed the party into a shell of its former self. The monolithic party designed by Lenin in *What is to be Done?*[10] was no more; what remained was a broken organization unable to provide a stable base of support for Gorbachev or anyone else.

Formally, the aim of establishing presidential rule had been achieved. But the big question now was where Gorbachev, extremely unpopular with the citizenry, could secure the supports needed to sustain presidential rule.

Although prospects for the Soviet system were even more uncertain after the Congress than before, Gorbachev had at least finessed his scheduling problem. Earlier settlement of the issue of Germany along lines dictated by circumstances would have provoked a firestorm at the Congress. Now, with the Congress safely over, Gorbachev could make the required sacrifices.

BETWEEN SCYLLA AND CHARYBDIS

Gorbachev had rejected the idea of German reunification in 1989 and, when such a development seemed inevitable in 1990, had insisted that a united Germany could not have NATO membership. In June, Gorbachev had proposed associate membership for Germany in both NATO and the Warsaw Pact, but the idea had been rejected out of hand by the NATO allies.

Following the XXVIII CPSU Congress, Gorbachev met with German Chancellor Helmut Kohl and hammered out a deal. United Germany would be allowed to have NATO membership but no foreign troops could be stationed on the territory of the former GDR. The German army would be limited to 370,000 troops in contrast to the 480,000 currently in the Bundeswehr and the period of military service would be reduced from fifteen to twelve months. Soviet troops would be withdrawn from East Germany over a period of three to five years and Bonn would pay the costs of relocation.

The key to the deal was Kohl's agreement to grant the U.S.S.R. $3 billion in credits and to pay $750 million for the stationing of Soviet troops in Germany during the remainder of 1990. The FRG would also pay for housing in the U.S.S.R. for returning Soviet troops and would fulfill all of the GDR's existing economic commitments to Moscow. [11] The last obstacle to German reunification was removed when the "two" (the two Germanys) plus "four" (United States, Britain, France, U.S.S.R.) conferees, meeting in Paris immediately after the Kohl-Gorbachev summit, announced a treaty guaranteeing the Oder-Neisse line as the border between Germany and Poland.

It appeared that Gorbachev had accepted a bribe from Kohl, and appearances were not deceiving. The spectacle of the U.S.S.R., until recently the donor of billions to client states, now receiving foreign aid was not lost on political elites in Moscow. And the Kohl-Gorbachev agreement marked the definitive end of the Soviet bloc in Eastern Europe.

When Iraqi forces invaded Kuwait in August, Shevardnadze was meeting with U. S. Secretary of State James Baker in Irkutsk. The two diplomats flew back immediately to Moscow, where Shevardnadze issued a statement denouncing Iraq's aggression and supporting the United States and its allies. Moscow's curtailed position in the world was demonstrated by its willingness to dump one of its client states to firm up its new relationship with the United States. Gorbachev subsequently sought to recover some leverage in the Gulf region by dispatching Presidential Council member Evgenii Primakov, a longtime acquaintance of Saddam Hussein, to Baghdad to attempt mediation in the conflict. The effort failed and the U.S.S.R. would not be a major player in subsequent developments in the Persian Gulf crisis.

The U.S.S.R. had moved well beyond the point where its superpower status was questioned; it was now rather doubtful that the Soviets could exert any real influence on the international scene. Three short years before, Moscow had appeared to be the center of the international political system, as Gorbachev's initiatives dominated the interaction of the superpowers. Now Moscow seemed to be subordinated to Washington as a "junior partner" in its foreign policy and was heavily dependent upon Germany as well as the United States. By the end of the year, the dependence would extend to other countries. Domestic political fragmentation and economic crisis had greatly diminished the U.S.S.R.'s clout in world affairs. And Gorbachev could no longer play the personal role in which he had dazzled the world between 1985 and 1988 since his hold on domestic power was so tenuous. In the late summer of 1990, Gorbachev's problems at home seemed to be personalized in the rising political star of Boris Yeltsin.

Yeltsin had been elected to the executive presidency of the RSFSR in May under the new constitutional arrangements.[12] Gorbachev had attempted to have his close associate Aleksandr Vlasov installed in the Russian Republic presidency and had failed dismally; the autonomous structures that he had created would not respond to his bidding. In the final round of balloting in the RSFSR legislature, Yeltsin had easily defeated Ivan Polozkov, who would be elected in the following month as head of the new Russian Communist Party. Yeltsin's resignation from the CPSU at the Congress in July added to his popularity and he was now in late Summer the unquestioned leader of the anti-Soviet opposition.

Gorbachev was compelled to negotiate with Yeltsin as a virtual equal in a series of meetings in August. There were two major questions on which they sought to attain a consensus. First, what to do about the economy, rapidly descending into chaos? Second, what to do about the union, threatened with possible dissolution as the three predominantly Slavic republics joined others in throwing down the gauntlet to the Center? The two questions were closely interrelated in the negotiations between the two leaders.

Yeltsin had been outspoken in his criticisms of Prime Minister Ryzhkov, a fellow former protege of Andrei Kirilenko in that ex-hierarch's former fiefdom of Sverdlovsk, since his assumption of the RSFSR presidency in May. The main points of contention were the pace of economic reform and the extent of centralized control over the economy.

Yeltsin endorsed the so-called "Shatalin 500-day plan" which had been prepared by a team of economists under the direction of RSFSR deputy premier Grigorii Yavlinsky, with general guidance from radical reformer Stanislav Shatalin. The plan called for full transition to a market economy within five hundred days with strict budget controls; the plan was also projected as the basis for a new union treaty, which would grant greater freedom to the republics on the economy and other matters. Ryzhkov, representing the state economic bureaucracy, held out for a much slower pace on marketization and for continuing overall centralized control over the economy.

Under extreme pressure from the popular Yeltsin, Gorbachev agreed in early August to formulate a joint program for transition to a market economy based on the Shatalin plan. However, the Gorbachev-Yeltsin entente quickly broke down when the U.S.S.R. president on August 9 abrogated the RSFSR resolution on control of the republic's resources. Further talks between the two leaders on August 29 and 30 failed to produce any agreements.[13] But the question of a long-term plan for the economy remained open. All of the republics except Lithuania were willing to accept the Shatalin plan which would have devolved most powers over the economy to them.

Neither Yeltsin's proposals nor Ryzhkov's more conservative stance offered much hope for a solution of Gorbachev's political problems. The Shatalin plan would enhance prospects for aid from the industrialized democracies. However, it would also entail a short-run increase in unemployment, possibly massive price increases, and elimination of the subsidies upon which the Soviet consumer relied. A severe public backlash could be anticipated and it was doubtful that the weakened Gorbachev could survive it. Further, the decentralization envisioned in the Shatalin plan would effectively eliminate the economic basis for political control by the center. The Kremlin would be rendered superfluous.

On the other hand, Ryzhkov's approach held out no real hope for a long-range improvement of the economy, aiming only to hold the line for the present, and the line was rapidly disappearing. It would also cloud the prospects for aid from abroad. Given existing trends, such a limited strategy would surely lead to a further deterioration of the economy, for which Gorbachev would be blamed. If "shock therapy" was terrifying, the alternative was at least more than mildly frightening.

Gorbachev was now reduced to flowing with the strongest current. In early August, the strongest pressures were coming from Yeltsin. Subsequently, the industrial bureaucracies and supportive partocrats applied greater pressure. On September 24, the Supreme Soviet gave Gorbachev new emergency powers to control the economy and authorized him to work out a compromise plan for the economy by October 15.[14] On October 19, the Supreme Soviet approved by a vote of 333 to 12 a compromise plan calling for strict budget controls but less strict than the Shatalin plan, leaving the existing economic machinery in place.

Following the September Supreme Soviet vote, Yeltsin announced that the RSFSR would proceed with the 500-day plan. After passage of the government's plan in October, Gorbachev denounced Yeltsin as an opportunist. Yeltsin replied that Gorbachev's plan was catastrophic and reasserted the claim of the union-republics to direct economic reform.

The economy sputtered on in the direction of catastrophe. The distribution system had broken down and suffering was widespread. Although the farm harvest was down from the previous year, economists calculated that all-around production was sufficient to meet the minimal needs of the Soviet people. But minimal needs were not being met, even with the help of an expanding black market. The centralized economy had dissolved into competing units that undermined the "socialist division of labor." In late October and early November, Gorbachev went begging, touring Western capitals in search of aid, and this was followed in December by more urgent appeals.

Gorbachev signed a nonaggression treaty with West Germany but could obtain no further credits from Kohl; the costs of reunification were draining the West German treasury. The Soviet leader did, however, get $2 billion in aid from Italy and a $1.5 billion credit from Spain. France promised unspecified aid when the U.S.S.R. moved to a market economy and, in November, Italy added to its aid package, bringing its total promised assistance in direct loans and credits over five years to $6 billion.[15]

In December, the heads of government of the European Economic Community nations, meeting in Rome, agreed to send $1 billion in new emergency aid to the U.S.S.R.. By that time, the Soviet economy was in truly desperate straits and relief supplies for food and medicine poured in from various countries. Emergency aid from Western Europe was motivated partially by fear of a flood of refugees from the chaotic U.S.S.R. There were also fears, well founded, that much of the aid would vanish before getting to the intended recipients, given the rise of criminal activity and the debilitated condition of governmental authority within the country. Aid from the West amounted to a patchwork of bandages for the staggering economy but did provide some comfort for the hard-pressed consumers in major cities, and the country managed to struggle through the winter without the worst fears being realized.

Alongside the physical suffering, a profound sense of national humiliation pervaded the country, a sickening awareness of how far the mighty

U.S.S.R. had fallen. Gorbachev's retention of office for another year in these strained circumstances was his last remarkable trick.

RESURGENCE OF THE RIGHT

There were other signs of trouble. At the end of the May Day parade in Red Square, a group of demonstrators unfurled banners denouncing Gorbachev and the leadership, causing Gorbachev and other Politburo members to retreat from the Lenin Mausoleum. On November 7, a man armed with a shotgun fired from about 100 yards away at the mausoleum, where Gorbachev, Yeltsin, and Moscow Mayor Popov, among others, were reviewing the parade. The May Day protest was the first such action in the U.S.S.R. since 1927, when Trotsky had led street demonstrations against Stalin. There had been an attempt by an army officer to assassinate Brezhnev at one of the Kremlin gates in 1969. Like the 1990 shooting, which police said posed no real threat, it had been a botched effort by a single individual. But the marring of both of the main showcase events in the same year constituted a unique connection of circumstances and many Soviet observers regarded this as symptomatic of the general breakdown of authority.

There had been an alarming increase in ordinary street crime and *perestroika* had opened up new possibilities for corruption in the economic sphere. Both kinds of illicit activity were far short of the level they would attain a few years later in the new Russia under Yeltsin but were sufficient to cause ordinary Russians grave concern.

Nationalities and labor unrest added to the impression of a country that was becoming ungovernable. The ancient Russian fear of anarchy resurfaced, leading to speculation about a possible army coup to restore order. The rumors were fueled by major troop movements in and around Moscow and in other areas during the last two weeks of September. Defense Minister Yazov denied rumors of a coup, saying that the troop movements were related to harvest assistance or to preparations for the November 7 parade in Red Square. Most observers regarded the explanations as ludicrous. Subsequently, the September military exercises would be viewed generally as the first dress rehearsal for the coup attempt eleven months later.

November 15 may have been the turning point for a clear rightward movement by the Soviet president. Gorbachev reportedly met with a rebellious group of mid-level military officers, who warned him that, if he did not take steps to assure order, they would do it for him. Over a two-day period, the press was filled with criticism and threats. On November 14, the leading Moscow evening newspaper carried a headline "Revolt in the Kremlin,"[16] and on the following morning, *Izvestia* carried an editorial criticizing the governmental disarray.[17] Most ominous was an article by Marshal Akhromeyev which warned that while the army would respect legitimate political authority, it was "ready to protect our federal and socialist state" from violent and illegal efforts to dismember it.[18]

Faced with a serious threat to his authority, Gorbachev again displayed his skills as an improviser, designing an emergency restructuring plan. Under the plan, the Council of Ministers would be directly subordinate to the president and the Federation Council, composed of presidents of the fifteen republics, would be the chief executive agency. A new security agency under the president would oversee the army, police, and KGB and a Presidential Supreme State Inspectorate would be set up to oversee compliance with orders from the center. The Supreme Soviet gave overwhelming preliminary approval and in December the Congress of People's Deputies agreed to most aspects of the plan but refused to establish the Inspectorate oversight body. The Congress also abolished the Presidential Council.

On December 2, Vadim Bakatin was replaced as minister of the interior by Boris Pugo, head of the Party Control Commission and former party first secretary and head of the KGB in Latvia. Col. Gen. Boris Gromov, the former commander in Afghanistan, was named as his deputy. In effect, the KGB and the army had taken over the civilian police. Viktor Alksnis and his fellow "young colonels" boasted openly that they were responsible for Bakatin's ouster and vowed that they would push Shevardnadze out next. The foreign minister was incensed and also upset over reports that Gorbachev wanted to move him from his important post to the vice-presidency. On December 20, he dropped his own bomb, announcing his resignation to the Congress of People's Deputies, warning that "dictatorship is coming."[19] He spoke of a campaign of vilification against him, complained of lack of support by the leadership in regard to the attacks, and characterized the "young colonels" as "boys with shoulder boards." Gorbachev, visibly upset, denounced Shevardnadze for quitting at a most difficult time; the foreign minister agreed to stay on until a replacement could be found.

More bad news for reformers followed four days later. Gorbachev nominated the conservative Gennadi Yanaev, a veteran party *apparatchik* and former trade-union official, for the vice-presidency. Yanaev failed to win a majority and Gorbachev, insisting that he needed a vice-president in whom he had full confidence, forced another vote confirming the nondescript nominee. Further, Valentin Pavlov, the finance minister whose easy-money policy had spurred inflation, became premier. The original November plan had called for abolition of the premiership and Ryzhkov had been the prime candidate for scapegoat in the economic crisis. In December, Ryzhkov suffered a heart attack, providing a convenient excuse for his "retirement."

Gorbachev's government was now in the hands of hard-line opponents of reform. Along with Bakatin and Shevardnadze, the reformer economists had been cast into darkness. Even Yakovlev was in limbo; it seemed unlikely that he would have any role in the new order of things. The drive for *perestroika* had been replaced by a commitment to *poryadok* (order). Lest there be any doubt about the sea change in policy, Gorbachev pledged to impose direct presidential rule on rebellious areas.

A major test came soon. On January 10, Gorbachev called on Lithuania to end its resistance to central authority. A Committee for National Salvation, which had close ties to Alksnis and the rightist *Soyuz* (union) faction in parliament, made common cause with the army and KGB in an attempt to overthrow the Lithuanian government. On January 13, troops seized the radio and television center in Vilnius, killing fifteen civilians and wounding more than a hundred. Representatives of seven other republics arrived in Vilnius to show support for the Lithuanian government and Yeltsin came himself, signing mutual assistance treaties with the three Baltic republics.

On January 20 Black Beret troops stormed the Ministry of Interior building in Latvia's capital, Riga, killing four people. Gorbachev denied advance knowledge of both attacks but the violence was sufficient to produce a postponement of a planned summit between Gorbachev and U.S. President George Bush. When the summit meeting was eventually held, at the end of July, it was marred by news that six Lithuanian border guards had been murdered execution-style, probably in an effort to embarrass Gorbachev during the conference with Bush.

Circumstantial and other evidence pointed convincingly toward Interior Minister Pugo and KGB head Kriuchkov as major instigators, abetted by the army, of the violence in the Baltic states. Gorbachev did not disavow any of the agencies involved and one conclusion was inescapable: either he approved or he was too weak politically to control the coercive forces formally under his command. Willing or not, he had entrusted the government to those who now pushed policy in all areas sharply rightward.

As these events unfolded, there was speculation among Western observers that Gorbachev, like Alexander II in the 1860s, had become disillusioned due to the failure of reform and decline of central imperial control, causing him to seek more authoritarian solutions. Gorbachev's public statements lent credence to this view. Perhaps more plausible is the idea that Gorbachev was pursuing a strategy of trying to preserve his own position and the union in any way possible. Having alienated virtually all other elements that might have sustained him, he was compelled to ally with conservative forces, mainly Russian, at the steadily shrinking center. These forces were not yet capable of assuming power outright and needed Gorbachev as a front man. Yet he still possessed enormous formal authority and this gave him room to maneuver, making possible one more exercise of his renowned tactical flexibility.

TOWARD A LESS PERFECT UNION?

In the early months of 1991, there were some indications that forces opposed to the new conservative government might be too strong to be ignored. On March 1, the all-union miners organization, a strong supporter of Yeltsin, went on strike, demanding the resignations of Gorbachev and Pavlov. The strike further damaged the economy and the work stoppage continued into May. When conservative deputies in the Russian Congress of People's Deputies tried to oust Yeltsin by parliamentary vote, a quarter of a million people rallied in the streets of Moscow in support of the RSFSR president, defying a Gorbachev ban on demonstrations.

Utilizing his presidential powers, Gorbachev called a referendum for March 17 on the question: "Do you support the preservation of the union as a renewed federation of sovereign republics in which the rights of a person of any nationality are fully guaranteed?"[20] Seventy-seven percent of voters approved, including 71 percent in the RSFSR. However, the Baltic states, Moldavia, Armenia, and Georgia did not participate and voters in Russia, polled at the same time on another question, over-whelmingly endorsed the popular election of the republic's president. The popularly elected president, it was generally assumed, would almost cer-tainly be Yeltsin.

On a number of occasions, Gorbachev said that there were two points on which he would not compromise: the public ownership of land and mainte-nance of the union. The leasing of land eroded the principle of public owner-ship and radical economists were pushing for a full-scale free market in the sale of land. But this was not now a pressing issue; maintenance of the union was Gorbachev's urgent concern.

The president's new Rightist allies might assure him a very tenuous authority at the center but they could not hold the union together. The Baltic states had been chosen as subjects for coercion precisely because they were pushing for independence. Far from being an object lesson to the other republics, the violence in Latvia and Lithuania had driven some of the others into solidarity with the Baltic republics and had given an impetus to inde-pendence or sovereignty claims generally. Gorbachev would not counte-nance a wide-ranging effort to secure the union by force and, in any case, such an effort seemed likely to provoke a civil war. The alternative was nego-tiation, in which Russia played a key role. If the RSFSR adamantly rejected the union, the center would surely collapse. This meant, of course, that Gorbachev was once more obliged to deal with Yeltsin.

Renewed negotiations led to the "nine plus one" agreement concluded at Gorbachev's dacha in Novo-ogarevo near Moscow on April 23. The "nine" (the three Slavic republics, the five Central Asian republics, and Azerbaijan agreed with the "one" (Gorbachev) on the broad principles of a union treaty that would grant extensive new powers to the republics, whose leaders also pledged to accelerate economic reform.

Yeltsin was already aggressively pushing economic reform in the RSFSR.[21] In June, he won an overwhelming victory in the election for the republic presidency, becoming the first popularly elected leader in Russia's history. An ominous note for the future was the six million votes cast for the neo-fascist Vladimir Zhirinovsky, leader of the inappropriately named Liberal Democratic party. This was a substantial protest vote for an extremist party but, at the time, Yeltsin's showing, which also represented a protest against the central leadership, was far more important. As a uniquely representative figure in Russian history, Yeltsin now loomed as an enormous presence in U.S.S.R. politics, his victory emphasizing the vulnerability of both Gorbachev and the conservative partocrats. Without Yeltsin, Gorbachev could produce no union treaty on any terms. The greater Gorbachev's dependence upon Yeltsin, the more suspicious the conservatives would be of the U.S.S.R.'s president. Sensing that the Soviet system as they had known it was in imminent danger, the traditional forces began organizing feverishly to try to prevent completion of the process initiated at Novo-ogarevo.

THE COUP

In June, Prime Minister Pavlov tried unsuccessfully to win parliamentary approval for his assumption of full powers over the economy, bypassing Gorbachev.[22] In July, twelve prominent political and military figures issued a manifesto deploring the "unprecedented misfortune" of the country, denouncing the leadership, and calling for restoration of the unity of the U.S.S.R.. Some of the exact phrases used in the manifesto were to reappear in the proclamations of the August coup leaders. Also in July, Yeltsin issued a decree banning Communist Party organizations within enterprises in the RSFSR.

As preparations for signing of a new union treaty proceeded, the threat from the Right became more palpable. Some of Gorbachev's closest associates, including Aleksandr Yakovlev, warned him about the likelihood of an attempted police-military takeover, as did U.S. President Bush. All such warnings were ignored by Gorbachev, who in mid-August was enjoying a vacation with his family in the Crimea.

Some of the plotters would claim, following failure of the takeover attempt, that Gorbachev himself was a party to the coup. As late as February 1994, former CPSU secretary Oleg Shenin, while still facing charges of coup participation before a parliamentary amnesty freed all of the plotters, claimed that Gorbachev had given approval for a state of emergency in parts of the U.S.S.R. to GKChP (the State Emergency Committee) emissaries Valentin Varennikov and Oleg Baklanov on August 18, 1991.[23] This version of events seems highly implausible, particularly in view of the fact that Gorbachev was placed under house arrest immediately following the Varennikov-Baklanov visit. Rather, it seems likely that Gorbachev was genuinely surprised by the GKChP and that he rejected its demands out of hand, just as he claimed.

Gorbachev's unwillingness to credit rumors of a coup probably can be explained by his confidence that restructuring had eliminated any possibility of a palace revolution. The party had been reduced to impotence, so no threat was anticipated from that quarter. The army and KGB had been placed under the authority of the Security Council (set up in November 1990) and the Law Enforcement Committee (established in May 1991), both of which reported directly to Gorbachev.[24] Further, Gorbachev appears to have been fatuously confident of the loyalty of some of the conspirators.

Clearly, the conservatives preferred to use Gorbachev's formal authority as a cover. When this proved impossible, they acted on their own. Three events spurred the August coup. First, there was the failure of Pavlov's attempt to take over the economy in July. Second, and perhaps more important, was the Central Committee's approval of a new Draft Program in the last week of July. The Draft Program rejected Marxism-Leninism and endorsed the principles of private property, freedom of religion, and a pluralistic political system.[25] Finally, negotiations on the new union treaty had proceeded to the point where it was possible to schedule a signing ceremony.

Gorbachev was due to return to Moscow on August 18 to prepare for the ceremony, set for August 20. Five of the Novo-ogarevo states would be represented, including key players Russia and Kazakhstan. Others were expected to follow suit. As the hard-liners saw it, implementation of the union treaty would mean the end of the Soviet system and they decided to act.

After the delegation from the Moscow group failed to obtain Gorbachev's cooperation, he was prevented from returning to Moscow and he and his family were placed under armed guard. In Moscow, Yanaev called a press conference at which he announced that Gorbachev was too ill to continue as president and that he was assuming the office under Article 127 of the U.S.S.R. constitution. The press conference was also attended by several other members of the junta, who were introduced as appointees to the State Emergency Committee, which would enforce a state of emergency for six months in unspecified localities. Anatolii Lukyanov was subsequently identified as one of the participants in the plot. However, during the coup he stayed in the background, presumably available as an alternate leader should the need arise. Foreign Minister Aleksandr Bessmertnykh simply disappeared; his later protestations that he was ill during the coup were given no credence.

The coup quickly assumed a comic-opera quality. The operation was poorly organized and its leaders made several elementary mistakes, the most glaring of which was the failure to arrest Yeltsin immediately upon announcement of the state of emergency. The colorless Yanaev provided no leadership. Pavlov reportedly spent the entire period of the coup in a drunken stupor. Yazov, Kriuchkov, and Pugo were unable to rally all the forces under their command and Yazov dropped out, supposedly due to illness. Above all, the members of the Emergency Committee conveyed an impression of indecisiveness and lack of direction which encouraged their opponents.

Yeltsin was able to establish a defensive headquarters at the White House, the Russian parliament building, where he was joined by Shevardnadze and other democrats. Mostly unarmed civilians set up a perimeter defense around the White House and some army troops joined them, bringing ten tanks to oppose any assault. Three civilians were killed in clashes with pro-coup forces but the expected major confrontation never came. Pro-coup forces occupied some government buildings in Estonia and Latvia but in St. Petersburg, Mayor Anatolii Sobchak persuaded the local military commander to refrain from action.

The turning point probably came when army forces that were headed for the White House turned back. Yazov and Pugo could not even control their immediate subordinates. As the tide turned, some military and police units switched over to support Yeltsin. Throughout, the Russian KGB was mainly loyal to Yeltsin, keeping him informed of Kriuchkov's plans.

By August 22, it was all over. Pugo committed suicide, as a did Marshal Sergei Akhromeyev. Pugo's fellow major conspirators were all placed under arrest. Massive crowds celebrated the victory in Moscow and other cities.[26]

The outcome was hailed both in the U.S.S.R. and abroad as a popular triumph against hard-line Communists. This was partially true, as the crowds outside the White House did inhibit the coup leaders. However, in the early stages most Muscovites went about their business as usual and the other capitals were quiet. Both political leaders and populace generally assumed an attitude of watchful waiting, making no commitment pending signs of the probable denouement. Prior to the coup, a successful takeover of the entire U.S.S.R. had seemed highly improbable, given the expected resistance by the republics. But the result could have been far different, with better leadership and disciplined cohesion of the pro-GKChP forces. The real determinants of the outcome were, first, the fact that the divisiveness and fragmentation that were affecting Soviet society had infiltrated the coercive instrumentalities; and second, the significant inroads that Yeltsin had made in the military and security agencies.

When Gorbachev returned to Moscow, courtesy of Yeltsin, he appeared stunned, unable to grasp the alteration of the political landscape, still professing to be a Communist, unwilling to blame the Communist Party. But he was soon compelled to face the profoundly different political reality, particularly the vastly enhanced role of Boris Yeltsin.

AFTER THE COUP

In the week following defeat of the coup, several steps were taken that effectively wrote *finis* to the U.S.S.R. The Baltic republics were recognized *de facto* as independent states; Gorbachev resigned as general secretary of the CPSU and dissolved the Central Committee apparatus; and Yeltsin unilaterally banned the Communist Party in Russia.

As late as August 27, Gorbachev still felt able to employ his tactic of threatened resignation, saying that he would quit if the republics did not complete the project of a renewed union.[27] It was an empty threat; Gorbachev's authority had faded to the vanishing point. The failed coup had also resulted in the final discrediting of both the Communist Party and the other central institutions of control. These political structures had lost all valid claims to legitimacy. Under the circumstances, it was rather surprising that four months were required for the playing out of the drama of dissolution.

A shell of central government survived briefly because hope remained for working out a revised union that would satisfy republican leaders and Gorbachev was useful as a mediator and representative of a formal, if largely empty, central authority. Real power had passed to Yeltsin, whose voice was decisive on all major appointments. His RSFSR premier, Ivan Silaev, was named as coordinator of the national economy. In this takeover of the center, the power of the purse was crucial; the discredited central government was unable to pay its bills and the RSFSR central bank assumed the role of U.S.S.R. paymaster. Russia's dominance of the central government produced a new complication in efforts to forge a renewed union. Nevertheless, work on a new federal structure went forward, spurred mainly by Yeltsin and Kazakhstan's president, Nursultan Nazarbaev.

Several new institutions were created, notably a Supreme Soviet representing the republics, replacing the Congress of People's Deputies, and a State Council made up of the presidents of the eleven cooperating republics and the U.S.S.R. president. In November, the participating republics (Georgia still refused to take part) agreed on a draft protocol for a Union of Sovereign States. However, the project was stillborn. On December 1, Ukraine voted overwhelmingly for independence, opting out of the proposed U.S.S. Even a majority of ethnic Russians in the republic voted for independence.

Without Ukraine, the U.S.S. was doomed. Taking account of the new situation, the leaders of Russia, Ukraine, and Belorussia met near Minsk on December 6 and announced formation of a Commonwealth of Independent States, with its "capital" at Minsk. Unwilling to be left out, the Central Asian presidents met in Turkmenistan on December 12 and demanded admission. Finally, on December 21, presidents of the eleven republics met in Alma Ata and signed agreements making them all founding members of the C.I.S. Since all of the constituent republics had left the old union, the U.S.S.R. government was now rendered entirely superfluous.

On December 25, Gorbachev stepped down and the Russian tricolor replaced the hammer and sickle atop the Kremlin walls. Yeltsin took possession of Gorbachev's office in the Council of Ministers building and, finally exacting revenge for the October 1987 humiliation, did not allow Gorbachev time to remove his papers and personal effects. On December 31, the U.S.S.R. was formally dissolved.

ENDNOTES

1. *Pravda*, February 7, 1990, p. 1.

2. Ibid, March 14, 1990, p. 1.

3. Ibid, June 9, 1990, p. 1.

4. *Tass*, July 17, 1990.

5. Ibid, June 23, 1990.

6. *Pravda*, May 25, 1990, p. 1.

7. Lee, Gary, "Sic Transit Party Discipline," *International Herald Tribune*. July 4, 1990, p. 2.

8. *Pravda*, July 7, 1990, p. 4.

9. Ibid, July 10, 1990, pp. 1–2.

10. See Lenin, V. I. *What Is To Be Done?* New York: International Publishers, 1969, esp. p. 121.

11. *Pravda*, July 17, 1990, p. 1; July 18, 1990, p. 1.

12. *Izvestiia*, May 30, 1990, p. 1.

13. *Tass*, August 29–30, 1990.

14. *Izvestiia*, September 25, 1990, p. 1.

15. *Tass*, November 18, 1990.

16. *Vechernaia Moskva*, November 14, 1990, p. 1.

17. *Izvestiia*, November 15, 1990, p. 1.

18. *Sovetskaia Rossia*, November 14, 1990, p. 2.

19. Keller, Bill, "Shevardnadze Stuns Kremlin by Quitting Foreign Ministry and Warning of Dictatorship," *The New York Times*, December 21, 1990, pp. Al, A6.

20. Quoted in Green, Barbara B. *The Dynamics of Russian Society: A Short History*. Westport, Conn.: Praeger Publishers, 1994, p. 162.

21. See Tedstrom, John, "Russia's Radical Reform Program," in *Report on the U.S.S.R.* vol. 3, no. 20, May 17, 1991, pp. 22–26.

22. Mann, Dawn. "An Abortive Constitutional Coup d'Etat?," *Report on the U.S.S.R.* vol. 3, no. 27, July 5, 1991, pp. 1–6.

23. Tolz, Vera, "Defendant Says Gorbachev Approved of State of Emergency," *RFE/RL News Briefs,* February 14-18, 1994, p. 3.

24. Knight, Amy, "The Coup That Never Was: Gorbachev and the Forces of Reaction," *Problems of Communism,* vol. XL, no. 6, November-December 1991, pp. 37–38.

25. *Pravda,* July 27, 1991, p. 1.

26. Keller, Bill, "Gorbachev Says Coup Will Hasten Reform; Yeltsin Leads Celebration in Moscow," *The New York Times,* August 23, 1991, pp. Al, A6.

27. Bohlen, Celestine, "Gorbachev Threatens to Quit Unless Republics Find a Way to Preserve a Modified Union," *The New York Times,* August 28, 1991, pp. A1, A6.

Russia's Administrative Divisions

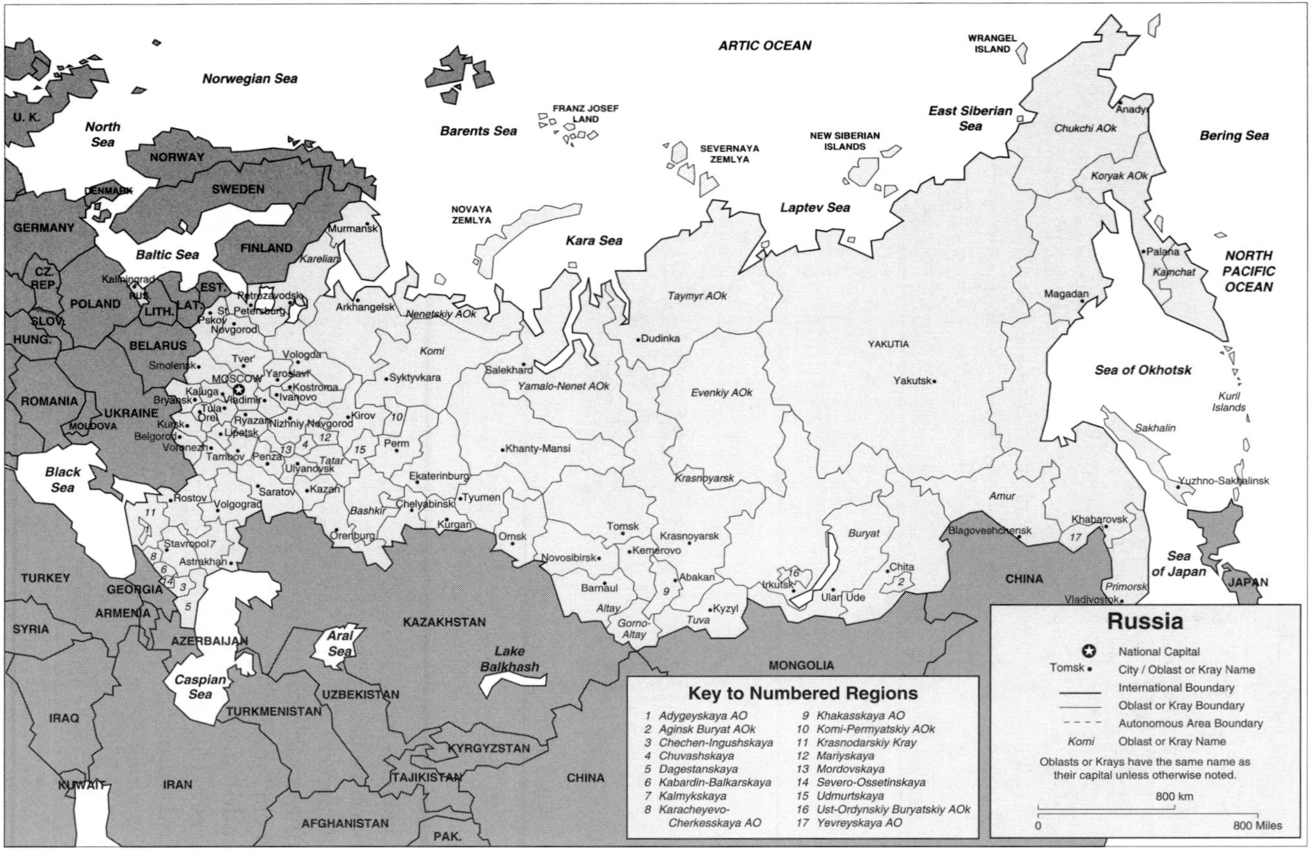

CHAPTER 5

Russia's Politics: The Struggle for Reform

Russia's politics in the post-Soviet period have been in a state of crisis. The obstacles to building a stable, effective, democratic system are formidable. Boris Yeltsin inherited a declining economy whose gross national product fell 40 percent during the period 1990–94. The government operated under an unworkable constitution that conferred absolute authority on a "superparliament." Facing conditions that required strong executive power, Russia was saddled with a constitution that made executive-legislative deadlock inevitable. On top of that, the country was severely divided politically. Yeltsin had crushed the Communist Party at the national level, but Communist forces remained influential at the local and regional levels. There did not exist a nationwide party or mass movement on which the President could rely for support. "Democratic Russia," which propelled Yeltsin and the reformers to power in the Soviet period, fell apart in 1992. The country was fragmented among diverse interests, some of which wanted radical transformation, some wanted limited reforms and some sought a restoration of the old order. But neither the forces for change nor those of reaction were organized nationally to mobilize support for a coherent program. Thus, for more than two years Russia lurched from crisis to crisis while the president attempted to reform the economy and his opponents sought to sabotage his efforts.

The overriding issue dominating Russian politics has been economic reform. On December 3, 1991 Boris Yeltsin decreed: "Starting January 2, 1992, a changeover is to be carried out, in the main, to the use of free (market) prices and rates, formed under the influence of supply and demand, for pro- duction-and-technical output, consumer goods, operations and services."[1] The basic elements of this reform were 1) decontrol of prices, 2) termination of government subsidies to inefficient industries, and 3) privatization of state- owned enterprises. Inevitably, efforts to transform a command economy into a market economy caused widespread hardship. Prices, which for decades had been held artificially low, rose sharply, diminishing the purchasing power of many. Pensioners on fixed income were especially hard hit. Officially, unemployment remained low, but hidden unemployment and underemployment rose steadily. A comparatively small number of entrepre- neurs prospered, some spectacularly so. A large segment of the public was outraged by the conspicuous wealth of the few and the affront to egalitarian- ism produced by nascent capitalism. The hardships produced by reform gave currency to the expression "shock therapy" for Yeltsin's program. During 1992 and 1993, the opposition to Yeltsin became organized in the two branch- es of parliament, the Congress of People's Deputies and the Supreme Soviet.

While economic reform was the main issue in Russian politics, it was by no means the only one. Corruption and crime became rampant. The term "mafiya" referred to the proliferation of gangs, smuggling and theft through- out the country.[2] There developed a strong nationalist backlash to the col- lapse of the Soviet Union and the decline of Soviet power and influence throughout the world. Many nationalists resented what they saw as Yeltsin's foreign policy of accommodation to the West and the United States in partic- ular. Some refused to accept the permanence of the independence of the non- Russian republics and demanded a stronger policy to bring the new states of "the near abroad" under Russian domination. Then there were those who criticized Yeltsin's style, his authoritarian actions, his refusal to consult and compromise. In a word, notwithstanding his immense popularity Yeltsin was a controversial figure, pursuing controversial policies in a political framework where there were no clearly established rules of the game.

YELTSIN VERSUS PARLIAMENT

The political structures that governed newly independent Russia were created in the Soviet era. Some were established by the 1978 constitution (a modified version of the 1977 Soviet constitution). Others were created by amendments to that constitution.[3] The result was a hodgepodge arrangement. The major institutions were the presidency, a two-tiered parliament (the Congress of People's Deputies and Supreme Soviet) and a Constitutional Court. Boris Yeltsin and Aleksandr Rutskoi were elected president and vice-president, respectively, in June 1991 for a term of five years. Both parliamentary bodies were elected in 1990, also for a five-year term. This parliamentary arrangement was created in the Soviet period and was modeled after corresponding structures for the U.S.S.R. The Congress of People's Deputies met only a few times annually and chose from among its membership a smaller body, the Supreme Soviet as the principal legislative organ of government. A Constitutional Court of fifteen judges (elected for life) was established in July 1991. Valerii Zorkin was selected to be its first chairman.

As suggested above, this constitutional arrangement was unworkable. It suffered from several serious flaws. First, it was a patchwork arrangement made over a period of years without any consistency or coherent constitutional principles. Russia's constitution came into being without a national debate, lacking consensus or national endorsement. Only Yeltsin's election as president brought a semblance of legitimacy to Russian government. Most seriously flawed was the legislative branch of government. The Congress of People's Deputies was legally supreme, the highest organ of state power. It alone could amend the constitution. The Congress could determine the general lines of foreign and domestic policy, and it elected from its membership the Supreme Soviet, which both legislated and controlled the government. The president's cabinet (the Council of Ministers) had to be approved by the Supreme Soviet. The Congress could enlarge or diminish presidential power, or even do away with the office entirely. It could also impeach the president.

The Congress was too unwieldy to be an effective legislature. Its full complement of members totaled approximately 1,050. The Supreme Soviet, which sat from six to eight months, numbered 250 deputies. Elected in 1990 when the Communist Party still dominated Soviet politics, the Congress of People's Deputies and Supreme Soviet suffered from the illegitimacy that attached to all Soviet-era institutions.

There existed no mechanisms by which differences between the executive and legislative branches of government could become reconciled. A party system might have done the job, but none existed. Inevitably, as the Yeltsin-Gaidar reforms adversely affected economic interests (bureaucrats, industrial managers, Communists), all strongly represented in the parliament, the conditions were created for a fierce struggle between the two branches of government.

Leading the opposition to Yeltsin were Ruslan Khasbulatov, speaker of the Russian parliament, and Vice-President Aleksandr Rutskoi. There was some irony in the fact that these two politicians became bitter opponents of

the president because both had achieved high political office as Yeltsin's protegés. Khasbulatov was Yeltsin's hand-picked successor and parliamentary
speaker in 1991, and Rutskoi was Yeltsin's choice for vice-presidential candidate. Less than a fortnight after the beginning of economic reform,
Khasbulatov called for the replacement of the government by the Supreme
Soviet. On January 30, Rutskoi joined in the attack: "The country today is not
simply in a state of crisis but in a political and, most importantly, an economic and social impasse caused . . . by the government."[4] For Rutskoi the
central economic problem was damage to the industries of the military-
industrial complex due to the termination of government subsidies; for
Khasbulatov it was the harm to the public of rapidly rising prices. Ultimately,
Yeltsin's reforms threatened to change the structure of property ownership in
Russia and to transfer the wealth and privileges of the old *nomenklatura* to a
new class of entrepreneurs. Parliament became the vehicle for resistance to
this transformation.

But more than economic transformation was at stake. Khasbulatov
increasingly became the spokesman for the constitutional position that government should be controlled not by the executive, but the legislature. He
was particularly critical of Yeltsin's assumption of the office of prime minister as well as president. Rutskoi initially supported Yeltsin on the constitutional issue, but as the struggle over policy grew more intense, he eventually
threw in his lot with the parliament against the president.

This struggle was fought out intensely in four sessions of the Congress of
People's Deputies, the sixth and seventh in 1992 and the eighth and ninth in
1993. On April 6, 1992 the Congress of People's Deputies convened its sixth
Congress, the first to be held since the Soviet collapse.[5] The deputies formed
four blocs: one, composed of approximately 300 deputies, supported the
president's reforms; another, numbering about 310 deputies, opposed the
government; a centrist group of approximately 150 deputies favored some
reform but less than Yeltsin; and a group of 285 shifted position in the voting
and were referred to as "the swamp."[6] Yeltsin opponents wanted to termi-
nate the special powers given to him in 1991, to force him to give up the office
of prime minister and to force a modification of the reforms. In the end they
failed to achieve any of these objectives because they were outmaneuvered by
Yeltsin and his supporters. Yeltsin vigorously defended his program, admit-
ting, "No breakthrough has taken place as yet." He called for a strong executive branch as the "guarantor of the preservation of Russia's integrity . . ."[7]
When the Congress threatened to lower taxes and increase social benefits
the cabinet said it would resign. The ploy worked. In the end, the Congress
was forced to accommodate the government because Yeltsin's prestige at
home and abroad remained high and there was no real alternative to his
leadership. On some issues it remained obdurate, such as defeating a measure that would have permitted the buying and selling of land. But Yeltsin

was victorious on the major issues. His emergency powers were left intact and he secured endorsement of his economic reforms. Even the choice of name for the country proved to be highly contentious, so the Congress produced a hybrid compromise—"Russian Federation-Russia."

Although he prevailed, Yeltsin's victory was only temporary. Clearly a substantial core of opponents existed. The issue of a new constitution proved to be so contentious that it had to be deferred. The question of presidential powers was not settled, only postponed. *Izvestiya* described the sixth Congress as "a two-week political spectacle that was by turns a drama, a farce, and, in effect, a theater of the absurd . . . This government and this Congress are incompatible."[8]

As a strategist, Yeltsin eluded simple description. He could be decisive and aggressive as when he attacked the Communist Party in 1987 and left it in 1990 or when he resisted the August coup in 1991. But his record shows also a capacity to compromise and, if necessary, back down. In the aftermath of the sixth Congress he found it expedient to accommodate his critics in the parliament.

In the face of a powerful coalition of Communist and nationalist forces—commonly referred to as the "red-brown" alliance—Yeltsin attempted to maintain parliamentary support by aligning with a new centrist group known as the Civic Union. Formed by the coalition of three centrist political parties in June, the Civic Union represented the industrialists of Russia who wanted above all to maintain state support for the nation's industries.[9] While not opposed to reform per se, the Civic Union sought to water down the economic reform program. This new political force viewed itself as a loyal opposition, professing full loyalty to President Yeltsin and the idea of democracy. It aimed its criticism at the government, particularly Gaidar. While unwilling to sacrifice Gaidar, Yeltsin did agree to bring three of the Civic Union's representatives (one of whom was Viktor Chernomyrdin) into the Cabinet. In addition Yeltsin, in deference to the Civic Union, abandoned plans under consideration to dissolve parliament and hold new elections. In June, Yeltsin gave up the office of prime minister and made Egor Gaidar acting prime minister. The fact that earlier Gaidar had supported granting 200 billion rubles in additional subsidies to industries assuaged some of his critics.

These concessions notwithstanding, Yeltsin's attempts to build a supporting coalition in the Supreme Soviet failed. Part of the problem was the shifting demands of his critics; they were constantly pushing for more and more positions in the government. But more fundamentally, the political struggle was waged between forces that simply did not agree upon the rules of the game. Until a constitutional consensus could be forged, the struggle would continue.

Most constitutional systems provide for an impartial arbiter over the institutions of government. That function might have been served by the

Constitutional Court that in 1992 gave promise of contributing toward a law-based state. In January, the Court issued an important decision overturning a presidential decree merging the KGB with the Ministry of Internal Affairs. An even more important decision was rendered in November when it ruled that the constitutional ban on the Communist Party of the Soviet Union imposed by Yeltsin in 1991 was only partially valid. The Court upheld the suspension of the Communist Party at the national level but ruled unconstitutional the ban on grassroots Communist Party activity. These decisions were important steps toward checking executive power which, from the long perspective of Russian history, was a promising sign for the future. However, the crisis of the post-Soviet period was arguably aggravated as much by the weakness as the preponderance of executive power. The Constitutional Court did play an important mediating role in the dramatic clash that dominated the Seventh Congress of People's Deputies in December 1992.

Domestic politics in the summer and fall of 1992 were dominated by the anticipation of the coming Congress at which the central issues would be the questions of the President's extraordinary powers to implement reform and the composition of his government. Yeltsin was vulnerable on several counts: The improvement in the standard of living promised remained unfulfilled. Nor had the economy stabilized. In September, inflation reached 20 percent; industrial output in the first three quarters fell 17.6 percent. The ruble failed to gain strength and the budget deficit loomed as large as ever. Yeltsin bemoaned before the fall session of the Supreme Soviet, "the momentum of senseless political confrontation . . . is diverting colossal amounts of energy and resources."[10]

To strengthen his position vis-a-vis parliament, Yeltsin experimented with creating state structures that he could control and which presumably would circumvent parliament. The most important of these was the Russian Security Council whose function was to oversee executive policy in a wide range of fields and whose structures were intended to reach deep into the Russian heartland. To oversee the work of the Security Council, Yeltsin appointed as its secretary Yurii Skokov, a representative of the military-industrial lobby.[11] Another state structure created was the Council of Heads of Republics in the Russian Federation. Ostensibly, the Council was to work on political and social policies within the republics. Interestingly, Skokov was made Secretary of that body as well. These structures were potentially important instruments of governance should Yeltsin choose to dismiss parliament and establish presidential rule.

A giant step toward desocializing Russia's economic institutions was made by Yeltsin on August 19 when he introduced an ambitious voucher scheme for transferring ownership of certain industries to private individuals. Every Russian citizen was to be given a voucher (or "privatization check") with a nominal value of ten thousand rubles. Citizens could use the vouchers to bid for shares in companies, join with others in creating privatization investment funds or simply sell the vouchers for whatever they would bring in cash on the open market. In announcing this plan Yeltsin proclaimed: "We need millions of property owners, not just a handful of millionaires."[12] Distribution was scheduled to begin in October.

As December 1, the date of the seventh Congress approached, the pace of criticism of Gaidar and the government quickened. In September the parliamentary bloc "Russian Unity" announced an "Agreement of the Right and Left Opposition" combining communist and nationalist forces. Their goal: "the removal of Yeltsin's ruling clique from power." Though Khasbulatov was not among their numbers, they sought to enlist his support by opposing the efforts of the reformers to remove Khasbulatov as speaker of the Supreme Soviet. Hoping to defer a showdown, in October, Yeltsin asked the Supreme Soviet to postpone convocation of the Congress until the spring of 1993. The proposal was rejected.

In short order the president and parliament were engaged in a series of tit-for-tat measures to secure the upper hand. After the defeat on postponement of the Congress, Yeltsin banned the parliamentary guards formed by the parliament for protection of the deputies. On October 24 the National Salvation Front was formed in Moscow to serve as the popular arm for Russian Unity. Its objective was to form support groups throughout the country—in apartments, places of work and social organizations—for the purpose of mobilizing popular opposition to the president. Within days the National Salvation Front was banned by Yeltsin as a "threat to the integrity of the Russian Federation . . ."[13] In November, the Supreme Soviet voted to require every minister to present personally an annual accounting to parliament. Yeltsin was denied his request that an annual report of the prime minister suffice; so he vetoed the bill entirely.

Some of Yeltsin's closest advisers, fearful of his impending loss of powers, urged the president to suspend parliament altogether and govern by presidential rule. Ironically many of these advocates of presidential rule were among the leaders of the democratic movement, such as Gennadi Burbulis, Andrei Kozyrev, Anatolii Sobchak and Gavril Popov. Egor Gaidar, the principal target of parliamentary wrath, however, opposed the authoritarian proposal and Yeltsin himself rejected (for the time) the option. As a sop to the Civic Union (which opposed presidential rule) he demoted aides Mikhail Poltoranin and Gennadi Burbulis, two of his staunchist reformers. But it was clear to all that a bitter fight was in the offing and Yeltsin took the precaution of cultivating the political support of regional and republican leaders as well as the army and leadership of the Ministry of the Interior.

The Seventh Congress of People's Deputies convened on December 1 in an atmosphere bitterly hostile to the president. Yeltsin requested, but was denied, a bill to assign the president a powerful role in the legislative process.

He also proposed a referendum on a new constitution to create a strong presidential form of government. Instead, he received from the assembled deputies a blistering critique of his reform measures and the adoption of several constitutional amendments to curb the powers of the president. Hardliners in the Congress secured another victory with the adoption of a constitutional amendment which would automatically strip the president of all powers if he ordered a dissolution of the Congress or the Supreme Soviet. Feelings were so antagonistic between the reformers and the conservatives that fighting broke out on the floor of the Congress.

To the surprise of his enemies and the chagrin of his supporters, Yeltsin conveyed a willingness to compromise. In an effort to obtain congressional approval of Egor Gaidar as prime minister Yeltsin agreed to let the parliament have the right of confirmation over four critical ministries: defense, security, internal affairs (the "power" ministries) and foreign affairs. In the words of one newspaper report, "B. Yeltsin Sacrifices Four Chess Pieces In Order to Save the Queen."[14] But the queen was not saved. The Congress accepted control over the four ministries and then proceeded to reject Gaidar's nomination by a vote of 486 to 467. Yeltsin thought he had a deal with Congress, but numerous Civic Union deputies joined with the hardliners to inflict a stinging defeat on the president.

Boris Yeltsin counterattacked with vigor. On December 10, he addressed the nation from the rostrum of the Congress. "I blame myself for the fact that, for the sake of achieving political concord, I repeatedly made unwarranted concessions." Accusing the Congress of carrying out a "creeping coup," he declared, "It has become impossible to go on working with such a Congress." He proposed a nationwide referendum in January 1993 worded as follows: "To whom do you entrust the task of extricating the country from economic and political crisis and reviving the Russian Federation: the Congress and the Supreme Soviet as now constituted, or the President of Russia?"[15]

Confrontation had produced yet another crisis. There were demonstrations in the streets of Moscow; military authorities affirmed the neutrality of the armed forces. The Congress erupted in anger. It did not object to the idea of a referendum so much as to the wording of Yeltsin's proposal, which appeared to pit the two branches of government against each other. If a referendum were to be held, the Congress wanted it to be on the question of holding early elections for both President and the parliament. Valerii Zorkin speaking for the Constitutional Court offered to mediate negotiations between Yeltsin and Khasbulatov. Both accepted, and a multifaceted compromise was reached. The referendum was deferred until April 1993 and would focus on a new constitution. All the constitutional amendments adopted by the sixth Congress limiting presidential power were put on hold until after the referendum. Yeltsin agreed to demote his top aide Gennadi Burbulis and to accept as prime minister a candidate acceptable to the parliament.

He chose Viktor Chernomyrdin, endorsed by the Civic Union. There was some grumbling among the deputies of Russian Unity and other rightists over the compromise, but the centrists joined by the reformers approved the agreement. The crisis was diffused though none of the long-term issues had been resolved.

THE APRIL REFERENDUM

In the winter and spring of 1993, Russian politics were, if anything, more chaotic than before the seventh Congress of People's Deputies. The parliament under the leadership of Ruslan Khasbulatov was determined to strip the president of his powers and reduce him to a figurehead. Yeltsin appeared to be vulnerable. There were signs of exhaustion caused by years of incessant political battles. The principal bulwarks of his power were his determination, his popularity and the support of the military and security apparatus. Early in 1993 all three seemed to be uncertain.[16] Yeltsin retained two potential weapons against his adversaries: the imposition of direct presidential rule, which he had considered before the seventh Congress of People's Deputies, and submitting the issue of his governance before the public in a referendum. There were risks with either tactic. It was by no means certain that he could carry out presidential rule without violence or that his position in a referendum would prevail. Although a referendum had been a part of the political compromise in December, the Supreme Soviet and Khasbulatov had a change of mind in December and came to oppose the idea. Yeltsin suggested that he might hold the referendum without parliamentary approval even if the results had no legally binding authority.

A serious weakness of Khasbulatov's campaign was that he possessed no alternative program to Yeltsin's. Lacking a popular base of support, Khasbulatov was dependent upon the parliament that he headed. Thus, he could not afford to alienate any sizeable bloc in the parliament, which pushing an alternative program might do. Yeltsin, on the other hand, though forced to abandon Egor Gaidar as prime minister, remained committed as fully as before to transforming Russia into a market economy. Indeed, Chernomyrdin's new Cabinet not only retained the core of Gaidar's reformist team, it added Boris Fyodorov as deputy prime minister. Fyodorov (only thirty-five years old) was one of the authors of the "500 days" plan that Gorbachev failed to implement in 1990. As overseer of the ministries of finance and economics, Fyodorov could be expected to intensify radical economic reform, fight inflation, and curb subsidies to inefficient state industries.

Since Chernomyrdin was known to favor some government control over the economy, there was uncertainty regarding how he and Fyodorov would work together. Indeed, the objective of forcing Gaidar's removal in the first place was primarily to slow down the reform. By 1993, whatever his political failures, Yeltsin had created a fundamental change in the Russian economy. He had abolished the bureaucratic allocation of goods and services and replaced that system with real markets. The transformation had been costly in declining production, inflation and deteriorating standards of living. And it covered only a segment of the national economy; but it was real. What impact on the transformation would Chernomyrdin have? The prime minister began with a misstep. One of the first substantive documents signed by him was a resolution "On the State Regulation of Prices for Certain Types of Products and Goods." This was price control and a major deviation from reform. Fyodorov called the resolution a mistake, demanding that it be revoked. While not formally revoked, the resolution was modified to provide that prices would be essentially governed by the market. As prime minister, Chernomyrdin proved to be not an adversary of Yeltsin, but more of a partner. Like his predecessors he came to see the issuance of credits by the government and inflation as dire threats to reform.

Dominating the political debate early in 1993 was the issue of the April referendum. Should it be conducted in the first place? If so, what should be the wording of the referendum? And, if held, what conditions should apply? Within weeks after he had agreed to the referendum, Khasbulatov began to criticize the idea as an ineffective instrument for working out the complicated legal issues of a new constitution. It was clear that many parliamentary deputies were fearful of the outcome of a referendum. Joining the forces calling for a postponement of the referendum was Constitutional Court Chairman Valerii Zorkin. As the legislative and executive branches became more and more polarized, Zorkin aligned himself with the former.

Responsibility for formulating the questions of a referendum lay with the Supreme Soviet. But in the face of a balking parliament, Yeltsin warned that if the Supreme Soviet did not come up with acceptable questions, he would determine the wording himself. Khasbulatov responded by proposing a referendum on the issue of early elections for the president and parliament. That was acceptable to Yeltsin but only if the parliamentary elections were held before presidential elections. Under then-existing law, the parliament would normally be elected in 1995 and the president in 1996. In mid-February, a working group of representatives from both sides met to draft a compromise acceptable to Yeltsin and the parliament. However, even before the working group finished its task, the Supreme Soviet voted to convoke an extraordinary Congress of People's Deputies. The conservative forces led by Khasbulatov had decided to force a showdown with Yeltsin in a forum they considered favorable.

The eighth Congress of People's Deputies met from March 10–13. Yeltsin pleaded in vain for cooperation between the legislative and executive branches of government. At the same time, he reaffirmed his argument that only "strong presidential power" could save Russia because only the popularly elected president could implement tough but necessary reform measures. From its inception the Congress was defiant. On March 12 it inflicted a blow against Yeltsin by stripping him of the emergency powers that it had granted him in 1991 and which were the basis for legislating economic change. The Congress affirmed that it was the "supreme power" while the president was merely the "highest official." It also formally annulled the compromise agreed upon at the previous Congress and voted not to hold a referendum. Several of the constitutional amendments limiting the president's powers that were put on hold in December were now formally approved. Enraged, Yeltsin declared that he would not return to the Congress.[17]

Immediately, demands were voiced within the Democratic camp for a suspension of the constitution and the introduction of direct presidential rule. Support for presidential rule was given by a majority of the Presidential Council, an advisory body consisting mainly of liberal and centrists politicians and academics. Yeltsin had renounced publicly the option of presidential rule, threatening the Congress instead with an appeal to the public in a referendum. The weakness of this threat was that a referendum was binding only if requested by a third of the parliamentary deputies or endorsed by the signatures of one million citizens. Otherwise a referendum was only advisory.

Apparently, Yeltsin agonized over what to do because what he did next revealed confusion and uncertainty. On March 20 he informed the nation via television that he was establishing "special rule." Exactly what "special rule" meant was unclear since neither the Congress nor the Supreme Soviet was suspended. The parliament, however, would be prohibited from interfering with any decrees or orders of the president or resolutions of the government. He also announced that a vote would be held on April 25 on confidence in the president and on a draft of a new constitution.[18] His actions were immediately endorsed by the government, including Prime Minister Viktor Chernomyrdin who himself had not been consulted or informed about the "special rule," even though others (including U.S. President Bill Clinton and British Prime Minister John Major) had been given advanced information of the decision.

But the vehemence of the opposition must have given Yeltsin pause. Not surprisingly, Khasbulatov and Valerii Zorkin criticized the action as unconstitutional. So did Vice-President Aleksandr Rutskoi, who would become president should Yeltsin be impeached. Though outward appearances suggested that the country was behind him, Yeltsin suddenly backed away from further confrontation. On March 23 his decree was published (thus becoming official) and it contained no reference to "special rule." It reaffirmed the April 25 vote but also acknowledged the validity of challenges to executive action by the Constitutional Court.[19] The presidential backdown, however, did not spare Yeltsin yet another parliamentary confrontation. On the day following publication of Yeltsin's decree the Supreme Soviet voted to convene a ninth (extraordinary) Congress of People's Deputies on March 26.

The ninth Congress opened in an atmosphere of extreme crisis. In their opening addresses to the Congress both Ruslan Khasbulatov and Boris Yeltsin acknowledged that the fundamental issue behind the crisis was economic reform. The speaker of the parliament accused the president of monopolizing all power and demanded that parliament have a voice in economic policy. In reply the president said that the search for a compromise between the legislative and executive branches "came to a dead end at the Eighth Congress." Notwithstanding their sharp differences, the two leaders feared pushing the crisis beyond the brink and agreed on March 27 on a plan to hold early elections for both branches of government. But the Congress would have none of it. On the next day the Congress unexpectedly voted on the question of removing both Yeltsin and Khasbulatov from office. The vote to impeach Yeltsin failed because it fell seventy-two votes short of the required two-thirds vote; but the measure of antagonism to him was reflected in the number of votes to remove him (617) as compared to the 268 deputies who supported the president. Khasbulatov too survived removal from office, with a vote of 558 to 339. At the same time, the deputies rejected the compromise deal for early elections in the fall and adopted instead several laws designed to further weaken presidential power. The last act of the ninth Congress was to approve the April 25 referendum, but on its terms. Four questions were to be submitted:

1. Do you have confidence in B. N. Yeltsin, President of the Russian Federation?
2. Do you approve of the social and economic policy that has been conducted by the Russian Federation President and the Russian Federation government since 1992?
3. Do you consider it necessary to hold an early election for president of the Russian Federation?
4. Do you consider it necessary to hold early elections for Russian Federation People's Deputies?

To be considered adopted, an affirmative vote of more than 50 percent of all registered voters had to be recorded.[20] The cards were being stacked against the president. In disgust, Vyacheslav Kostikov, Yeltsin's press secretary, issued a statement accusing the Congress of violating "all conceivable standards of political decency and human morality."[21]

Everyone understood that the ninth Congress did nothing to resolve the ongoing political crisis in Russia. Each side subsequently hoped to bolster its position through the referendum. Boris Yeltsin apparently felt secure enough to leave the country to meet with President Clinton at a summit meeting in Vancouver on April 2–4. Barely a week before the summit, the Russian president had told the Congress that "excessive hopes of foreign aid" had been a mistake of his administration. Presumably he expected to convert expectation into reality with the promise of $1.6 billion in American aid made by President Clinton. Certainly one of the arrows in his quiver was his claim that he alone among the contenders for power had the capacity to extract significant Western aid.

Yeltsin's campaign strategy for the referendum was to urge a "yes" vote on all four propositions, though some of his supporters argued that he should have advised a "no" vote on early president elections. Indeed, Yeltsin's campaign supporters plastered Moscow and other cities with posters encouraging a vote of "Da, Da, Nyet, Da" (Yes, Yes, No, Yes). Some of Yeltsin's campaign tactics were strikingly similar to ploys practiced in the United States and other democracies. Thus, in the weeks leading up to the referendum Yeltsin issued decrees and made promises that would, if implemented, prove to be costly to the treasury. He rescinded recent gasoline price increases, raised stipends for students and pensions for pensioners, and ordered better working conditions for miners. To woo leaders of Russia's republics, Yeltsin promised that the new constitution would provide for extensive autonomy for the political subdivisions of the Federation. Aleksandr Rutskoi, now an outspoken opponent of the president, accused the administration (of which he was nominally vice-president) of promoting and dismissing military personnel on the basis of political considerations rather than merit.

On April 25, the Russian electorate gave Yeltsin a strong show of support. Overall, turnout was 64.5 percent of an electorate of 107 million. Of those voting 58.7 percent supported Yeltsin's leadership and 53 percent backed his policies. Slightly less than half (49 percent) wanted new presidential elections while 67.2 percent called for new parliamentary elections.[22] A victory had been anticipated by the government, but not by such a strong margin. Perhaps most surprising was the size of the support for Yeltsin's economic reforms despite skyrocketing prices and plunging living standards.

Politically the referendum was a decisive turning point in the struggle between the executive and legislative branches of government. Prior to the vote, Yeltsin had threatened to resign if he lost. Certainly a defeat would have emboldened his opponents to renew their effort to remove him from office. As it was, the hard-liners opposing Yeltsin refused to accept the verdict of the vote. On May Day the National Salvation Front and the Russian Communist Worker's Party organized a demonstration against Yeltsin. The numbers involved were estimated at between ten and fifty thousand people.

The government had no hesitancy in using police force to contain the demonstration.

Yeltsin now determined to exploit his victory by adopting a new constitution that would sharply curtail the governing powers of the parliament. To achieve this objective, Yeltsin had to bypass the Congress of People's Deputies that legally could block the adoption of any new constitution. In a word, he had to pursue an extra-legal process. He thus announced the convocation of a Constituent Assembly to begin work in June. In so doing, he fell back on the political argument that the people were the ultimate repository of sovereignty and that he—not the parliament—represented that sovereignty. The referendum was the third popular endorsement he had been given (the first being his election and the second popular reaction to his stand against the August 1991 coup) and these he believed overrode the mandate given the Congress of People's Deputies in 1990.

THE CONSTITUTIONAL ASSEMBLY

The discussion of the constitutional debate in Russia has focused to this point on the struggle between the president and parliament. But in fact there were three major parties contending for power in the early years of Russia's renewed statehood. In addition to the above parties there were the republics and regions of Russia. Thus, the two central questions that had to be resolved by the Constitutional Assembly were: 1) whether Russia was to be a presidential or parliamentary system, and 2) what would be the division of powers between the government in Moscow and the republics and regions. The political elites in several of Russia's administrative subdivisions wanted considerable autonomy. A few wanted outright independence. The power struggle between the executive and legislative branches of government offered them an opportunity to obtain new power in their own territories. Both Yeltsin and Khasbulatov courted regional leaders with the consequence that the periphery received significant concessions.

As the Constitutional Assembly began its deliberations in the summer of 1993, the Russian Federation was made up of eighty-nine administrative subdivisions which were of two types. Twenty-one were republics identified by a particular ethnic or national group.[23] Sixty-eight were diverse regional subdivisions that included one autonomous *oblast* (region), ten autonomous *okrugs* (areas), forty-nine administration *oblasts*, six *krais* (territories), and the cities of St. Petersburg and Moscow. Among these political subdivisions, the pressures for autonomy and decentralization were greater among the republics than the regions (though in general the regions sought to have the same constitutional status as the republics). Just as the awakening of political consciousness among the non-Russian republics in the Gorbachev era led to the disintegration of the Soviet Union, non-Russian nationalism in some of Russia's republics threatened the integrity of the Russian Federation. The very name "Russian Federation" recognized the existence of other nationalities in the polity. Though Yeltsin and his opponents both courted republican leaders they were in agreement that the territorial integrity of Russia had to be maintained. And though a few republics did want some form of independence, there was little likelihood that Russia would disintegrate as had the U.S.S.R. Three factors undermined the likelihood of secession: 1) Russians constituted a majority or a plurality in many of the republics; 2) geographically most of the territories were enclaves surrounded by Russia; and 3) economically the regions and republics were interdependent with Russia.[24]

The Constitutional Assembly opened on June 5, 1993. It was composed of 750 delegates from the regions and republics, political parties and social organizations. Generally reflective of the diverse social and political forces in Russian society, the Assembly was a moderate and balanced body of representatives. In undertaking to draft a new constitution for the nation, the Assembly had a considerable body of constitutional proposals and analysis upon which to draw. Three years earlier on June 16, the First Congress of People's Deputies created a Constitutional Commission of 102 deputies and legal experts. The chairman of the Russian Supreme Soviet, Boris Yeltsin, headed the Commission assisted by Ruslan Khasbulatov as deputy chairman and Oleg Rumyantsev as executive secretary. A draft constitution supported by Yeltsin was proposed for debate in the fall of 1990, but failed to be approved because of resistance by communist deputies. The draft firmly rejected the notion of communism, offering instead "the indisputable priority of individual rights and liberties."[25] It provided for a presidential republic with the president exercising extensive powers independent of parliament. The Congress of People's Deputies would be abolished in favor of a single legislative assembly.

A second draft was published in October 1991 under different political conditions from the previous year. Yeltsin was now in firmer control in the aftermath of the August coup and the collapse of the Communist Party. During 1991 differences in the Commission focused more sharply on the problem of the distribution of power between Moscow and the political subdivisions of Russia and between the president and parliament. The 1991 draft affirmed the federal character of the Russian state, denying the republics the right of secession. Particularly controversial were the differences in status between the republics and regions. At the Fifth Congress in November 1991 Yeltsin urged adoption of the draft but he again failed to overcome parliamentary objections.

At the Sixth Congress in March 1992 a third Commission draft was considered along with two other drafts. The alternative draft constitutions were offered by a group of neo-Communists and the Russian Democratic Reform

Movement. Again, no decision was reached and again, it was largely because of opposition from the republics. Republican opposition stemmed from the fact the third draft failed to incorporate rights given to them by a Federal Treaty signed on March 31, 1992.[26] Yeltsin himself had objection to this draft because it did not give him as much presidential power as he wanted. A fourth official draft issued in November 1992 also became enmeshed in the increasingly bitter struggle between the president and parliament.

As noted above the political balance between Yeltsin and parliament shifted significantly after the April 25 referendum. Though legally the referendum conferred no additional power on the president, Yeltsin felt confident enough to publish four days later the text of a new constitutional draft authored by a group of legal experts who supported the concept of a presidential republic. The Assembly had before it the so-called "presidential draft" and a revised draft of the Constitutional Commission. Yeltsin preferred the former. Both drafts would have replaced the two-tiered Congress of People's Deputies and Supreme Soviet with a simple bicameral legislature. A major difference was the inclusion in the presidential draft of the entire Federal Treaty. This reflected Yeltsin's determination to win the support of the republics and regions. That support, however, did not come easily. What the republics wanted was explicit acknowledgment that they were "sovereign states" with the right of secession. What the regions wanted was equal constitutional status with the republics. There were strong objections to these demands by those who feared they would convert Russia from a federation to a confederation. Compounding those differences were sharp disagreements among the delegates regarding the method of adopting a new constitution.

On July 12th, the Constitutional Assembly approved a draft constitution by a vote of 433 (74 percent) of 585 participating delegates. The draft gave the president power to dissolve parliament and call for elections. It also eliminated the vice-presidency. On the critical question of the status of the members of the Federation, the draft contained contradictory elements, which Boris Yeltsin admitted needed clarification. The republics were identified as "sovereign states" as they wished, but at the same time, the draft asserted that the federal constitution and federal laws had priority over republican laws. Clearly, sovereignty was qualified. Many regions objected to their lack of status as truly sovereign entities; and they were not appeased by the fact that they were accorded equality in the economic field. Republican dissatisfaction was reflected in the final vote which garnered the support of only five republics.

One concern among Russia's leaders was that the regions and provinces would ultimately attempt to change their status to that of republics. That is precisely what the Sverdlovsk and Vologda provinces did while the Constitutional Assembly was working. In July, the Sverdlovsk province Soviet of People's Deputies proclaimed itself to be the "Urals Republic" while the Vologda province gave itself quasi-republic states. Cautiously, Yeltsin condemned these actions as "hasty" and "untimely." "The integrity of Russia," he said, "is something that no one can put at risk."[27]

There remained the problem of ratification of the draft constitution. Four methods were considered by the media: 1) by the Congress of People's Deputies (the legal method under the existing constitution), 2) by a popular referendum, 3) by a newly elected parliament, and 4) by a constitutional assembly. Each method served different purposes. Yeltsin wanted rapid approval, which he knew he would not get from the Congress. The republics and regions wanted approval, by their respective soviets. The Congress wanted to strengthen parliamentary control through amendments. No sooner did the Assembly finish its work than political maneuvering began in earnest. About seventy heads of territory, province and republic soviets met in Ruslan Khasbulatov's office and agreed informally that the new constitutional draft should be ratified by soviets in each of the eighty-nine members of the Federation. A more definitive preemptive step was taken by the Supreme Soviet in July with the adoption of a law "on the procedure for adopting the new constitution." Under this law ratification could be done only by the Congress of People's Deputies or by a national referendum under rules established by the parliament. If a referendum should be used, ratification would require approval by 50 percent of all registered voters as well as two-thirds of the members of the Federation.[28] Complying with parliament, Yeltsin submitted the draft constitution to the parliament, requesting it to eschew turning the debate into a political struggle.

THE COLLAPSE OF CONSTITUTIONAL ORDER

The disintegration of political authority and institutions that began in the late Gorbachev era continued unabated during the early years of the Yeltsin era. Nothing emerged to replace the discredited Communist Party. The many political parties and movements that proliferated under freedom failed to lead to a multiparty system, producing instead what Richard Sakwa has described as "pseudoparties".[29] Nor had Russia's leaders and political movements produced workable governing institutions to replace those of the Soviet era. After a year in office, President Yeltsin concluded that only a new constitution could create workable institutions of governance. But a consensus or even the clear-cut majority needed to draft one eluded him. His effort with the April referendum and Constituent Assembly achieved only limited success. The constitutional process reached a stalemate when Yeltsin referred the constitutional draft to the republics and regions for further consideration.

In the summer and fall of 1993, the parliament resumed its assault on Yeltsin's policies. Some members of the parliament (notably Nikolai Ryabov, deputy chairman of the Supreme Soviet Presidium) saw the April referendum as a mandate for Yeltsin and attempted to curb Khasbulatov's strident opposition. But adroit maneuvering by the speaker quelled an incipient revolt and he was able to forge a solid majority of conservative deputies who saw themselves threatened by either a new constitution or early elections. Parliament sought to undermine the pro-Western foreign policies of Foreign Minister Andrei Kozyrev. Legislators condemned the United States raid on Iraq despite endorsement by the foreign minister. Against Yeltsin's wishes it asserted Russian sovereignty over the Crimean port of Sevastopol. The parliament rejected a compromise agreed to by the United States and Russia that would have halted a proposed sale of rocket engines to India in return for greater Russian involvement in the US space program.

Even more relentless was parliament's challenge to the government's economic program. Parliament's revision of the annual budget sharply increased expenditures on defense and pensions, throwing the government's fiscal policies into disarray. In July, an attempt to slow privatization was made by repealing a presidential decree that had set a timetable for selling state assets to the public. These and other measures were accompanied by parliamentary criticisms of prominent reformers and attempts to force many Yeltsin aides from office. At the same time that parliament seemed to be more invigorated, the president appeared to be in a state of malaise. As has occurred from time to time with Yeltsin, there were rumors that he was seriously ill. Yeltsin even found it necessary in early August to deny in public that he had any health problems.

By late summer, government in Russia was moving toward deadlock. Reminiscent of the "war of laws" between Gorbachev and Yeltsin in 1991 the parliament and Yeltsin in 1993 were issuing decrees of dubious legality and often in total contradiction to each other. On occasion, as with the notorious case of the Central Bank cancellation of pre-1993 paper currency, there was confusion as to who the real author of government policy was. Even Prime Minister Chernomyrdin complained of conflicts between ministerial directives and presidential decrees.

A particularly sordid manifestation of the slugfest that Moscow politics had become were the accusations of corruption made by senior officials against each other. On the eve of the April referendum, Vice-President Aleksandr Rutskoi made a dramatic and emotional speech accusing several key reformers of corruption. Those accused included, among others, Igor Gaidar (the accusation was later retracted), Gennadi Burbulis, First Deputy Prime Minister Vladimir Shumeiko, Deputy Prime Minister Aleksandr Shokhin, Anatoli Chubais (administrator for privatization), Deputy Prime Minister Mikhail Poltoranin and Sergei Filatov, Yeltsin's chief of administration. In the months that followed, accusations of all kinds of wrongdoing were made by authorities in several branches of government, including the

charge that Rutskoi himself was guilty of corruption. One of the most sensational of the charges was that Prosecutor General Valentin Stepankov had
conspired to commit murder. The impact of these charges was to increase
popular cynicism in government and disgust with all authorities including
Yeltsin himself. On September 1, the Russian President temporarily suspended both his adversary Rutskoi and his ally Shumeiko from the performance of their duties. Parliament immediately voted to suspend that part of
Yeltsin's decree as it applied to the vice-president pending a review by the
Constitutional Court.[30]

One of the more serious examples of government paralysis was the deadlock on the budget. In the late summer Yeltsin vetoed a Supreme Soviet
budget that Finance Minister Boris Fyodorov claimed created a 26 trillion
ruble deficit and would lead to hyperinflation. His veto was overturned by
the Supreme Soviet, only to be vetoed a second time. That Yeltsin was not
backing down on this issue was made clear on September 16 with the
announcement that Egor Gaidar would be returning to the Cabinet as first
deputy prime minister for economic policy. That announcement was made
during a visit to a military formation, the Dzerzhinsky Division.

By September, relations between Yeltsin and the parliament were so
antagonistic that rumors circulated in the media about an impending presidential coup. Khasbulatov was preparing legislation that would, in *Izvestiya*'s
words, reduce the president to a "figurehead." Analyzing the stalemate
newspapers supporting both sides agreed that the country was governed by
a "dual power" which had produced almost complete paralysis in government. On September 21, Yeltsin ended dual power with a decree dissolving
parliament, calling for elections to a new Federal Assembly in December and
establishing presidential rule as the basis for governance until then. In a televised address to the nation, Yeltsin said:

> *The past few days have destroyed, once and for all, hopes for the restoration*
> *of any sort of constructive cooperation. The majority of the Supreme Soviet*
> *is moving toward the outright flouting of the will of Russia's people and is*
> *pursuing a course aimed at weakening and eventually removing the*
> *President and at disorganizing the work of the present government.*[31]

Thus began a showdown between Yeltsin and parliament that ended on
October 4 in the bloodiest confrontation of his administration.

Almost immediately, battle lines formed to oppose and support Yeltsin's
action. Not surprisingly Khasbulatov condemned the action as a "coup
d'etat." The Constitutional Court ruled the president's action to be unconstitutional and grounds for his removal from office. The parliament promptly
voted to impeach Yeltsin and replace him with Vice-President Aleksandr
Rutskoi. But Yeltsin had the bigger guns. He was supported by the government (Chernomyrdin and the cabinet) and more importantly by the "power

ministries"—Defense, Security and Internal Affairs. Even four judges of the Constitutional Court sided with Yeltsin. Also, Yeltsin had the backing of the Western governments and nearly all of the former Soviet republics.

More uncertain, though, was the response of the general public, the republics, and regions. Opinion was divided in the outlying areas. Most of the executive bodies of Russia's regions sided with the president while most of the legislative bodies viewed the presidential decree as unconstitutional. The leadership of Russia's republics was also divided. Generally the response of the outlying areas in September resembled the reaction to Yeltsin's call for "special rule" the previous March.

It was indicative of the state of public opinion in Russia throughout the ongoing post-Soviet political crisis that so little popular reaction to what was going on in Moscow was manifested. Public opinion appeared to be basically indifferent. Supporters of both sides attempted to mobilize public demonstrations with a notable lack of success. Several thousand anti-Yeltsin demonstrators took to the streets in Moscow and St. Petersburg while between eight thousand and fifteen thousand supporters cheered the President when he attended a performance of Tschaikovsky's "1812 Overture" in Red Square. Most of the people interviewed in provincial cities claimed to be uninterested in what was going on in Moscow.[32]

For about two weeks, a mood of high tension permeated the political atmosphere in Moscow. Yeltsin ignored parliament's attempt to remove him from office. Instead he put all buildings, property and finances of the Supreme Soviet under presidential control and transferred the Parliamentary Guard from parliamentary jurisdiction to the Ministry of the Interior. The Supreme Soviet was cut off from heat, electricity, and telephone, and its occupants told to go home. An attempt was made to convene an Extraordinary Tenth Congress of People's Deputies on September 23 only to find that it lacked a quorum.

Several attempts were made to find a way out of the impasse. One widely circulated proposal—endorsed by regional leaders, many liberals and the Constitutional Court—was to hold parliamentary and presidential elections simultaneously. Rutskoi accepted this plan as did many in the parliament, but Yeltsin refused to go along. He had the upper hand and he knew it. On September 29, he demanded that those deputies still holding out in the White House (the parliamentary building) leave by October 4. The threat of violence loomed large in late September as it became known that the approximately 180 remaining deputies were acquiring fire arms, including machine guns. Although Yeltsin promised not to use force against the parliament, he ordered forces of the interior ministry to blockade the White House.[33]

In the afternoon of October 3, the showdown turned violent. A rally outside the White House was addressed by Aleksandr Rutskoi who urged his supporters to storm the municipal administration building and the Ostankino television station. From within the White House Ruslan Khasbulatov called for seizure of the Kremlin. Breaking through the police cordon the demonstrators seized and destroyed five stories of the Moscow Mayor's office. That evening anti-Yeltsin protestors, armed with grenades, seized the Ostankino broadcast center temporarily shutting down the first Russian TV channel. On October 3 and 4, there was sporadic fighting in the city as the main action centered around the mayor's office, the television center and the parliamentary building itself. Calling the riots an "armed fascist-communist rebellion" Yeltsin declared a state of emergency and ordered a massive military response. On October 4, a full assault was made on the White House with artillery firing pointblank into the building. In all about two hundred people died in the three days of fighting. Rutskoi and Khasbulatov were arrested and imprisoned in the Ministry of Security's Lefortovo prison.

Was Yeltsin's suppression of parliament justified? In so acting he violated Article 121-6 of the Constitution as well as the law establishing the presidency. Yeltsin acknowledged as much in his memoirs: "And here I was, the first popularly elected president breaking the law . . ."[34] Albeit, he added, "a bad law." The clear fact was that the constitution and laws under which Russia operated were unworkable. The Soviet era constitution had been amended hundreds of times and produced a chaotic structure of incompatible institutions. There existed a "dual power" which produced not a system of checks and balances but stalemate. Yeltsin had tried vigorously by legal means to amend the constitution but was thwarted by his political opponents.

The system of government advocated by Khasbulatov and Rutskoi—parliamentary supremacy—was alien to Russian history and its political traditions. The weight of historical evidence argued for the need of a strong executive, not a dictator, but an administration capable of acting decisively. Khasbulatov's theory of parliamentarianism was one "in which parliament plays a prominent role not only as a legislative body but also as the supreme body supervising executive power."[35] He defended his concept of parliamentary supremacy with the example of Great Britain citing Blackstone's words that parliament can "change the entire state structure and create a new one; it can even completely reform itself; it can do anything within the bounds of the possible, and whatever is done by parliament cannot be undone by any power on Earth."[36] But Khasbulatov ignored a central feature of Britain's parliamentary system, namely its party structure which in fact permitted the chief executive (the prime minister) to have great power. Indeed, because of the two-party system, the British prime minister can in fact dominate parliament. Russia does not have a party system and thus lacks a mechanism for creating a strong executive within a parliamentary framework.

The case for Yeltsin can further be supported by the political objectives of the two sides in conflict. Yeltsin was committed to democracy and its economic concomitant, a market economy. Over time his parliamentary opponents came increasingly to oppose economic reform. And within the parliament there was a large segment—possibly a majority—which rejected democracy as well. During the course of his presidency, Yeltsin had bent over backward to avoid the use of force and had repeatedly sought to compromise with parliament. But the Supreme Soviet and its parent, the Congress of People's Deputies, had often spurned the president's efforts to find a middle ground. Finally, it is clear that during the early years of Yeltsin's presidency the Russian people preferred his positions to those of parliament. That was indicated by the voting in the presidential election of 1991 and the referendum in 1993. So while parliament had the legality in the September-October crisis Yeltsin had the legitimacy. Students of American politics may recall that when the American founding fathers met in 1787 to amend the Articles of Confederation they proceeded without legal mandate to discard the Articles of Confederation altogether and write a new constitution.[37] Because the democracies of the world recognized that Yeltsin was at that time Russia's best hope for democracy, they overwhelmingly supported him in his forceful suppression of the parliament.[38]

THE DECEMBER ELECTIONS

The suppression of parliament paved the way for Yeltsin to initiate the constitutional changes he long desired. Most of the existing structures of the government (except the presidency) were abolished or modified. The Supreme Soviet and Congress of People's Deputies were to be replaced by a bicameral Federal Assembly whose lower house, the State Duma, would consist of 450 deputies, half elected by party lists and half by single-member districts. The upper house, the Council of the Federation, was to consist of two representatives from each of Russia's eighty-nine republics and regions. Initially, those representatives were to be the chief executive and legislative officers of each region. These deputies were to be chief executive and legislative officers from the republic or region which they represented. To strengthen presidential control over the regions—and by extension over the Council of the Federation itself—Yeltsin in 1994 decreed that the governors of Russia's regions be approved and dismissed by the president. Another source of opposition, the Constitutional Court, was suspended pending the adoption of a new constitution.

The campaign for a new parliament and constitution dominated Russian politics throughout the fall of 1993. These, the first post-Soviet general elections, were conducted under conditions of uncertainty, confusion and acrimony. Some bitterness was caused by authoritarian measures taken by

Yeltsin to punish his enemies or limit their power. Several extremist political organizations were barred outright and a few opposition newspapers were closed temporarily. On October 9, Yeltsin dissolved all soviets at the city, district and village level, transferring their power of governance to local executives appointed by himself. Although not formally disbanded regional soviets were "invited" to dissolve themselves. Many did so.

Also alarming to many was the favoritism shown by the Russian media to the party—Russia's Choice—most sympathetic to the government's reform program. Television had become the main source of information for 85 percent of the Russian population with the decline of newspaper circulation. Despite a presidential decree calling for equal access to radio and television for all political parties and blocs the state-owned Ostankino and Russian Television companies actively propagandized for Egor Gaidar, leader of Russia's Choice.[39] Media bias, however, did not determine the electoral outcome as evidenced by the unexpectedly poor showing of Gaidar's party when the votes were counted.

A serious problem confronting the electorate was the multiplicity of new political parties with programs that were difficult to differentiate. In part, this was the result of the suddenness of the call for elections. Many political parties and their leaders were taken by surprise with the announcement that elections would be held on December 11 and 12. To qualify for the ballot, a party or bloc had to collect one hundred thousand signatures in at least seven republics or regions. Thirteen parties met the requirement but several had difficulty getting their message across to the public. A survey conducted by Russian Public Opinion and Market Research in November found that only one-quarter of the electorate was familiar with the programs of the parties contesting the elections.[40]

The qualifying parties fell into three general categories: reform, centrist and extremist. Besides Russia's Choice the reformers included the Yavlinsky-Boldyrev-Lukin bloc, Sergei Sakhrai's Party of Russian Unity and Concord and the Movement for Democratic Reform led by Anatolii Sobchak and Gavriil Popov. In the center were Aleksandr Volsky's Civic Union and Nikolai Travkin's Democratic Party of Russia. The extremes reflected Communist and nationalist views. The Communist Party was led by Gennadi Zyuganov and the rightist Liberal Democratic Party was headed by Vladimir Zhirinovsky. Many of the party programs were similar making the choice difficult for the voters.

In addition to electing 628 deputies to a new Federal Assembly from among a multitude of candidates most of whom were unknown to the public, the voters were asked to approve or reject a new constitution. The text of the constitution, long and complicated, did not even become available until November 10, barely a month before the election. In all, the obstacles to achieving an outcome genuinely representative of the electorate were formidable.

But the campaign and election did meet the basic tenet of fairness. Yeltsin had invited foreign observers to monitor the elections, and some one thousand came from all over the world. The Helsinki Commission of the CSCE reported that "Russian voters were able to express their political will freely and fairly."[41] That political will came as a surprise. Most pre-election polls showed strong support for Gaidar's Russia's Choice and Yavlinsky's bloc. Those same polls showed weak support for Zhirinovsky's Liberal Democratic Party. They were wrong. Yeltsin was not the first political leader who was unable to convert personal popularity into support for his program.

In the State Duma, the lower house of the Federal Assembly, the antireform group did particularly well in those seats allotted proportionally by party vote. Figures released by ITAR-TASS, Russia's official news agency, showed that Zhirinovsky's Liberal Democratic Party won almost 23 percent compared to a little over 15 percent for Russia's Choice. In declining order came the Communists, Women of Russia, the Agrarian Union, the Yavlinksy-Boldyrev-Lukin Bloc, the Russian Party of Unity and Accord, and the Democratic Party. However, when the 225 single member seats were added to the party seats the outcome was somewhat more favorable to Yeltsin. The exact figures for political party and factions in the Federal Assembly have changed over time because of vacancies and party changes. As of late 1994, the breakdown was as follows:[42]

- Liberal Democratic Party: 65 seats
- Russia's Choice: 65 seats
- Communist Party of Russia: 48 seats
- Agrarian Party of Russia: 33 seats
- Women of Russia: 23 seats
- Yavlinsky-Boldyrev-Lukin Bloc: (Yabloko) 22 seats
- Russian Party of Unity and Accord: 19 seats
- Democratic Party of Russia 15 seats

On balance, the State Duma as a body boded ill for the president. He could expect resistance to his reform program from the Liberal Democratic Party, Communist Party, Agrarian Party, and from some of the lesser parties as well. In the Council of the Federation, the upper house, the antireform parties did poorly though an exact measure was difficult because most deputies did not indicate party affiliation.

The biggest winner of the parliamentary elections was Vladimir Zhirinovsky, a personality known to the Russian voter. His Liberal Democratic Party, founded in March 1990, was the first political party to be registered in the Soviet Union after the Communist Party was forced to abandon its monopoly of power. In June 1991, Zhirinovsky ran against Yeltsin for the Russian presidency and came in third with eight million votes. Zhirinovsky's rhetoric categorized him as an extreme nationalist. He claimed that the dissolution of the U.S.S.R. was an unlawful act which must be avenged. He promised to restore Russia to its status as a great power and in the process recover territories in the Ukraine, the Baltic States, Kazakhstan, Turkmenistan and Finland. He championed himself as the protector of the twenty-five million Russians living outside of present-day Russia. His domestic program was vague. At times he advocated a market economy but on some occasions he criticized privatization which he saw benefitting "Zionists" and the "mafiya."[43]

Zhirinovsky's success in 1993 was the result of several factors. He successfully manipulated the populist theme that "I am one of you." He appealed to those who were hurt by rising prices, the specter of unemployment and declining living standards. He also appealed to those nationalistic elements who felt humiliated by the decline of their country in the world at large. Perhaps most fundamental was the image that he would bring strong government to a society experiencing disintegration. Part of his success resulted from the ineptness of his main opponents, the democratic reformers. The electorate was put off by the divisions among the reformers and the inability of their ambitious and egotistic leaders to cooperate. Gaidar proved to be a poor campaigner, Zhirinovsky a brilliant one with a talent for demagoguery.

THE RUSSIAN CONSTITUTION

If the results of the State Duma elections were disappointing to Yeltsin, he could draw some consolation with the adoption of a new constitution. Russia's 1993 constitution was the first ever to be endorsed by popular vote, although it could hardly be said to represent a consensus of the nation. Of the 54 percent of the eligible electorate who voted, only 58.4 percent approved the constitution, which meant that less than one-third of the entire voting population approved of the document.[44] Nevertheless, Yeltsin finally replaced the Soviet-era constitution that gave primacy to the parliament with one establishing a strong presidential republic.[45]

A central constitutional bone of contention between Yeltsin and Khasbulatov had been over who would control the government, that is, the prime minister and the Cabinet. That issue is resolved in favor of the President who proposes candidates for the posts of prime minister and deputy prime minister as well as chairman of the Central Bank, high court judges and the procurator-general. Appointments to the Cabinet are confirmed by the State Duma and high court judges and the procurator-general are confirmed by the Federation Council. If the State Duma rejects the president's choice of a prime minister three times, the president may dissolve the Duma and call for new elections. For its part, the State Duma has the power to vote "no confidence" in the government, but the president does not have to accept this vote. If a second vote of no confidence is made within three months, the president must respond but he may choose either to dismiss the government or to dissolve the State Duma. Great Britain and France both empower the chief executive (prime minister or president) to dissolve the parliament but in those two countries this power is exercised very infrequently due to the party structures of those regimes. Russia has yet to develop a party system to ensure that the government represents a parliamentary majority, so it is uncertain how the provisions of the Russian constitution are likely to work out in practice. If the president is dissatisfied with the government, he may dismiss it without the approval of the State Duma.

In addition, the president has control over foreign and defense policy and can declare war and a state of emergency. In the exercise of these powers he must inform the Federal Assembly, but is not bound by its response. The president can issue "decrees and directives" which are binding so long as they are not in conflict with federal law or the constitution.

The Federal Assembly consists of the State Duma and the Council of the Federation. Except for the first Assembly, which lasts for two years, the normal life of the parliament is four years. The State Duma can adopt federal laws. Laws are considered by the Council of the Federation. If the Council rejects a decision of the Duma, then the federal law requires a two-thirds vote by the Duma for adoption. The president can veto federal laws, and a veto can be overridden by a two-thirds vote of both houses of the Assembly. There are four exceptions to the presidential power to dissolve parliament. The State Duma may not be dissolved during the first year of its four-year life; nor if it is considering impeachment of the president; nor during a state of emergency; nor within the six-month period before the president's term expires. The government (prime minister and cabinet) determines the budget and monetary policy though the parliament must approve of those policies. The Constitutional Court is to resolve disputes between the President, the government and parliament. However, in the relationship between the federal and regional organs of government it is the President who mediates disputes.

The federal structure is composed of twenty-one ethnic republics and a combination of sixty-eight territories, provinces, the Jewish Autonomous Province, regions and the federal cities of Moscow and St. Petersburg.[46] The overall thrust of the constitution is toward federal supremacy. Thus, the definition of the republics as sovereign states is not included (though it was in an earlier constitutional draft). Nor do republics have special status or citizenship. The distribution of governmental powers between Russia and its subdivisions is specified in articles that distinguish between powers possessed solely by the Russian Federation (the central government) and those that it shares with its subdivisions. There is no enumeration of powers belonging exclusively to the subdivisions, although the constitution does empower the regions to "exercise their own legal regulation, including the adoption of laws . . ."[47] The constitution fails to clearly delineate the powers between the center and the members of the Federation, and it will be years before a delineation is worked out in practice. If the tradition of Russian and Soviet politics prevails, the likelihood is that decision making will be concentrated in Moscow.

COHABITATION—RUSSIAN STYLE

The closest Western model for the Russian constitution is the 1958 constitution Charles DeGaulle created for France's Fifth Republic. Both constitutions were fashioned by strong leaders to create order in a time of crisis. Both regimes mix elements of a presidential and parliamentary system. Both subordinate the government to parliament but empower an independently elected president to exercise considerable leverage over the parliament. There is a potential for confrontation should parliament fall under the control of political forces hostile to the president. That is what happened in France during the 1980s and again in the 1990s when the Socialist president, Francois Mitterand, faced a parliament dominated by conservative forces. This period of his administration, known as "cohabitation", produced more cooperation than conflict (to the surprise of many).

Russia's elections in 1993 created a quandary for President Yeltsin. The electorate had given him a parliament almost as unsympathetic to his program as the previous legislature, but it also gave him constitutional powers to run roughshod over that parliament. He could secure his reforms but at the expense of democracy. If he were to respect the popular will, he would have to step back from his reforms. Democracy or reform: but not both. Yeltsin chose democracy. His response to cohabitation was to move to the right, away from reform. Having suspended the parliament only months before, he was not inclined to repeat that act soon. "On no account should anyone think in terms of dissolving the new parliament," Yeltsin said in a press conference.[48]

Yeltsin's decision to retain Viktor Chernomyrdin as prime minister meant that he intended to pursue a moderate course toward reform. Chernomyrdin's position in the government was strengthened with the resignations in January 1994 of Egor Gaidar and Boris Fyodorov, two of the country's staunchest advocates of radical reform. By giving Chernomyrdin a free hand over the government, Yeltsin was acquiescing in the policy of continuing credits to powerful industrialists and agrarian lobbies whose backing he wanted to have. Chernomyrdin's clout with the State Duma gave him clout with the president.

The opening sessions of the Federal Assembly provided an interesting contrast of the two chambers. Yeltsin addressed the Council of the

Federation, after which it proceeded to elect Vladimir Shumeiko, an ally of Yeltsin, to be speaker. Viktor Chernomyrdin addressed the State Duma, promising the deputies that there would be no "shocks." As its speaker the Duma chose Ivan Rybkin, a leader of the Agrarian Party (beating Yurii Vlasov, a former Olympic weightlifting champion). In accordance with the constitution, the new parliament was opened by its eldest Liberal deputy, Gregory Lukava, who was a Communist turned Democrat. He urged the fledgling parliament to base its work "on the legacy of Aristotle, Beethoven and Timiryazev." As reported in the press:

> *Mr. Lukava easily and quickly brought the Duma to a furor that was close to collective hysteria, with chaotic shouting into the microphone and a menacing crowd of people all talking at once near the presidium . . . In the end, 190 Deputies, threatening to refuse to register and to boycott the meeting, demanded that Lukava be relieved of the burden of chairmanship, which was beyond him . . ."*[49]

Indeed, the large number of extremist deputies in the Duma, led by the demagogue of demagogues, Vladimir Zhirinovsky, foreshadowed a turbulent legislature. There were occasions when Zhirinovsky did get out of hand to create a degree of disorder. But as the Duma began its work, there was sufficient cooperation among the moderate deputies to prevent extremists from achieving positions of importance in the committees that ran the business of the Duma.

Cohabitation faced a major test early in the life of the State Duma. On February 23, the parliament voted to amnesty all those individuals involved in the August 1991 coup and the uprisings of September-October 1993. Initiated by speaker Ivan Rybkin, the action had the enthusiastic endorsement of Zhirinovsky who even described the amnesty as a fulfillment of a preelection promise. But most viewed the action as an act of national reconciliation. The vote of 252 in favor and 67 opposed saw Russia's Choice as the only faction not in favor of the amnesty.[50] Yeltsin considered the amnesty as a usurpation of his right of pardon, but in the end he acquiesced. It was certainly galling to him to see the unconditional release of Aleksander Rutskoi and Ruslan Khasbulatov, particularly with the expectation that the former might be a candidate in the next presidential election. On the other hand, he could take some consolation with the likelihood that a Rutskoi candidacy would divide the conservative opposition, since Zhirinosvky had made clear his intention to seek Yeltsin's position in the next presidential election.

In the late winter and spring of 1994 Yeltsin appeared to be faltering politically again. There were reports that his health was deteriorating as he spent lengthy periods at his *dacha* or on vacation at the Black Sea. In March, rumors were rife of an impending coup. His opponents began a campaign for early presidential elections instead of waiting until the scheduled date of 1996. With the adoption of the new constitution, Yeltsin's opponents adopted a radically different strategy from that of his earlier critics in the former Congress of People's Deputies. Where rivals like Rutskoi and Khasbulatov sought to weaken the presidency and take power via the parliament, Yeltsin's opponents now thought in terms of capturing the presidency itself. No longer was there any strong desire to install a powerful parliamentary system.

A change in tactics came with the change in strategy of this continuing struggle. Where previously the focus had been on the constitutional issue of parliamentary or presidential supremacy, now it was on the question of who would be president. Where before it was fought largely within the confines of government and over legal issues, now it shifted to the broader domain of public opinion and influences over the electorate. In this contest Yeltsin had the advantage over most of his adversaries of his relative popularity. Certainly he overshadowed the Rightists like Zhirinovsky and Rutskoi and also his moderate critics such as Gregorii Yavlinsky and Sergei Shakrai. But his popularity was a waning asset as crime, inflation, and domestic disarray bred disillusionment in the public at large. *Nezavisimaya Gazeta*'s authoritative list of Russia's one hundred most influential politicians in early 1994 placed Viktor Chernomyrdin as first with Yeltsin in second place.[51]

In this political environment Yeltsin resorted to an unorthodox tactic to bring about political stability and some relief from his rivals' incessant attacks. He proposed a pact on Civic Accord which for a two-year period would commit the nation's political forces to put aside their differences and cooperate for the benefit of economic and political stability. In order to obtain the largest possible adherence to this pact he made numerous concessions to his critics during the course of weeks of intensive negotiations.

The terms of the Civic Accord committed the president not to initiate early parliamentary elections in return for which other politicians promised not to demand early presidential elections. All signatories were prohibited from introducing "destabilizing" constitutional amendments. The Council of the Federation was committed to adopting new laws defining the respective powers of the central government and the constituent regions of the Federation. For its part the government promised to curb inflation and ensure financial stability and promote economic growth. Trade unions pledged not to engage in strikes aimed at the redistribution of budget monies. The regions and republics committed themselves to insure the collection of taxes and the proper remittance of taxes to the federal budget. Leaders of political parties and movements were prohibited from establishing paramilitary units and from attempting to involve the country's military forces in political struggles.[52]

Dubbed by one newspaper as "a Mutual Nonaggression Pact," the Accord was received skeptically by many. It had no legal standing and contained no sanctions against those who violated its provisions. Nevertheless, Yeltsin viewed this Civic Accord as an important instrument of political conciliation, and it received a surprisingly widespread response despite predictions that few politicians would cooperate. On April 28, 245 individuals representing most political factions signed the Accord in a ceremony in the Kremlin. Among the signatories were politicians as different as Egor Gaidar and Vladimir Zhirinovsky (the latter at one point offered to sell his signature to the highest bidder). Of particular importance to Yeltsin was the adherence of every regional leader but two and of every republic except Chechnya.[53] Subsequently, more than one hundred leading businessmen and bankers also endorsed the document. Notable among those who refused to sign the Accord were such disparate political personalities as Gregorii Yavlinsky of the Yabloko parliamentary faction who dismissed the accord as meaningless and Gennadi Zyuganov, the Communist leader who demanded that Yeltsin form a coalition government including Communists.

The Civic Accord did not change Russia's political climate. Such stability as existed reflected the fact that Yeltsin was for the time in control but that he was not attempting to use that control to implement radical reform. Recognizing his own limits, the Russian president accepted a division of labor in which he maintained control over foreign policy while domestic policy rested in the hands of his prime minister, Viktor Chernomyrdin, who worked closely with the leaders of the parliament, Ivan Rybkin and Vladimir Shumeiko.

The year 1994 was notable for the absence of the contentiousness between the legislature and president that had so dominated Russian politics in the previous two years. The parliament, whose first session ended in the summer, acknowledged that it had very little control over public policy. That was because of the legislative constraints built into the new constitution and because of the fragmentation of the Duma into several blocs which could not easily be mobilized to form a working majority. In the view of one member of parliament, "the essence of the matter is not the current Duma but the barely flickering flame of parliamentarianism that it symbolizes . . ."[54]

CHECHNYA AND THE RENEWAL OF CRISIS

The stability that calmed Russian politics during 1994 was more apparent than real. On December 11 Russia sent troops into Chechnya, one of the smaller components of the Russian Federation bordering Georgia in the Caucasus. The Chechen Republic had declared itself independent in 1991, but that independence was recognized neither by the Russian government nor any other state. Under the constitution adopted in 1993 unilateral succession was denied to any of the eighty-nine subjects of the Federation. Earlier, Yeltsin had sought to oust Chechen President Dzokhar Dudaev by supporting a "Provisional Council" led by the dissident Umar Avturkhanov, but that effort proved unsuccessful. Exactly why Yeltsin chose to suppress Chechen succession when he did was never publicly revealed. The stated reason for the invasion was to establish constitutional order over the breakaway republic and to eliminate the crime and corruption allegedly widespread in Chechnya. This move constituted a radical (and widely viewed as misguided) departure from Yeltsin's previous approach to national and regional problems. Until the Chechen misadventure, the Russian government had pursued a strategy of entering into special arrangements with individual republics and permitting a substantial amount of regional autonomy.[55] Prior to the Chechen war, Yeltsin had successfully negotiated broad agreements with most of the eighty-nine "subjects" of the Federation including a special bilateral accord with the obstreperous Tartarstan Republic. Under these arrangements, the subject territories were given considerable control over their economic resources, but at the same time they remained subject to federal law and particularly federal taxation. With Dudaev's government Yeltsin was unable to reach any kind of an accommodation.

Politically and militarily, the assault on Chechnya proved to be a disaster. For one thing, the war was brutally fought with high casualties on both sides. Grozny, the capital, was virtually destroyed by Russian forces. The wanton destruction of the civilian population and their homes produced dismay on both sides. The forces deployed by the Russian military proved to be unprepared and inept. Several Russian generals simply refused to lead their forces into combat. Thus, Chechnya immediately resulted in a sharp decline in the prestige of the Russian military.

It also brought a precipitous decline in the popularity of Yeltsin himself. Chechnya was the first televised war ever viewed by the Russian people. In contrast to the Soviet experience, this event was well covered by the media and widely watched by the viewing public. Perhaps the only bright spot in a gloomy situation was the vivid demonstration that the country had a free press. But that did not bring good news to the president. Public reaction to the war was overwhelmingly negative. A national poll early in 1995 found a 72 percent disapproval rate of the president's action and only a 16 percent approval rate.[56] A direct consequence was a catastrophic decline in the overall approval rating of Yeltsin's presidency. In February 1955, only 8 percent gave full confidence to Yeltsin. In a comparison with other political leaders, Yeltsin's approval rating for the first time dropped to fourth place.[57]

Politically Yeltsin found himself more isolated than at any time during his presidency. Many of his former democratic allies condemned his Chechen policy and many announced their intention to oppose his reelection should he decide to run for a second term in 1996. "Yeltsin has no political future," observed Sergei Yushenkov, the Chairman of the Parliament's Defense Committee and a member of the liberal Russia's Choice Party.[58] Ironically, it fell to right-wing nationalists to defend Yeltsin's war policy, though in the end they would hardly be reliable political allies because they differed from the president on so many other issues.

We have seen that throughout his presidency Yeltsin shifted back and forth between authoritarian and democratic practices. The Chechen decision and the way it was made marked a shift toward authoritarianism. Yeltsin's decision to invade Chechnya was made within the framework of a small executive body known as the Security Council. Created in 1992, the Security Council consisted of five permanent voting members and nine nonpermanent, non-voting members. The permanent members are the president, prime minister, security council secretary and the chairmen of the two houses of the Federal Assembly.[59] The two parliamentarians, Vladimir Shumeiko, the Chairman of the Council of the Federation, and Ivan Rybkin, the State Duma Chairman, were made full members after the war in Chechnya began. Ostensibly intended to bring the parliament into the decision-making process, the real reason for their inclusion was to co-opt their support and through them to garner support in parliament. Every indication was that Yeltsin had consulted with a very small number of advisers and that the most influential were from the military and the intelligence community as well as his body guard Aleksander V. Korzhakov.[60]

One of the most damaging consequences of Chechnya was that it sparked a new power struggle between the legislative and executive branches of government. We have already noted that the constitution strongly favors the latter over the former. Chechnya further undermined the capacity of parliament to exercise any check on the president when he made a costly and unpopular decision. In December, the Duma had overwhelmingly but futilely passed a resolution urging the Kremlin to stop the war. Yeltsin deliberately avoided parliamentary oversight by refusing to declare an emergency in the Chechen Republic. Such a declaration would have required approval by the Council of the Federation. Making Rybkin and Shumeiko full Security Council members helped to dampen parliamentary hostility to Yeltsin as both legislative leaders condoned Yeltsin's refusal to declare a state of emergency.

Early in 1995, efforts were made to force an end to the war by legislative means, but these failed to win a majority in parliament. The only party factions consistently supporting an anti-war position were Russia's Choice, Yabloko, and Women of Russia.[61] As the war proceeded inconclusively through the winter and spring, opposition grew throughout the country. It required only a dramatic event to crystalize that opposition and that event came in mid-June when a gang of two hundred guerrillas led by Shamil

Basayev seized some two thousand hostages in the Russian city of Budyonnovsk.

Several features of this assault provoked widespread concern and criticism. The fact that terrorist operations on such a large scale could happen inside Russia fostered a sense of vulnerability. Budyonnovsk was almost one hundred miles from the Chechen border. A desperate attempt to storm the hospital where the hostages were held failed completely and resulted in casualties among the victims. Overall the performance of the military seemed to parallel the ineptness of the Russian soldiers in Chechnya itself.

Within the Parliament, almost every party faction demanded the resignation of Minister of Defense Pavel Grachev. Over time, the criticism was extended to the Minister of the Interior, Viktor Yerin, to the Head of the Federal Security Council, Sergei Stepashin, and to others responsible for state security. Yeltsin was criticized for not being on top of the situation. He was in Halifax, Canada at the time meeting with the G-7 leaders. In the end, the crisis was ended by the successful negotiation of Prime Minister Chernomyrdin who in order to secure the release of the hostages permitted Basayev and his guerrillas to escape.

Notwithstanding Chernomyrdin's successful diplomacy, the Duma was outraged by the overall performance of the government and on June 21 voted 241 to 72 (with 20 abstentions) no confidence in the government.[62] (A motion of no confidence requires only a simple majority of 226 votes.) This was the first successful vote of no confidence under the new constitution. The constitution permits Yeltsin to ignore a Duma vote of no confidence unless a second vote is taken within a period of three months. If that happens, the president is required either to form a new government or to dismiss parliament and call for elections. Yeltsin had indicated his intentions to do the latter, if pressed. The Duma wanted to express its dissatisfaction, but it did not want face early elections. Yeltsin, too, wanted to avoid a showdown. As he had so often in the past, Yeltsin compromised with his critics and agreed to fire his ministers of security, interior and nationalities. He did not dismiss the principal target of Duma wrath, the Minister of Defense, presumably because of Grachev's long history of loyalty to Yeltsin. It worked. On July 1, the Duma voted again and this time failed to muster a majority for a vote of no confidence. Equally unsuccessful was an effort to institute impeachment proceedings against Yeltsin.[63]

What did all this maneuvering mean for Russian government and politics? In institutional terms it meant that the parliament had not yet established itself as a successful balance to the president, that is, a workable separation of powers had yet to be constructed. It also demonstrated the weakness of the party system in Russia. There existed a multiplicity of party factions in the Duma, but there was little connection between their activities and social forces outside of parliament. There was no party discipline and no party responsibility. The factions in opposition to the government could not mobilize as a counterforce to those that supported the government. In part this was because the parties were built around personalities rather than programs and party positions on issues frequently changed at the whim of those leaders. Political power continued to rest in the hands of the president, but Yeltsin was increasingly viewed as a lame duck president. By the latter half of 1995, political activity focused on the coming elections for a new parliament and president.

Parliamentary elections were scheduled for December 17, 1995. Yeltsin attempted to change the law regarding the number of Duma members chosen by party list. Believing that he would do better with deputies elected by single member districts, he proposed that three hundred deputies be elected by single member districts and 150 from party lists. But the Duma refused to go along and the law that was approved in the summer retained the same ratio of 225 from each category as was originally established.

Even before the election campaign officially started, in the summer every imaginable interest and political group began organizing a political party to seek representation in the Duma. By July, 260 political parties and blocs had organized. From that group, forty-three parties obtained the requisite number of signatures and were officially registered in November. They included all the major parties—Russia's Democratic Choice, Yabloko, the Communist Party, the Agrarians, Our Home Is Russia, the Congress of Russian Communities and the Liberal Democratic Party—as well as many lesser known specialized groups such as the Beer Lovers Party, Common Cause, Party of Economic Freedom, Association of Lawyers of Russia, Generation of the Frontier, and Power to the People. Recognizing that many would not win the necessary 5 percent of the vote to qualify for representation in the Duma, some of the parties formed coalitions or blocs. Yeltsin himself encouraged the formation of two centrist coalitions, one center right led by Viktor Chernomyrdin ("Our Home Is Russia") and one center left led by Ivan Rybkin. After Chechnya Yeltsin was abandoned by most of his former democratic liberal allies (such as Gaidar and Yavlinsky). He was even less popular with the communists and ultra-nationalists (the "reds and browns") who reflected the extremist elements of left and right. Thus, Yeltsin moved toward the center in hopes of getting a parliament with which he could work. He explicitly stated that the main goal of Chernomyrdin-Rybkin blocs was "to cut off the extremists on the flanks."[64]

Yeltsin's strategy failed. The results of the December parliamentary elections did not auger well either for adoption of his economic reforms or for his re-election prospects. The major parliamentary winner was the Communist Party. Led by Gennadi Zyuganov, it won 22.3 percent of the popular vote. Vladimir Zhirinovsky's Liberal Democratic Party was second with 11.18 percent of the vote. Viktor Chernomyrdin's Russia Is Our Home garnered only

10.13 percent, and Gregorii Yavlinsky's Yobloko was fourth with 6.39 percent. No other party gained the necessary 5 percent minimum to be represented in the Duma by those deputies selected according to the rule of proportional representation. [65]

As the campaign for the election of a new president on June 16, 1996, went into high gear, it seemed likely that Yeltsin's principal opponent would be Gennadi Zyuganov. A combination of factors—a decline in living standards, crime, the war in Chechnya, and even his health—made the Russian president an underdog in the presidential race. Boris Yeltsin's administration had begun a remarkable transformation of Russia's politics, but it was clearly the beginning, not the end. Russia had not yet emerged from the politics of transition. In the last chapter we will consider the prospects for a stable democratic system. But first we look at Russia's post-Soviet foreign policy and the Commonwealth of Independent States.

ENDNOTES

1. The full text of the decree is in *The Current Digest of the Post-Soviet Press (CDPSP)*, Vol. XLIII, No. 52, January 29, 1992, p. 6.

2. According to the Russian Ministry of Internal Affairs the "mafiya" controlled as much as 40 percent of the turnover in goods and services by 1993. Stephen Handelman, "The Russian 'Mafiya'", *Foreign Affairs*, Vol. 73, No. 2, March/April 1994, p. 84.

3. For a good analysis of the Soviet constitution and its modifications see Robert Sharlet, *Soviet Constitutional Crisis from De-Stalinization to Disintegration*. New York: M. E. Sharpe, 1992.

4. *Pravda*, January 30, 1992, p. 1.

5. Each session of the Congress of People's Deputies was numbered consecutively from the first in the summer of 1990.

6. This breakdown was made by Anatoly Karpychev in *Kuranty*. See *CDPSP*, Vol. XLIV, No. 16, May 20, 1992, p. 9. A more detailed breakdown of the factions at the Sixth Congress was made by Igor Yakovenko in *Nezavisimaya Gazeta*, 24, 1992, as reported in Ibid., p. 10.

7. *CDPSP*, Vol. XLIV, No. 14, May 6, 1992, pp. 6, 8.

8. *CDPSP*, Vol. XLIV, No. 16, May 20, 1992.

9. The Civic Union was formed by a coalition of the Democratic Party of Russia led by Nikolai Travkin, the People's Party of Free Russia founded by Aleksandr Rutskoi, and the All-Russian Renewal Union led by Arkady Volsky. See "The Civic Union: The Birth of a New Opposition in Russia?" by Elizabeth Teague and Vera Tolz, *RFE/RL Research Report (RFE/RL)*, Vol. 1, No. 30, July 24, 1992.

10. *CDPSP*, Vol. XLIV, No. 40, November 4, 1992, p. 1.

11. Yurii Skokov, an important member of the Civic Union, was considered by some to be the number-two man in government. For the powers of the Security Council, which continues to exist under the 1993 constitution see *CDPSP*, Vol. XLIV, No. 28, August 12, 1992, pp. 1–5.

12. *CDPSP,* Vol. XLIV, No. 33, September 16, 1992, p. 3. See also Bozidar Djelic, "Mass Privatization in Russian: The Role of Vouchers," in *RFE/RL,* Vol. 1, No. 41, October 16, 1992, pp. 41–44. Many of the vouchers were entrusted to investment funds which numbered in the hundreds. Some of these funds were used by swindlers to cheat the recipients. See Celestine Bohlen, "For New Russia, a New Brand of Swindler," *The New York Times,* March 17, 1994, pp. 1, 5.

13. *CDPSP,* Vol. XLIV, No. 43, November 25, 1992, p. 9.

14. *CDPSP,* Vol. XLIV, No. 49, January 6, 1993, p. 13.

15. *Izvestiya,* December 10, 1992 in *CDPSP,* Vol. XLIV, No. 50, January 13, 1993, p. 3.

16. A survey conducted in European Russia in the fall of 1992 showed Aleksandr Rutskoi with a broader base of support than Yeltsin. Amy Corning, "How Russians View Yeltsin and Rutskoi," *RFE/RL,* Vol. 2, No. 12, March 19, 1993, p. 57.

17. See Julia Wishnevsky, "Constitutional Crisis Deepens after Russian Congress," Ibid., Vol. 2, No. 13, March 26, 1993.

18. See *CDPSP,* Vol. XLV, No. 12, April 21, 1993, pp. 1–2.

19. *Izvestiya,* March 25, 1993, p. 1.

20. Ibid., March 30, 1993, pp. 1–2. The Constitutional Court subsequently ruled that only questions 3 and 4 required a vote of at least 50 percent of the entire electorate in order to be binding. Questions 1 and 2 were expressions of opinion only and required no specific action.

21. Ibid., March 30, p. 1.

22. Special Commission on Security and Cooperation in Europe, "Report on the April 25, 1993 Referendum in Russia," May 12, 1993, p. 11.

23. The twenty-one ethnic republics are Adygeya, Altai, Bashkortostan, Buryatia, Chechnya, Chuvashia, Dagestan, Ingushetia, Kabardino-Balkaria, Kalmykia, Karachaevo-Cherkessia, Karelia, Khakassia, Komi, Marii-El, Mordovia, North Ossetia, Sakha, Tartarstan, Tuva, Udmurtia.

24. See Ann Sheehy, "Russia's Republics: A Threat to Its Territorial Integrity?", *RFE/RL,* Vol. 2, No. 20, May 14, 1993, p. 34.

25. Richard Sakwa, *Russia's Politics and Society.* London: Routledge, 1993, pp. 79–83.

26. The text of the Federal Treaty is in *CDPSP,* Vol. XLIV, No. 13, April 29, 1992, pp. 15–16. Only Tartarstan and Chechnya refused to sign the Federal Treaty. Chechnya declared itself to be independent in 1991, and Tartarstan voted to be a sovereign republic in March 1992.

27. *Izvestiya,* July 13, 1993, pp. 1–2.

28. *CDPSP,* Vol. XLV, No. 28, August 11, 1993, pp. 4–5.

29. Richard Sakwa, "Parties and the Multiparty System in Russia," in *RFE/RL,* Vol. 2, No. 31, July 30, 1993, pp. 7–15. See also his *Russian Politics and Society,* chapter 4.

30. See Julia Wishnevsky, "Corruption Allegations Undermine Russia's Leaders," *RFE/RL,* Vol. 2, No. 37, September 17, 1993 and *CDPSP,* "Yeltsin Temporarily Suspends Rutskoi and Shumeiko," Vol. XLV, No. 35, September 29, 1993, pp. 1–8.

31. *Nezavisimaya Gazeta,* September 23, 1993, p. 1.

32. See report of Rubinfein, *The Wall Street Journal,* September 23, 1993, p. A12.

33. *Nezavisimaya Gazeta,* September 29, 1993, p. 1. An exception was made for American journalists who were permitted to enter the White House by agreement with the United States embassy.

34. Boris Yeltsin, *The Struggle for Russia.* Translated by Catherine A. Fitzpatrick. New York: Random House, 1994, p. 242. Yeltsin and Khasbulatov chose the same title for their memoirs.

35. Ruslan Khasbulatov, *The Struggle for Russia.* Edited by Richard Sakwa. New York: Routledge, 1993, p. 229.

36. Ibid.

37. The Congressional invitation to the states to send delegates to the Philadelphia Convention in 1787 was "for the sole and express purpose of revising the Articles of Confederation." Samuel Eliot Morison, *The Oxford History of the American People.* New York: Oxford University Press, 1965, p. 305.

38. Bill Clinton said, "It is clear that the violence was perpetrated by the Rutskoi-Khasbulatov forces . . . it is also clear that President Yeltsin bent over backwards to avoid the use of force . . ." *The New York Times,* October 4, 1993, p. 11.

39. See Julia Wishnevsky, "The Role of the Media in the Parliamentary Election Campaign," *RFE/RL,*Vol. 2, No. 46, November 19, 1993, p. 8.

40. Amy Corning, "Public Opinion and the Russian Parliamentary Elections," Ibid., Vol. 2, No. 48, December 3, 1993, pp. 18–19.

41. Commission on Security and Cooperation in Europe, "Russia's Parliamentary Election and Constitutional Referendum, December 12, 1993," Washington, January 1993, p. 1.

42. *Russian Government Today.* Washington, D. C.,: Carroll Publishing, 1994, pp. 3–18.

43. See Michael Specter, "Why Russia Loves this Man," *The New York Times Magazine,* June 19, 1994, pp. 26–33, 44–5, 52, 56.

44. In fact, the real number is almost certainly considerably less. A special group of election experts (part of the President's staff) reported widespread election fraud. Among its findings was that the election turnout was only 46 percent, which if true, would invalidate the constitution. They also found fraud in the election of members of the Federal Assembly. The major beneficiary of the fraud was Zhirinovsky's Liberal Democratic Party and the principal loser was Russia's Choice. However, except for a small number of district complaints, no one has chosen to challenge the legality of the December elections as a whole, so they stand as originally reported. See *CDPSP,* Vol. XLVI, No. 18, June 1, 1994, pp. 1–3.

45. The text of the 1993 constitution is in *CDPSP,* Vol. XLV, No. 45, December 8, 1993, pp. 4–16.

46. Art. 65. The Chechen Republic refused to accept its status as a member of the Russian Federation. The latter, for its part, does not recognize the independence of Chechnya (nor does anyone else). Practically, it is a part of Russia.

47. Art. 76.

48. *Nezavisimaya Gazeta,* December 23, 1993, p. 1.

49. *CDPSP,* Vol. XLVI, No. 2, February 9, 1994, p. 10.

50. Ibid., Vol. XLVI, No. 8, March 23, 1994, p. 1.

51. Alexander Rahr, "Russia's Future: With or Without Yeltsin," *RFE/RL,* Vol. 3, No. 17, April 29, 1994, p. 7.

52. See *CDPSP*, Vol. XLVI, No. 15, May 11, 1994, p. 13; Ibid., Vol. XLVI, No. 16, May 18, 1994, pp. 12–13; Ibid., Vol. XLVI, No. 17, May 25, 1994, pp. 1–4.

53. See Vera Tolz, "The Civil Accord: Contributing to Russia's Stability?", *RFE/RL*, Vol. 3, No. 19, May 13, 1994, pp. 3–4.

54. *CDPSP*, Vol. XLVI, No. 30, August 24, 1994, p. 9.

55. Edward W. Walker, "Federalism—Russian Style: The Federation Provisions in Russia's New Constitution," *Problems of Post-Communism*, Vol. 42, No. 4, July-August 1995, p. 4. See also Robert Sharlet, "The New Russian Constitution and Its Political Impact," Ibid., Vol. 42, No. 1, January-February 1995, pp. 6–7.

56. The poll was conducted by the Open Media Research Institute (OMRI) and reported by Michael Haney in "Russia's First Televised War: Public Opinion on the Crisis," *Transition*, April 14, 1995, p. 7.

57. See "Polls Track Plummeting Confidence in Yeltsin," *CDPSP*, Vol. XLVII, No. 14, May 3, 1995, pp. 1-6.

58. Steven Erlanger, "War's Political Price," *The New York Times*, January 1, 1995, p. 5.

59. See "Security Council: Just How Powerful Is It?", *CDPSP*, Vol. XLVII, No. 8, March 22, 1995, pp. 7–9.

60. *Izvestiya*, December 22, 1994, p. 1. See also Allesandra Stanley, "The Man at Yeltsin's Side: Some Russians See a Sinister Role," *The New York Times*, January 5, 1995.

61. "Duma Majority Votes Support of War," *CDPSP*, Vol. XLVII, No. 4, February 22, 1995, p. 12.

62. This was the first successful vote of no confidence under the new constitution. Michael Specter, "Angry Russian Parliament Votes to Rebuke Yeltsin Government," *The New York Times*, January 22, 1995.

63. The July vote of no confidence had the support of 193 deputies with 117 against and 48 abstentions. Allesandra Stanley, "Yeltsin Prevails in Second Vote on His Ouster," Ibid., July 2, 1995. 170 deputies voted for impeachment and 56 against. One abstained and 223 boycotted the vote. 300 votes would have been necessary to force a hearing. In this vote Yeltsin had the support of Russia's Choice and was opposed principally by the Communists and Zhirinovsky's nationalists. *Pravda*, June 28, 1995.

64. "Yeltsin Plans Left-Right-Center Blocs for Elections," *CDPSP*, Vol. XLVII, No. 17, May 24, 1995, p. 2.

65. The December 1995 election results can be found in "Official Election Results Confirms Communist Lead," *CDPSP*, Vol. XLVII, No. 52, January 24, 1996, pp. 9–10. See also, Robert W. Orttung, "Duma Elections Bolster Leftist Opposition," *Transition*, Vol. 2, No. 2, February 23, 1996, p. 7.

Commonwealth of Independent States

Occupied by the Soviet Union in 1945, administered by Russia, claimed by Japan.

Russia

CHAPTER 6

Commonwealth of Independent States

The Commonwealth of Independent States came into existence by accident. It was a system that no one in 1991 really wanted. After four years its future remains as problematic as it was at the beginning. While the Soviet Union was in the process of disintegration during 1990–91 there was a constitutional struggle over the shape of a successor structure to the U.S.S.R. The beginning of the end for the Soviet Union came as a result of the relatively free elections for the republic Supreme Soviets in March 1990. These elections brought to power nationalist movements determined to break free of Moscow's control. Beginning with the Baltic republics, all the constituent republics, of the union (and several autonomous republics of the Russian Federation) declared themselves to be sovereign and then proceeded to act as though they were in fact sovereign. Republican parliaments began a "war of laws" with the all-union government, enacting legislation in conflict with the Center. Following the coup attempt in August 1991, most of the republics declared themselves independent of the U.S.S.R.: Ukraine on August 24, Byelorussia on August 26, Moldova on August 27, Azerbaijan on August 30,

Uzbekistan on September 5, Tajikistan on September 9, Armenia on September 21, Turkmenistan on October 27.

Russia was in a different position. As early as June 12, 1990, the Russian Congress of People's Deputies had declared the Russian Federation (RSFSR) to be sovereign. But rather than break away from the center, President Boris Yeltsin sought during 1991 to have Russia take over the basic functions of government from the center. At the same time, he wanted to retain some form of union among the former Soviet republics. This position was shared with Belarus, Kazakhstan, and the four Central Asian republics, in contrast to Ukraine, Moldova, and the Transcaucasion republics, which were more independence minded. (Lithuania, Latvia and Estonia adamantly opposed any form of union with Russia.) Thus, in 1991 Yeltsin and Gorbachev agreed on the need for a new union treaty, but Gorbachev wanted the U.S.S.R. to be replaced by a federated state while the Russian president insisted upon a confederation. On April 23, Gorbachev and leaders of nine of the republics signed an agreement for a new union treaty that provided for a union of "sovereign states" rather than republics. It appeared that Yeltsin had prevailed.

All that, however, was before the aborted August coup. The impact of the coup was to intensify nationalistic demands for independence. When republican leaders sought in November to initial the text of a new union treaty, Ukrainian leader Leonid Kravchuk balked. On December 1, 1991 the people of Ukraine voted overwhelmingly for independence (90.3 percent) and that sealed the fate of a new union in any form. Yeltsin and Gorbachev had both agreed that a union without Ukraine was unthinkable.[1]

The Commonwealth of Independent States came into being because Boris Yeltsin was determined to preserve some form of union and the arrangement agreed upon at Belovezhskaia Pushcha on December 8, 1991 was the maximum President Leonid Kravchuk of Ukraine would accept.[2] For Ukraine, the commonwealth was a means to break away from the U.S.S.R. and establish its independence. The Belovezhskaia Pushcha agreement, signed by the heads of state and premiers of the three Slavic republics (Russia, Ukraine, and Belarus), created a loose federation with no powers of governance. Its central institutions, the Council of Heads of State and the Council of Heads of Government, lack authority to impose a decision on any commonwealth member. Such decisions as might be agreed upon require a consensus of all members. The Ukrainian government insisted that the commonwealth was not a state formation and therefore not a subject of international law. Nor was there a commonwealth citizenship. Indeed, in ratifying the Belovezhskaia Pushcha agreement, the Ukrainian parliament added amendments that further weakened the original text.

For his part, Boris Yeltsin, though anxious to be rid of Mikhail Gorbachev and his government, did want to maintain some form of unity among the former republics. So did several of the non-Slavic leaders, most particularly

Nursultan Nazarbaev, president of Kazakhstan. Not only did he and the leaders of the four Central Asian republics (Turkmenistan, Tajikistan, Kyrgystan, and Uzbekistan) want admission into the commonwealth, they demanded to be admitted as cofounders. Accordingly, on December 25, 1991 in Alma-Ata a protocol to the Belovezhskaia Pushcha agreement was signed expanding the commonwealth to eleven republics. Only the Baltic states and Georgia of the original fifteen republics chose not to join. Armenia, Azerbaijan and Moldova acceded notwithstanding strong sentiment in each to maintain full autonomy. Azerbaijan withdrew from the commonwealth in October 1992 but resumed membership in 1993.[3] An interesting feature of the commonwealth is that it was originally "open to accession by all member states of the former U.S.S.R. as well as for other states . . ."[4] One can only wonder what "other states" might have been candidates for membership.

The Commonwealth of Independent States is difficult to categorize as a political structure. It lacks the power of governance, so it is not a federation. Neither does it meet the conditions generally associated with a confederation. It does not have a charter or constitution. There are no general purposes acceptable to all its members. It is neither a political alliance nor an economic community. Nor is there a unifying symbol as the crown is for the British Commonwealth. Each member considers itself sovereign and independent. While the CIS has sponsored numerous agreements among its members, each state is free to choose which agreement to associate with and which to disregard. As a rule agreements signed by several or even all CIS members are not implemented. Kazakhstan's President Nazarbaev has more than once in exasperation described the CIS as a "president's club."

The purpose of the CIS is to unify states that were previously integrated tightly in a totalitarian structure and which broke away to become independent. There is neither historical nor theoretical evidence to guide such an endeavor. There is a voluminous literature examining the theoretical prerequisites for political integration of previously independent states.[5] And a few, Switzerland and the United States, for example, have succeeded. But to move in the opposite direction—from statehood to confederation—has no modern precedent. Thus, from its inception, the CIS has been struggling to define its purposes and groping for a means to achieve them.

Three factors account for the pressures to integrate the newly independent former Soviet republics into some form of a new union: economic, security and political. The most compelling were the economic factors. Seventy-five years of Soviet rule had created a high degree of economic interdependence among the republics of the former U.S.S.R. Russian oil and gas fueled the industries, homes and automobiles of the non-Russian republics; Ukraine supplied grain and other foodstuffs and rolled ferrous metal; Central Asia provided its cotton for the clothing industries in the western republics. Clearly there had to be agreed-upon rules to govern the exchange of goods and services among the various republics. Theoretically the best option would be a common market eliminating all internal borders to the free transit of goods, labor, resources and capital. But whether the economic space of the CIS was to be governed by free trade or by a more restrictive regime, there had to be unifying institutions to establish some uniformity in social and labor policies.

Then there was the ruble, each republic's unit of currency. Since Russia had the only presses for printing rubles, Moscow was in a position to determine each state's money supply and available credit. If the CIS countries wanted to remain a part of the "ruble zone," a central bank and policy-making institutions to maintain uniform fiscal policy would have to be created.

The military issue had two major components: the need to establish a command over nuclear weapons and to establish a joint CIS defense force. When the Soviet Union fell apart in 1991, nuclear weapons were possessed by Ukraine, Belarus, and Kazakhstan in addition to Russia. There were several possibilities for the disposition of these weapons: Each state could become an independent nuclear power; the nuclear weapons could be transferred to Russia; a joint command could be established by the four states with the bombs; or a larger, strategic command could be created among all the ex-Soviet republics. Nuclear proliferation—the first option—would have encountered strong international resistance and was quickly rejected by the nuclear weapons states themselves. The idea of transferring all nuclear weapons to Russia did not appeal to the other three—at least initially—so that left as the only feasible alternative some form of a joint CIS strategic command.

National security required also a joint military force to defend the newly independent states against foreign aggression. As the once formidable Red Army began to disintegrate, it seemed logical to many that it be replaced by a multinational force under a unified command as an alternative to a dozen or so separate armies. From the Russian perspective the prospect of having what once were internal borders defended by "foreign" armies was quite unpalatable.

A third factor for union was the hope that the successor to the Soviet Union could remain a "great power." Whatever its flaws, the Soviet Union had at least made the country a world power . . . indeed a superpower. Soviet citizens derived some satisfaction that they were members of a community respected or feared throughout the world. Thus, sentiments of nationalism spurred many ex-Soviets, Russian and non-Russian alike, to retain their status as citizens of a great power. These were some of the sentiments which induced the public and leadership of the newly independent states to make the CIS work and to strengthen it.

Nationalism, however, was a two-edged sword, and the edge of nationalism working against unification was much sharper than the forces for integration. Every republic staunchly defended its independence and sovereignty, but most particularly Ukraine, the Baltics, Moldova, and the Transcaucasian republics. As we have noted, the Baltic states and Georgia did not join the CIS and Moldova was slow to ratify its adherence. And, as we shall describe below, Ukraine vigorously resisted endowing the CIS with supranational authority. Among the Central Asian states there was support for the commonwealth, but not to the point where it infringed state sovereignty. The fact is that the memory of three-quarters of a century of Soviet power in Moscow was the most powerful factor undermining efforts to bring cohesion to the CIS.

After four years the forces for integration have been largely neutralized by the pressures for disintegration. The CIS survives, but it is virtually ineffective. Its first year was marked by frequent frustration though enough was accomplished for one observer to note that "the Commonwealth was a transitional organization which was developing rapidly."[6] In its second year, development slowed. Because of objections by Ukraine, Moldova and Azerbaijan no permanent forum was created to formulate policy.[7] The major responsibility fell to the Council of State and Council of Heads of Government, primarily the former. CIS summits meet irregularly, averaging less than once a month. And when they have met, some presidents failed to show up. Over a two-year period, approximately three hundred agreements were signed, but to the lament of CIS supporters virtually none of them were implemented.

ECONOMIC CHAOS

Several issues have dominated the CIS agenda. They can be grouped into three categories: 1) economic, 2) military and security, and 3) organizational.

Economic relations among the CIS members started off on a rocky road. President Yeltsin had determined that radical economic reform of Russia was to be a top priority of his government. In January 1992 he introduced a central feature of that reform, price control, without consulting his CIS partners notwithstanding his obligation under the CIS agreement to coordinate economic policy. Ukraine and some other states were outraged. But Moscow was not alone in pursuing economic practices unilaterally. Several CIS members placed restrictions on the export of goods to the Russian Federation, prompting Russia to retaliate. Within a short time, interrepublic trade became enmeshed in a web of trade restrictions. Efforts early in 1992 to resolve differences and establish a viable economic framework for the commonwealth proved to be futile as each state sought to protect its economy from external influence, particularly the instability emanating from Moscow.

Other problems developed as a result of the CIS commitment initially to retain the ruble as a common unit of currency (during 1992 Ukraine was the only CIS member to withdraw fully from the ruble zone). In July 1992 the Russian Central Bank tightened its rules governing the settlement of accounts with banks outside of Russia. Payments were processed only for banks that maintained a net positive balance with the Russian Central Bank. This requirement forced Russian enterprises to demand hard-currency payment for exports when a republic lacked a positive credit balance. Ukraine, Belarus, and Kazakh central banks protested the adoption of these payment rules without any prior consultation. Another complaint of the non-Russian banks was the concentration by the Russian Central Bank of cash emission inside Russia.

On the other hand, the Russians were victimized by the lax monetary and budget policies pursued by the other CIS governments, giving them what economists called a "free ride." The inflationary effects of policies pursued by CIS governments were spread throughout the ruble zone including Russia. While Moscow could regulate the cash emission inside Russia, it was unable to imposed fiscal discipline in the other republics.[8]

Notwithstanding the benefits of the "free ride," many CIS members wanted their own currency in order to secure more complete and independent control over their own economies. They were simply unwilling to subordinate their economies to Moscow. Thus Ukraine and Belarus introduced republic coupons to supplement ruble notes. This permitted them to run budget deficits, issue credits, and in general to pursue inflationary fiscal policies. While national currencies tended to complicate trade among CIS members in the short run, in the long run it forced some republics to take more responsibility for domestic macroeconomic policies.

Those republics that continued to use the ruble were pressured by Russia to subordinate monetary policy to the Russian Central Bank or to abandon the use of the ruble. In July 1993 the Russian government introduced a controversial currency reform prohibiting the use of pre-1993 ruble notes in Russia and allowing only Russian citizens, enterprises and foreign visitors to exchange old rubles for new ones. At that time, nine republics were still using the ruble either exclusively or together with a local currency. They were Belarus, Azerbaijan, Armenia, Georgia, Moldova, Kazakhstan, Tajikistan, Turkmenistan, and Uzbekistan. Kyrgyzstan had joined Ukraine in abandoning the ruble. Subsequently Azerbaijan, Turkmenistan, Moldova and Georgia decided to abandon the ruble. For Russia, the central concern was not who belonged in the ruble zone but how to control the value of the ruble.

One of the interesting contradictions between CIS economic policy during 1992–93 was the sharp contrast between rhetoric and behavior. On numerous occasions CIS leaders committed their governments to greater integration and cooperation at the same time they were pursuing unilateral policies. Thus at a meeting in Bishkek (Kyrgyzstan) on October 9, 1992, the CIS leaders signed an agreement on a Unified Monetary System. On May 14,

1993 in Moscow they signed a declaration of intent to increase economic integration. It envisioned a common market for the free transit of goods, services,
capital and labor. Two months later Russia, Ukraine and Belarus announced
their intention to integrate their economies in a "single economic space."[9] To
date only Russia and Belarus have begun integration.

Economic relations have yet to be normalized. In 1992, trade declined
sharply. A major problem was the chronic trade imbalance between Russia
and the other CIS members (particularly with Ukraine). To resolve this imbalance, Russia, as noted above, imposed a variety of payments and trade
restrictions. Inflation was rampant in 1992–93, and living standards declined.
The answer to these problems is supranational economic bodies imposing a
common policy on all. Leonid Kravchuk, former president of Ukraine,
summed up the problem and explained the contradiction between words
and deeds in observing, "We support economic integration, but the word
'union' will cause an allergic reaction among the population."[10]

MILITARY FRAGMENTATION

Military coordination proved to be as difficult as economic integration.
Differences over whether there should be unified armed forces erupted at the
very first CIS summit on December 30, 1991. Ukraine, fearing that a unified
force would threaten its sovereignty, demanded the right to create a national army. It also sought control over military assets on its territory including
the Black Sea Fleet headquartered in the Crimean city of Sevastopol.
Ukraine's position clashed sharply with the views of Russia's leadership,
particularly the military who sought a unified armed force with only minimal republic control over military affairs. Clearly Russia and Ukraine were
operating from differing conceptions of national security. Russians viewed
the probable threat to national security as coming from outside the territorial domain of the CIS. To the Ukrainians, the major concern was Russia itself.
President Kravchuk was pressured at home to take a hard line because the
million-man army in the Ukraine was only 40 percent ethnically Ukrainian
and was commanded by an officer corps that was 75 percent Russian.

As a concession to Ukraine, Moldova, and Azerbaijan, the CIS leaders
confirmed the right of each member state to create its own army. They also
established the Council of Defense Ministers, headquartered in Moscow, to
oversee security issues. At the third CIS summit in Minsk in February 1992,
the issue of whether a common military would be unified or joint and who
would participate was heatedly debated and not resolved, though there was
agreement to make Evgenii Shaposhnikov Commander-in-Chief of the CIS
Joint Armed Forces.[11]

During its first year no issue threatened to disrupt the CIS more than the military one, and the principal confrontation was between Ukraine and Moscow. One of Kravchuk's first acts as president was to subordinate all military formations in the Ukraine (except strategic forces) to the president and minister of defense. All military personnel in the country were required to take an oath of allegiance to the Ukraine. As will be discussed below, the sharpest point of contention was the Ukrainian demand for control over the "nonstrategic" component of the Black Sea Fleet. Ukraine was not alone in opposing a unified CIS army. In January the Belarus parliament voted to create a ministry of defense and to subordinate all former Soviet troops on its territory to Belarus authority.

The hope of the Russian military that the CIS might become a framework for a unified security system as a replacement for the Soviet armed forces proved to be illusory. Suspicion was deep among several members that the CIS High Command really took its orders from the Russian government and was in effect a surrogate for Russian power. The close personal relationship between President Yeltsin and Shaposhnikov did little to dispel that perception. Consequently support for a unified CIS command dwindled to only five members.

The lack of consensus regarding a CIS high command posed a problem for Moscow regarding control over former Soviet armed forces outside the territory of the Russian Federation. That problem was resolved on May 7, 1992 when the Russian government announced its decision to create an independent Russian army. With the development of national armies, the CIS command increasingly became obsolete except in one area: nuclear weapons. According to the original CIS compact, "The member states of the commonwealth will preserve and maintain under joint command a common military-strategic space, including unified control over nuclear weapons . . ."[12] For about a year, the Russian High Command and the CIS Joint Command coexisted in a relationship whose boundaries were far from clear. All that changed on June 15, 1993 when the abolition of the CIS Joint Military Command was announced in Moscow. Henceforth the security of each member rested on its own defense with relations between the military commands of CIS members determined by bilateral agreements.

The end of the CIS command confirmed Russia's intention to assume full control over all nuclear weapons in the commonwealth. Russia's military leaders had never reconciled themselves to the idea that Russia should be required to share with another government the decision to deploy or use nuclear weapons whether of the strategic or tactical variety. As Russian Defense Minister Pavel Grachev explained it, "The main command, as well as the CIS, is not a state and cannot have the right to control and use nuclear weapons."[13] However, it was one thing for Russia to demand control of strategic nuclear weapons and another to secure it. When the CIS was established, nuclear weapons were possessed by Belarus, Kazakhstan, Ukraine, and Russia. They included both tactical and strategic bombs. Belarus, Kazakhstan, and Ukraine agreed to dispose of the tactical weapons, and on May 6, 1992 the CIS command announced the completion of the withdrawal of all tactical nuclear weapons from the Ukraine. The disposal of strategic weapons proved to be more problematical. Although the Belovezhskaia Puscha Agreement of December 30, 1991 provided that the strategic forces of the CIS were to be under a joint command and Ukraine committed itself to eliminating all its nuclear weapons by the end of 1994, it did not specify who actually owned the weapons or how they should be disposed. In principle a unified control of strategic weapons was to be exercised by the CIS commander and the Russian president acting in agreement with the heads of states of the CIS nuclear states, but in fact the problem of control plagued Ukrainian-Russian relations throughout 1992 and 1993.

During this period the West pressured the three non-Russian nuclear states to accept unconditional nonnuclear status. Legally, that meant adherence to the nonproliferation treaty and ratification of the START I treaty. Practically, that would involve either destroying all strategic nuclear weapons or turning them over to Russia. A step in that direction was taken on May 23, 1992 when United States Secretary of State James Baker met with the foreign ministers of the CIS nuclear weapons states in Lisbon. They signed the Lisbon protocol to the START I treaty. This protocol committed Belarus, Kazakhstan, and Ukraine to ratify the nonproliferation treaty "in the shortest possible time."[14] But continued antagonism between Ukraine and Russia induced Ukraine to set conditions for the dismantling of its nuclear weapons. One condition was Kiev's demand that the West provide Ukraine with security guarantees. The West refused to meet Ukrainian requirements. Another condition was compensation for the value of the uranium and the cost of dismantling the bombs. On that issue the United States was prepared to negotiate. After Russia, Belarus, and Kazakhstan ratified the START I treaty (in November 1992, February 1993, and July 1992 respectively), pressure on Ukraine to do likewise increased. Ukraine was also reluctant to ratify the nonproliferation treaty.

In early September 1993, presidents Yeltsin and Kravchuk met in Massandra, Crimea to resolve the controversies over the Black Sea Fleet (see below) and the transfer of Ukraine's 1,656 remaining nuclear warheads to Russia. When reports surfaced that Kravchuk had agreed to turn over its nuclear weapons and its share of the Black Sea Fleet as a means of paying off its huge debt to Russia, there was a firestorm of criticism throughout the country, forcing Kravchuk to insist that no definitive decision had been made at Massandra. Vyacheslav Chornovil, leader of the main opposition party, Rukh, suggested impeachment of Kravchuk. Those elements in Ukraine opposed to giving up nuclear weapons were suspicious that Russia had not genuinely accepted the idea of an independent, sovereign Ukraine. In October, Kravchuk stated publicly that Ukraine was considering retaining forty-six SS-24 missiles (each capable of carrying up to ten nuclear warheads). To allay the fears of the United States, from whom he was seeking financial compensation in the billions of dollars for demobilizing the remaining nuclear warheads, Kravchuk promised that "they will not be aimed at the United States."[15]

THE BLACK SEA FLEET AND THE CRIMEA

We consider here the controversy over the Black Sea Fleet and the Crimea though technically they were not issues before the CIS. They were fundamentally bones of contention between Ukraine and Russia. But the ramifications for the CIS were serious because the survival of the commonwealth is closely linked to Russian-Ukrainian relations. In January 1992 when Leonid Kravchuk claimed jurisdiction over all general-purpose forces in Ukraine, he included the entire Black Sea Fleet, headquartered in the Crimean port of Sevastopol. Boris Yeltsin rejected Kravchuk's claim out of hand though his rationale was initially unclear. In statements made within days of each other, he asserted that the Black Sea Fleet was part of the CIS strategic forces and thus under the Joint Command, and that "The Black Sea Fleet has been, is and will continue to be Russia's."[16] Under nationalist pressure, Moscow increasingly pressed the latter argument. Vice-President Alexander Rutskoi was a particularly vehement spokesman for the Russian claim to the fleet.[17] Yeltsin however, anxious to avoid a rupture with Ukraine, worked out an arrangement in the summer of 1992 to divide the fleet into separate Russian and Ukrainian navies. Unable to agree on how to split the fleet, Kravchuk and Yeltsin worked out a temporary plan by which both states would jointly finance and use the fleet.

This temporary arrangement did not end the acrimony over ownership and control of the fleet. There continued to be sharp disagreements over the payments to sailors in the fleet, over Russian claims to basing rights in Sevastopol, and over the flag to be flown aboard the ships. Another summit meeting in the summer of 1993 produced an agreement to divide the fleet equally but nationalists in both the Russian and Ukrainian parliaments threatened to prevent ratification. Indeed, on July 9 the Russian Supreme Soviet outraged Ukrainian opinion when it passed a resolution asserting that Sevastopol, the home port of the Black Sea Fleet, was part of the territory of the Russian Federation. Yeltsin firmly rejected the Supreme Soviet's action stating that he was "ashamed of the decision,"[18] but Ukrainian fears were not mollified.

When Yeltsin and Kravchuk met yet again at Massandra on September 3, it appeared that a resolution of the controversy had been achieved. Yeltsin announced: "The Black Sea Fleet will be transferred entirely to Russia. Russia is to pay Ukraine half of the fleet's value."[19] Russian control over the entire fleet constituted a major victory for Russia in its contest with Ukraine and for Yeltsin in his struggle against the Russian parliament. There were reports of euphoria in Moscow. However, the negative reaction to the agreement back home produced qualifications from Ukrainian spokesmen that suggested that Ukraine was no more committed to giving up the fleet than it was to abandoning nuclear weapons. The political changes that took place in Moscow during September and October 1993 contributed to reducing tensions between the two governments.[20]

For Ukraine, both the nuclear and naval issues were linked fundamentally to a more basic issue which was the question of the territorial integrity and sovereignty of the country. The basic fact is that economically Ukraine cannot afford either nuclear weapons or a fleet in the Black Sea, nor does either serve her real national security needs. But Ukraine saw itself threatened by Russia (not necessarily a Yeltsin-led Russia but perhaps one led by a more aggressive nationalist leadership.) And no issue goes to the heart of Ukrainian fears more than the controversy over the Crimea.

Ukraine's role in bringing about the collapse of the Soviet Union followed by Kravchuk's disruptive behavior in the CIS provoked Russian nationalists to demand the restoration of the Crimea to Russia. The Crimea had been part of the Russian Federation (RSFSR) until 1954 when Nikita Khrushchev arbitrarily gave it to Ukraine to mark the three hundredth anniversary of the "reunification" of Ukraine with Russia. It was the only *oblast* in Ukraine (it is now an autonomous republic) with a Russian majority. As of 1989, Russians accounted for 67.04 percent and Ukrainians 24.75 percent of the Crimean population. Furthermore, almost half of the Ukrainians in the Crimea consider Russian to be their native language.[21] Barely a month into the life of the CIS, Russia's Supreme Soviet voted overwhelmingly to examine the constitutionality of Khrushchev's action in 1954. That act, said Sergei Stankevich, "has no legal basis. The Supreme Soviet will put an end to it."[22] And that is what the Supreme Soviet did on May 21 when it resolved that the 1954 transfer "had no legal force from the moment it was adopted.[23] The Supreme Soviet called for state-to-state negotiations between Russia and Ukraine along with the participation of the Crimea. Ukraine's response was immediate and unequivocal. It rejected talks of any kind on an issue deemed to be "Ukraine's internal affairs." Extremist statements flowed from both sides. Sergei Baburin, a militant in the Russian parliament, told the Ukrainian ambassador, "If we don't get the Crimea from you, there will be a war between Russia and the Ukraine." A Ukrainian legislator replied, "The Crimea will be Ukrainian or it will become totally depopulated."[24]

Yeltsin avoided taking a clear position on the questions but made it clear that he would do everything possible to avoid a rupture with Ukraine. To a *Pravda* interviewer in May he said, "We and Ukraine have a thousand-year history of relations, and what — are we going to fight now? No one would forgive us for that crime."[25] He demanded that a solution be found "by means of negotiation." Leonid Kravchuk too sought to cool passions. He reported to the Ukrainian Supreme Soviet, "Maximum efforts are being made to reduce the political tensions with Russia."[26] Both leaders were then encountering growing domestic political opposition and probably came to the same conclusion that their interests would be better served by cooperation rather than conflict.

In mid-1992 a dramatic change in the conflict between Russia and Ukraine took place. On June 23 Yeltsin and Kravchuk met in the Russian resort town of Dagomys and signed an accord that resolved a large number of issues particularly in the economic sphere. Agreements were reached on the contentious question of dividing property, including property abroad. State borders would be opened with visa-free access to citizens of both countries. Of particular significance, for the first time in months Kravchuk affirmed his country's intention not to withdraw from the CIS. A number of troubling issues were not covered in the Dagomys accord. One was the Crimea. However, both leaders affirmed that their countries had no territorial claims against each other. The failure to include the Crimean issue constituted a tacit acceptance on Russia's part that it was an internal affair of Ukraine.

As the struggle between Yeltsin and the Russian parliament heated up during 1992 and 1993, the ultranationalists in the legislature sought to challenge Yeltsin's credentials as a patriot. Led increasingly by Vice-President Rutskoi, they took a hard line on the Crimean issue. Even some liberals, such as Anatolii Sobchak, mayor of St. Petersburg, criticized the government for failing to defend Russia's claim to the Crimea. The Supreme Soviet resolution of July 9, 1993 asserting that Sevastopol, the Crimean home port for the Black See Fleet, was part of the territory of the Russian Federation was another blow in the struggle between president and parliament. Yeltsin's rejection of the resolution was thought at the time to be a risky move politically. However, Yeltsin's successful dismissal of the parliament in September gave him some leverage to work out Russia's difference with Ukraine on the Crimea and other issues.

PEACEKEEPING

One of the promises made by the CIS was to promote security through peacekeeping. At the fourth CIS summit in Kiev on March 20, 1992, ten of the CIS members signed an agreement spelling out the principles for the use of "collective peacekeeping forces" by CIS members. Mirroring the practices developed in United Nations peacekeeping operations, the CIS agreement required that peacekeeping forces be utilized only with the consent of all parties and after a ceasefire had been agreed upon, and that the peacekeeping forces not be used in combat against a party to a conflict. A decision to deploy peacekeeping forces could be made by the Council of the CIS Heads of State on a consensus basis. At the time, however, no provision was made for establishing peacekeeping forces. Russia's efforts to create such a force encountered resistance from several of the original signatories to the agreement including Ukraine, Belarus, and Azerbaijan. As a result, the Russian government took upon itself the responsibility for organizing peacekeeping operations outside of the CIS framework. As in other areas where the CIS has been unable to reach a consensus smaller groups of states have chosen to act on their own. Peacekeeping forces deployed to date have been primarily Russian. In the eyes of some, this has raised questions that Moscow was using peacekeeping forces to extend its influence over the former Soviet republics.

Peacekeeping operations were initially undertaken in Georgia and Moldova. Hostilities began in Georgia in the spring of 1989 between Ossetians seeking to unify their autonomous region with the North Ossetian Republic in the Russian Federation. In the summer of 1992, Georgian State Council Chairman Eduard Shevardnadze and Yeltsin agreed on a joint Russian-Georgian-Osset peacekeeping force to stop the fighting. Shevardnadze began to have second thoughts about Russians in South Ossetia after relations between Russia and Georgia deteriorated following the outbreak of rebellion in Abkhazia (another province of Georgia), amid suspicions that Moscow supported the Abkhaz secessionists.

Moldova is another former Soviet republic confronted with a secessionist movement. When Moldova proclaimed its independence in 1991 the Russians in the left bank of the Dnestr River declared the "Dnestr Republic" to be independent of Moldova. Comprising five districts and the city of Tiraspol, the Dnestr region has a mixed population of 40.1 percent Moldovan, 28.3 percent Ukrainian and 25.5 percent Russian. [27] The secessionists were aided by the Fourteenth Army, a component of the former Red Army headquartered in Tiraspol. Here, as in the Crimean case, nationalists in the Russian parliament supported the Russians seeking to break away from Moldova. Vice-President Rutskoi visited the Dnestr region in April 1992 to encourage a rally to press for "self-determination," a position that was endorsed by the Russian Congress of People's Deputies. Russian Foreign Minister Andrei Kozyrev proposed that the Fourteenth Army be used as a peacekeeping force, but Moldova, Ukraine and Rumania vetoed the idea.[28] Moldova eventually agreed to accept a peacekeeping force of Russians and Moldovans in return for Russian recognition that the "Dnestr Republic" be considered a part of Moldova. Only if Moldova itself should unite with Rumania would the "Dnestr Republic" be permitted to determine its own future.

The largest and most controversial of Russia's military operations on territories of the former Soviet Union is in Tajikistan. Following the outbreak of civil war, the president of Tajikistan worked out an arrangement with Evgenii Shaposhnikov, CIS commander, for the deployment of CIS peacekeeping forces in that state. There was no pretense of impartiality as Moscow joined with the Tajik government to suppress a coalition of Islamics, nationalists, and democrats to keep in power a regime of former Communists. Approximately twenty thousand Russian troops were engaged in combat in the deadliest civil war in any of the CIS states. In 1993, two Russian divisions were sent to patrol the rugged 900 mile Tajik-Afghan border in order to counter what Russia feared was an Islamic threat from the south. [29]

Russian spokesmen refer to the use of Russian forces in CIS states as CIS peacekeeping operations; and for the most part, they did reflect a desire to end ethnic and nationalist fighting along the periphery of Russia. But the fact that none of the operations has been in compliance with established CIS peacekeeping principles raises the question that Russia has been protecting its national interests under the guise of CIS peacekeeping.

Internal disorders were not the only threat to the security of CIS members. There was a widespread sense of insecurity among the newly independent states, particularly among the Central Asian republics. None of the Central Asian states possessed strong national defense forces, and each turned to Russia for assistance in building national armed forces. At a Heads of State summit in Tashket in May 1992, six CIS members put their signature to a collective security pact. Forming the new alliance were Armenia, Russia, Kazakhstan, Uzbekistan, Kyrgystan, and Tajikistan. Belarus, though an active supporter of the CIS, declined to sign on the grounds that its foreign policy was one of "neutrality." Leonid Kravchuk chose not even to attend the Tashkent meeting. According to the terms of the pact, the parties will not join alliances threatening a signatory; they will render aid should a signatory become the victim of an attack; and they agreed to hold regular consultations on security questions.

What the collective security pact really boils down to is whether or not Russia will assist one side or another in a conflict involving a CIS member. Armenia and Georgia have both sought Russian aid in their respective wars. Armenian President Levon Ter-Petrossyn invoked the Tashkent CIS security agreement in its struggle with Azerbaijan over the sovereignty of Nagorno-Karabakh. Moscow has supported the Armenians because of Azerbaijan's nationalist anti-Russian orientation, particularly under President Abulfaz Elchibey. With regard to Georgia's call for Russian aid against Abkhazian forces Moscow pointedly reminded the government in Tbilisi that Georgia was not a member of the CIS. Indeed, until late 1993, Georgia and Azerbaijan were the two hold-outs in the Caucasus on CIS membership. Both governments changed policies and decided to join the CIS and Moscow, not surprisingly, shifted its policies.[30]

INSTITUTIONAL DEVELOPMENTS

One measure of its uncertain prospects is the lack of CIS institutional development. In this regard there is some parallel between the CIS and the states that comprise its membership inasmuch as few of the post-Soviet republics have developed enduring political institutions. After four years, the CIS remains an amorphous body lacking a charter or constitution or any mechanism to ensure compliance with agreements reached. As noted above, the main obstacle to the creation of permanent structures is Ukraine. Fearing Russian domination, Ukraine consistently opposes any institutions that might become a nucleus for the recreation of the old "center". At a summit in 1992, there was limited agreement on the creation of a CIS Economic Arbitration Court and an Economic Council, but little was ever done to breathe life into the proposals.

Interrepublic differences were not the only impediment to CIS institutional growth. During 1993, Russian internal politics squashed the nascent development of an Interparliamentary Assembly (IPA). In March 1992, the IPA was founded to foster parliamentary cooperation among CIS members. Delegations from Armenia, Belarus, Kazakhstan, Kyrgystan, Russia, Tajikstan, and Uzbekistan signed the accord. Again Ukraine opted out. St. Petersburg was chosen as the IPA home, and as a gesture of support Mayor Anatolii Sobchak gave the Assembly the Tauride Palace for its permanent headquarters. The Council of the Assembly was created to organize the IPA's activities. The first chairman of the Council, unanimously picked, was Ruslan Khasbulatov, chairman of the Russian parliament. Khasbulatov proved to be a vigorous promoter of the IPA, but in so doing he attempted to make the institution an instrument of his struggle again Boris Yeltsin. He called upon the IPA to take over leadership of the CIS from the CIS presidents whose work he called "chaotic and unpredictable."[31] In December 1992, the Russian Congress of People's Deputies under Khasbulatov's guidance appealed to the IPA and CIS presidents to consider creating a confederation or another framework to unify the peoples of the former U.S.S.R. Fundamentally, Khasbulatov was using the IPA in his struggle with Yeltsin to assert the value of parliamentary supremacy over that of executive power. His downfall and arrest in October ended the movement for parliamentary supremacy within the CIS. Even before the events of October 1993, the CIS chief executives had created an alternative structure—the Coordinating Consultative

Committee and the Executive Secretariat—to oversee implementation of CIS declaration. However, most efforts to promote CIS integration have been put on hold pending the development of stable political institutions in Russia.

One obstacle to institutional development has been the lack of a CIS constitution. England is proof that political structures can be established without a written constitution, but the CIS states lack a history of cooperation—let alone a tradition of constitutionalism. Thus, from the beginning those members seeking a stronger, more integrated union pushed for the adoption of a CIS Charter or constitution. Early in 1993, the leaders of Kazakhstan and the four Central Asian republics met in Tashkent to consider common action in the face of CIS paralysis. It was a warning to the European republics that the Asian (and largely Moslem) states were considering going their own way. Yeltsin himself, not unsympathetic to the idea of a new CIS Charter, joined with six other CIS states at the Eighth CIS summit in Minsk on January 22, 1993 to recommend a draft CIS Charter for ratification by member parliaments. Ukraine, Turkmenistan, and Moldova were among the nonsignatories though they did sign a declaration indicating the possibility of signing in the future. The Agreement set one year as the time frame for parliamentary ratification.

The Charter provides for a commonwealth of sovereign and equal states essentially along the same lines as the Belovezhskaia Pushcha and Alma-Ata agreements creating the CIS. Members agree to cooperate in a wide range of areas including foreign policy, economics, collective security and human rights. A category of associate membership is recognized for those states that wish to participate in only "individual aspects" of commonwealth activity. The central guiding (but not governing) organs remain the Councils of Heads of States and Heads of Governments. Decisions are to be reached by consensus with the provision that any member can withdraw from an issue without impeding a consensus. A new arrangement for meetings specifies that the Council of Heads of State meet twice a year and the Council of Heads of Government four times annually. Minsk remains the capital of the commonwealth and Russian the working language.

Prospects

Commonwealth politics from the beginning have been overshadowed by the political struggles in Russia. It was clear that before a new constitutional order for the former Soviet Union could be established there would have to be a viable constitutional order in Russia. Yeltsin would have to unify his country before he could unify the commonwealth. Russian policy toward the CIS has been complex and at times contradictory. Yeltsin clearly has wanted a stronger commonwealth; but he was determined that it should include the active participation of the European and Transcaucasian republics, most particularly Ukraine. He has therefore gone to considerable lengths to cajole and even pressure Ukrainian participation. Toward this end he has sought to resolve and diffuse the points of contention between the two slavic states, notably on the issues of the Crimea and the Black Sea Fleet. Yeltsin has shown little interest in a Moslem-Russian union, although ironically the Moslem states have demonstrated the strongest interest in a genuine confederation.

Toward those states reluctant to join the CIS, Russia has exerted pressures. In the Caucasus that pressure took the form of support for the Abkhazians against Georgia and for Armenia in its war with Azerbaijan. In Moldova the presence of the fourteenth Army was pressure enough.[32] In September 1993, Eduard Shevardnadze in desperate need for Russian help announced, "I sent a telegram to Moscow saying Georgia will join the Commonwealth of Independent States, which I was against until the last moment."[33] Azerbaijan has also ratified the CIS agreement after holding out for almost two years. Only the Baltic states of the former Soviet Union are not in the commonwealth.

Yeltsin clearly views the CIS as a means to promote Russia's interests, and on many issues the Russian position at CIS summits has prevailed. But Russia does not control the CIS on all issues. At a summit in Ashgabat, Turkmenistan a proposal by Yeltsin to give Russians outside of Russia "special" status, including potential dual citizenship, was not approved. Nationalist sensitivities to national sovereignty still reign in the non-Russian republics.[34]

Although Russian efforts to use the CIS to reintegrate the former Soviet republics were unsuccessful, Moscow found an alternative function for the Commonwealth during the second half of Yeltsin's administration. As we will note in the chapter on Russia's foreign policy, Russia in 1994 and 1995 moved away from its initial pro-Western orientation and became more nationalist in outlook. One expression of this new orientation was increasing use of Russian forces for peacekeeping and peacemaking in the regions on the country's periphery. To do this with a minimum of outside interference, Moscow found it useful to organize peacekeeping operations within the framework of the CIS. To legitimize these activities, Russia actively promoted and sought recognition by the United Nations and the CSCE (after 1994 the OSCE) of the CIS as a "regional" and as an "international" organization. During the December 1993 summit meeting in Ashgabat, the CIS formally requested that the United Nations grant the CIS the status of an international organization. In February 1994, Foreign Minister Kozyrev requested that the CIS be granted observer status at the UN General Assembly.

Moscow sought to use the CIS status as an international organization to promote acceptance by the West of Russia's domination of peacekeeping in the CIS region. [35] Presumably, objections to the use of Russian troops unilaterally would be overcome by the use of Russian-dominated CIS forces. But Moscow was clear: UN or OSCE endorsement of CIS operations did not mean that Moscow had to seek permission before initiating them. Further, the Russian military was against any outside monitoring of its activities even though OSCE rules specifically authorized it to do just that for OSCE-endorsed operations. Another advantage of CIS peacekeeping was that it preempted peacekeeping by other outside forces. Russia, for example, opposed OSCE efforts to send its own peacekeepers to Nagorno-Karabakh. It also declined to permit free access for CSCE missions to peacekeeping facilities in Moldova and Georgia.[36]

Within CSCE/OSCE there has been strong resistance to endorsing CIS peacekeeping without some form of monitoring. This opposition reflects the concerns of some OSCE members (e.g., the Baltic republics, Ukraine Turkey) about Russian imperialism. By contrast, the United Nations has been more willing to approve of CIS peacekeeping. The Security Council tends to permit the major powers to police the areas of their greatest strategic interest.[37] To date, Russian-led peacekeeping operations within the CIS are mainly limited to those countries that signed the Tashkent accord on collective security in 1992: Russia, Armenia, Kyrgystan, Tajikistan, Uzbekistan, and later Azerbaijan, Belarus, and Georgia. Despite Russia's insistence, the OSCE refuses to recognize the CIS as within Russia's sphere of influence.

ENDNOTES

1. Gorbachev was devastated to learn that President Bush was prepared to recognize Ukrainian independence even before the December referendum. Michael Bechloss and Strobe Talbott, *At the Highest Levels: The Inside Story of the End of the Cold War*. Boston: Little, Brown, 1993, p. 449.

2. Kravchuk revealed on Russian television that he informed Yeltsin that Ukraine would not participate in any kind of confederation but only a commonwealth of states. See Roman Solchanyk, "Kravchuk Defines Ukraine-CIS Relations," *REF/RL Research Report*, Vol. 1, No. 1, March 13, 1992, p. 8.

3. The membership number has changed. Moldova never ratified the founding documents although it has participated in many of the CIS meetings and holds the special position of an associate. Azerbaijan, an original member, withdrew in 1992 but rejoined in 1993. Georgia, originally a holdout, also joined in 1993.

4. The text of the Agreement creating the CIS is in *The Current Digest*, Vol. XLIII, No. 49, January 8, 1992, pp. 10-11.

5. See, for example, Philip E. Jacob and James V. Toscano, eds. *The Integration of Political Communities*. New York: J. B. Lippincott, 1964 and the writings of Karl W. Deutsch including *Nationalism and Social Communication* (1953), *Political Community at the International Level* (1954), and *Political Community and the North Atlantic Area* (1957).

6. Jan S. Adams, "Will the Post-Soviet Commonwealth Survive?", *Occasional Paper* for the Mershon Center, The Ohio State University, 1993, p. 15.

7. Daniel C. Diller, ed. "Russia and the Independent States," *Congressional Quarterly*, 1993.

8. John Tedstrom, "CIS: Kiev Summit Yields Few Economic Results," *RFE/RL Research Report*, Vol. 1, No. 15, April 10, 1992, p. 27. See also Keith Bush, "Little Progress Registered Toward Economic Integration," Vol. 1, No. 8, February 21, 1992; Philip Hanson, "The End of the Ruble Zone?", Vol. 1, No. 30, July 24, 1992; Erik Whitlock, "The CIS Economy," Vol. 2, No. 1, January 1, 1993; Erik Whitlock, "Obstacles to CIS Economic Integration," Vol. 2, No. 27, July 2, 1993.

9. Steven Erlanger, "Russia, Ukraine and Belarus Agree to Press Efforts for Economic and Customs Union," *The New York Times*, July 15, 1993. Also *The Current Digest*, Vol. XLIV, No. 41, November 11, 1992, pp. 6–9 and Ibid., Vol. XLIV, No. 42, November 18, 1992, pp. 1-4.

10. Ibid., Vol. XLV, No. 20, June 16, 1993, p. 9.

11. Ibid., Vol. XLIV, No. 7, March 18, 1992, p. 2.

12. *RFE/RL Research Report*, Vol. 1, No. 4, January 24, 1992, p. 52. On the military issues see Stephen Foye, "The CIS Armed Forces," Ibid., Vol. 2, No. 1, January 1, 1993 and "End of the CIS Command Heralds New Russian Defense Policy?," Ibid.,Vol. 2, No. 27, July 2, 1993.

13. Quoted in Ibid., p. 47.

14. The Lisbon Protocol did not resolve questions concerning the ownership and control of nuclear weapons. For the text see *Arms Control Today*, June 1992, pp. 34–37.

15. *The New York Times*, October 20, 1993.

16. *The Current Digest*, Vol. XLIV, No. 1, February 5, 1992, pp. 13, 35. At the same time he reminded his audience that "we should not quarrel with Ukraine . . ." Ibid., p. 35.

17. Douglas L. Clarke, "The Battle for the Black Sea Fleet," *RFE/RL Research Report*, Vol. 1, No. 5, p. 55. See also *The Current Digest*, Vol. XLIV, No. 4, February 26, 1992, p. 8 and Vol. XLIV, No. 13, May 6, 1992, p. 13.

18. *Nezavisimaya Gazeta*, July 13, 1993, p. 1.

19. *The Current Digest*, Vol. XLV, No. 36, October 6, 1993, p. 1.

20. See Bohdan Hahaylo, "The Massandra Summit and Ukraine," in *RFE/RL Research Report*, Vol. 2, No. 37, September 17, 1993. Also John W.R. Leppingwell, "The Black Sea Fleet Agreement: Progress or Empty Promises?", Ibid., Vol. 2, No. 28, July 9, 1993.

21. Roman Solchanyk, "Ukrainian-Russian Confrontation over the Crimea," Ibid., Vol. 1, No. 8, February 21, 1992, p. 28.

22. *The Current Digest*, Vol. XLIV, No. 14, May 6, 1992, p. 13.

23. Ibid., Vol. XLIV, No. 21, June 24, 1992, p. 4.

24. Ibid., p. 5.

25. Ibid., p. 7.

26. Ibid., Vol. XLIV, No. 22, July 1, 1992, p. 22.

27. This is according to the 1989 census.

28. Ethnically and linguistically Moldovans and Romanians are very close. Part of Moldova belonged to Romania before it was seized by Stalin in 1940. There is sentiment in Romania and Moldova for a merger of the two states, but there is also opposition to that idea.

29. Raymond Donner, "Why All Eyes Are on a Place Called Tajikistan," *The New York Times*, November 7, 1993.

30. See Serge Schmemann, "In Heavy Blow to Georgia, Separatists Seize Key City," *The New York Times,* September 28, 1993.

31. Jan S. Adams, "CIS: The Interplanetary Assembly and Khasbulatov," *RFE/RL Research Report,* Vol. 2, No. 36, January 25, 1993, p. 21.

32. See Thomas Goltz, "The Hidden Russian Hand," *Foreign Policy,* No. 92, Fall 1993.

33. *The New York Times,* September 28, 1993. See also, "Eduard Shevardnadze," *The New York Times Magazine,* December 26, 1993, p. 19.

34. Steven Erlanger, "Yeltsin Rebuffed in Russia's Role in Ex-Soviet Lands," *The New York Times,* December 25, 1993, p. l.

35. Suzanne Crow, "Russia Promotes the CIS as an International Organization." *RFE/RL Research Report,* Vol. 3, No. 11, March 18, 1994, pp. 35-36.

36. Heather F. Hurlburt, "Russia Plays a Double Game." *Transition,* Vol. 1, No. 11, June 30, 1995, pp. 12, 14.

37. The United States ambassador referred to this as "sphere-of-influence-peace-keeping." See Michael Mihalka, "Trawling for Legitimacy." Ibid, p. 19.

CHAPTER 7

Russia's Foreign Policy

Foreign policy is the product of both domestic and external influences. These influences explain both continuity and changes in a state's foreign policy. An important contribution to the continuity in the foreign policy behavior of states is what political scientists call the international system. The international system determines the conditions under which foreign policy is made. The international system is composed of sovereign states whose power relationship is constantly changing. Sovereignty gives states the right, at least in principle, to determine the policies they will pursue, including the use of force. The international system is decentralized, lacking a central political authority like a world government. In effect, state sovereignty gives international politics an anarchic character.

There are a number of important consequences of the decentralized or anarchic character of the international system. One of the most important is that each state is compelled to look after its own security and to advance its interests as best it can. This condition gives rise to what Hans Morgenthau referred to as the "struggle for power" between states, a struggle that often results in the use of force. Kenneth Waltz explains this tendency as follows:

> *Each state pursues its own interests, however defined, in ways it judges best. Force is a means of achieving the external ends of states because there exists no consistent, reliable process of reconciling the conflicts of interest that inevitably arise among similar units in a condition of anarchy.*[1]

"Balance of power" is the term that Waltz and other theorists use to describe the behavior of states pursuing their interests in a decentralized political system. Balance of power policies take many different forms but the most common is the tendency of states to align themselves with other states to promote their interests or to enhance their security. In a general sense all great powers, whatever their domestic political order, must exercise a degree of reserve and caution vis-a-vis other great powers. The Soviet Union and post-Soviet Russia both had interests which were achieved by balance of power policies. This explains in a general way some of the points of conflict between Russia and the West in the latter period of Yeltsin's administration.

Nevertheless, between the Gorbachev and Yeltsin administrations there were significant differences in relations with the West. It could not be otherwise because of the fundamental domestic changes that took place in post-Soviet Russia. During the Gorbachev administration, Soviet foreign policy changed dramatically, culminating in the abandonment of Eastern Europe, the dissolution of the Warsaw Pact and the end of the Cold War. But just as there was always a fundamental ambiguity in his domestic policies—seeking change in order to preserve what he inherited—so in foreign policy Gorbachev could never completely abandon the notion that the U.S.S.R. and the United States were rivals. As expressed in his book, *Perestroika, New Thinking for Our Country and the World*, "Economic, political and ideological competition between capitalist and socialist countries is inevitable."[1a] Gorbachev did, in fact, revolutionize Soviet foreign policy by ending the antagonism whose roots went back to Lenin. Yeltsin went further. Building upon Gorbachev's foreign policy achievements, Yeltsin sought to create a genuine partnership with the United States. He told the United States Congress on June 17, 1992, "In joining the world community, we wish to preserve our identity and history . . . at the same time Russia does not aspire to remake the world in its own image."[2] Russia's new foreign minister, Andrei Kozyrev, expressed the new policy succinctly, "The developed countries of the West are Russia's natural allies."[3]

This change was not simply the result of a new leadership, though Yeltsin did repudiate explicitly the ideological baggage of his predecessor. There were many factors involved in Russia's move toward reconciliation with the West. One important consideration was the transformation of the economy and Russia's almost desperate need for assistance. Another was Yeltsin's desire for Western support against domestic reaction. In both the August 1991 and October 1993 crises, he relied on political support from the United States. Looking at international politics from a systemic perspective, the bipolarity of the Cold War had broken down and neither government felt compelled to view their relationship as a "zero-sum-game." Russia and Europe ceased to see each other as a military threat. In sum, Yeltsin's foreign policies were determined by both conviction and necessity.

Not all Russians shared the Yeltsin-Kozyrev vision. Indeed, post-Soviet politics witnessed a proliferation of views regarding every important issue both domestic and foreign. Throughout the period of Yeltsin's struggle with the parliament, a particularly vigorous debate developed between two schools of thought regarding the fundamental direction Russian foreign policy should take. They were known at the time as the "Atlanticist" and "Eurasian" schools, a distinction attributed to Russian State Counselor Sergei Stankevich.[4] The Atlanticists, led by Yeltsin and Kozyrev, wanted Russia to join in partnership with the West in the creation of a new world order based upon the principles of democracy, a market economy and respect for human rights. Ultimately they hoped to gain membership for Russia in the G-7 group of industrial democracies and possibly even NATO. They supported active participation in the United Nations, the Conference on Security and Cooperation in Europe, the International Monetary Fund, and World Bank. Within the Commonwealth of Independent States they sought to placate and encourage the participation of Ukraine because it was viewed as an important link with the West. Andrei Kozyrev, one of the staunchest of the Atlanticists, in arguing for Western support warned that democratic Russia's course toward rapproachment with the West was "not yet the mentality of the entire society . . ."[5]

The Eurasians contended that Russia should look south and east, not west. China, India, and the Moslem world were more natural allies than Europe and the United States. Russia's political and economic interests were viewed as more connected to the Pacific Rim and the Middle East. Among those countries Russia could be an ally, even a leader. With the West, they argued, Russia would never be more than a second-class citizen. The Eurasians criticized Yeltsin's government for neglecting ties between Russia and the commonwealth states of Central Asia. They believed that Yeltsin devoted too much effort to keeping Ukraine in the CIS while neglecting states like Kazakhstan that wanted to pursue their traditional ties with Russia.

Although the Eurasian school reflected the views of the opposition it did receive support among some senior Russians in government, notably Russian State Counselor Sergei Stankevich. In March 1992 he wrote, "It is obvious that we will have to look for a new balance of Western and Eastern orientations that is distinctive to today's Russia and our times. Initially, however, we will most likely have to devote special attention to the strengthening of our positions in the East, rectifying the obvious distortion caused by the creators of the conceptions of the 'common European home.'"[6] Some scholars viewed this debate as a modern variant of the historic struggle between "Westerners" and "Slavophiles" that was waged among Russia's intellectuals in the nineteenth century.[7] The post-Soviet debate, unlike its earlier counterpart, reflected widespread uncertainty among politicians, intellectuals, and the public at large over Russia's new place in a very new world.

Russia's foreign policy debate was more complex than simply two sides opposed to each other. Not all Eurasians were anti-West and some Atlanticists were critical of the administration's concessions to the United States. There were also issues that cut across both of these sides. An important crosscutting issue was that of nationalism. Nationalists—sometimes referred to as "national patriots"—deplored the disintegration of the Soviet Union and considered Yeltsin as responsible as Gorbachev and Shevardnadze for making it happen. The most extreme nationalists wanted to restore the Soviet Union. Until that happened they demanded that Russia vigorously prosecute the interests of the state and the protection of Russians throughout the former Soviet territory. They thus demanded support for Russians fighting to create the Dnestr Republic out of Moldova and for protection of the civil rights of Russians in the Baltic states. They opposed the surrender of any territory such as the Kurile Islands to Japan, or recognition of Ukrainian sovereignty over the Crimea. Yevgeny Ambartsumov, Chairman of the Supreme Soviet's Joint Committee on International Affairs and Foreign Economic Relations expressed the nationalist view in a report to the Russian parliament:

> As the internationally recognized legal successor to the U.S.S.R., the Russian Federation should base its foreign policy on a doctrine declaring the entire geopolitical space of the former Union to be the sphere of its vital interests (like the US's Monroe Doctrine in Latin America) and should strive to achieve understanding and recognition from the world community of its special interests in this space. Russia should also strive to achieve from the world community recognition of its role as political and military guarantor of stability in the entire former space of the U.S.S.R.[8]

Support for the nationalist position permeates Russian society and had powerful representation in both the pre- and post-1993 parliaments. In June 1992, the Russian National Assembly was created under the leadership of Alexander Sterligov, a former KGB officer, to mobilize support for "the re-creation of Russia within the border of the former Soviet Union."[9] Working with the nationalists in the old Russian parliament were pro-Communists elements, thus giving rise to the label "the Red-Brown alliance." In the old Russian parliament, the nationalist faction took the label "Russian Unity."

Headed by parliamentary deputies Sergei Baburin, Vladimir Isakov and Nikolai Pavlov, Russian Unity condemned Yeltsin's foreign policy, particularly its pro-Western orientation. In the State Duma the most outspoken bearer of nationalist views was the leader of the Liberal Democratic Party, Vladimir Zhirinovsky.

Nationalist sentiment was particularly strong in the military. Yeltsin's first minister of defense, Pavel Grachev, though loyal to his boss, frequently supported the nationalist position, particularly with regard to protecting Russian-speaking minorities in other republics and the territorial integrity of Russia. Shortly after his appointment, Grachev promised that he would "not allow the honor and dignity of Russians to be insulted on the territory of any state."[10]

In opposition to the nationalists were the "liberals" or "moderates" who deplored the aggressive threats and strong-arm tactics of the nationalists. Emphasizing the importance of good relations between Russia and its neighbors they stressed the need for compromise and negotiations of differences. This sentiment reflected the views of most of the democratic activists in Russian politics. It was also closer to the public's view of Russian foreign policy than the nationalist position. In 1992, a survey of public attitudes regarding the means that should be used to resolve conflicts between Russia and the "near abroad" countries showed that 46 percent supported the use of peaceful means only compared to 19 percent who accepted the nationalist argument that Russia should use any means necessary, including war.[11]

These two schools, Atlanticist-Eurasian and liberal-nationalist, often merged into a single liberal-conservative dichotomy, though the full mosaic of opinion in Russian politics was in fact more diverse and complicated.

Yeltsin's administration reflected his commitment to the Atlanticist-liberal position just described. Yet there were frequent contradictions as when he adopted a tough, nationalist line on one issue or another. His foreign policy (and domestic as well) accommodated changing domestic pressures. Just as Gorbachev had moved to the right in the fall and winter of 1990-91 in response to conservative pressures, so Yeltsin found it necessary to make some accommodation to nationalist forces that emerged from the 1993 and 1995 parliamentary elections. The complex interplay of ideology and domestic policy was evident in the two broad issues that have dominated Russian foreign policy in the post-Soviet period: 1) relations with the West and 2) relations with the former Soviet republics, commonly referred to as the "near abroad."

RELATIONS WITH THE WEST

An underlying consistency in Yeltsin's early foreign policy was the pursuit of accommodation with the West in general and the United States in particular. On no issue was this clearer than that of disarmament and arms control.

Here Yeltsin built upon policies established by Gorbachev, notably the INF agreement in 1987, the CFE treaty of 1990, and the START agreement in 1991.[12] On September 21, 1991, President George Bush introduced a new initiative that became known by the acronym GPALS (for Global Protection Against Limited Strikes). Bush proposed that the Unites States and Russia jointly deploy a limited number of nonnuclear missile defenses to protect both countries against limited ballistic missile strikes whatever their source. GPALS was endorsed by the U.S. Congress in the Missile Defense Act of 1991. Boris Yeltsin somewhat unexpectedly expressed interest in GPALS before the United Nations in January 1992. He was attracted to the idea of cooperating on missile defense because it provided an opportunity to strengthen the foundations of American-Soviet cooperation, particularly in a field where Russia would be a genuine partner, not a supplicant. At the June 1992 summit in Washington, Yeltsin and Bush signed a statement on GPALS that referred to "the potential for sharing of early warning information through the establishment of an early warning center."[13]

Though nothing came of GPALS, the Washington summit in June 1992 produced an arms control agreement of considerably greater importance to Washington. Yeltsin agreed with Bush to reduce strategic weapons well beyond the numbers specified in the 1991 START Treaty. Under START, the United States and the former Soviet Union agreed to reduce their strategic nuclear inventory from 11,602 for the United States to 8,592 and from 10,877 to 6,940 for the Soviets. When the Soviet Union disbanded and Yeltsin took responsibility for continuing the arms-control negotiations, he quickly challenged the United States to even deeper cuts. In January 1992 he proposed reducing nuclear warheads in long-range missiles to between 2,000 and 2,500 each. That figure was considerably below the number of 4,500 to 5,000 being proposed by President Bush.[14]

Negotiations toward strategic-arms reduction began in the winter. The biggest difficulty was not the number of warheads to be reduced but which delivery systems to destroy. The bulk of the Russian strategic arsenal consisted of land-based ICBMs with multiple warheads (SS-18, SS-19, SS-24 behemoths). For years, Washington had sought to eliminate these weapons because of their "first strike" potential. In a crisis the Soviet Union would have had a theoretical incentive to use these weapons or risk their destruction in a surprise attack. The United States itself has a portion of its strategic inventory in land-based MIRV'D (multiple independently targeted vehicles) missiles (the Minuteman III and MX missiles), but the bulk of the U.S. missiles are in submarines deep in the oceans. United States doctrine considered the submarine-launched ballistic missiles to be more stabilizing because they could not be destroyed in a surprise attack and were not accurate enough for a "first strike." Thus, there was no incentive to preempt in a crisis. What the Bush administration wanted Russia to accept was a plan that eliminated all land-based MIRV'D missiles but permitted the United States to retain the bulk of its sea-based deterrent. Russia's military resisted this deal as asymmetrical in favor of the United States.

Yet in the end, the Bush administration got exactly what it wanted: both a reduction in the numbers (but not too great) and, more importantly, agreement to eliminate the backbone of the Russian arsenal, their land-based ballistic missiles. START II, signed on January 3, 1993, committed the two sides to reduce their nuclear warheads to three thousand on the Russian side and 3,500 for the United States by the year 2003. More importantly, the United States was permitted to retain the core of its most potent weapon, the sea-based ballistic missile. For the first time, Russia abandoned its goal of parity with the United States. Yeltsin explained his reasons as follows: to give tangible "expression of the fundamental change in the political and economic relations between the United States of America and Russia." But also, "We are departing from the ominous parity where each country was exerting every effort to stay in line, which has led to Russia . . . having half of its population living below the poverty line. We cannot afford it . . ."[15]

The fate of START II, however, became linked to the separate issue of Russia's relations with Ukraine. Before START II could be implemented (or even ratified), Belarus, Kazakhstan, and Ukraine had to agree to give up all the nuclear weapons they inherited from the U.S.S.R. Legally that entailed ratification of both the START I Treaty and the Nonproliferation Treaty by the three newly endowed nuclear states. On May 23, 1992, all three signed the Lisbon Protocol to the START Treaty, agreeing to ratify START I and become nonnuclear-weapons states. Ukrainian President Leonid Kravchuk, however, failed to follow up on this commitment because nationalist sentiment at home, particularly in the parliament, sought some quid pro quo for giving up the country's 1,800 strategic nuclear warheads. During 1992 and 1993, Kravchuk pressed both Russia and the United States for security guarantees against military threats or blackmail. In addition Ukraine sought substantial Western financial assistance to pay for the costs of dismantling its nuclear weapons and from Russia compensation for the value of the nuclear fuel.

On September 3, 1993, presidents Kravchuk and Yeltsin met at Massandra to resolve their nuclear differences. They appeared to do so in an accord that provided for the return of Ukrainian nuclear weapons to Russia and Russian compensation in the form of nuclear fuel for peaceful uses. Subsequent bickering on both sides over the details of the Massandra Accord revealed that Ukraine was still unwilling to abandon the nuclear option.

Ukraine was subjected to strong pressure by both the West and Russia to give up its nuclear weapons. A massive debt to Russia for energy supplies coupled with a rapidly worsening economy in 1993 rendered Ukraine vulnerable to these pressures. In addition, Leonid Kravchuk was particularly anxious to obtain political and economic support from the Clinton administration and to prevent his country from becoming isolated politically over this issue. Following the collapse of the Massandra Accords in late 1993, the United States undertook to mediate Russian-Ukrainian differences. This effort led to a Moscow summit where presidents Bill Clinton, Leonid Kravchuk and Boris Yeltsin on January 14, 1994 signed the Trilateral Agreement. Under its terms Kravchuk agreed that measures would be taken to bring START I into force and for Ukraine to "accede to the Nuclear Non-Proliferation Treaty as a nonnuclear-weapon state in the shortest possible time."[16] In compensation Ukraine, Belarus and Kazakhstan would be paid for the highly enriched uranium in the warheads and Ukraine was given security assurances by both Russia and the United States. Like the Lisbon Protocol and Massandra Accord, the Trilateral Agreement became enmeshed in Ukrainian domestic politics. It fell to Kravchuk's successor, Leonid Kuchma (elected president in June 1994), to obtain parliamentary consent to nonnuclear status. In November the parliament agreed by the surprisingly strong vote of 301 to eight to accede to the Non-Proliferation Treaty.[17] Belarus and Kazakhstan having already ratified START I and the Non-Proliferation Treaty, the way was finally opened to ratification of START II by Russia and the United States. Nationalist opposition in the Russian parliament guaranteed that this would not be an easy task for the Yeltsin administration.

One issue thought to have been resolved during the Soviet period but whose terms the Russian military subsequently attempted to change was the Conventional Forces in Europe (CFE) Treaty signed in November 1990. That treaty established allocations for a variety of conventional weapons in NATO and Warsaw Pact states. But there are restrictions on the internal distribution of forces in Russia and Ukraine. Specifically, in Russia the size of military forces is limited in two military districts, the Leningrad and North Caucasus Military districts. When the CFE Treaty was signed these two districts were essentially rear-echelon regions. But with the collapse of the Warsaw Pact and the breakup of the U.S.S.R., these districts unexpectedly emerged as part of Russia's first line of defense. The Russian military, never happy with the CFE Treaty in the first place, insisted that the CFE limits be revised upward to reflect the fact that they are now border districts. The North Caucasus has assumed particular importance because of instability in Georgia, Armenia, and Azerbaijan and the need to bring Russian peacekeeping forces into the area. In addition, the Russians have pointed to the growing threat of militant Islamic fundamentalism in the region as an argument for raising the CFE limits in the southern flank. NATO was not inclined to accommodate the Russian demands.[18]

Russia has asserted itself more vigorously on other security issues. One of these involves the export of arms. Here the problem is more economic than political; arms exports are an important source of much-needed hard currency. In addition, arms exports helped to cushion the deterioration of Russia's defense-industrial complex.

Yeltsin's arms-export policies balanced elements of cooperation and competition with the West. Thus, even in the face of strident nationalistic criticism, Russia supported United Nations sanctions against Libya, Iraq, and Yugoslavia and in so doing forfeited billions of dollars in arms sales. On the other hand, Yeltsin urged his government to push exports in the Middle East and Asia where for years the United States and other Western countries had been the dominant suppliers of arms. Early in his administration Yeltsin promised the First All-Army Officers Assembly that he would use the proceeds from arms sales to improve living conditions for military personnel.[19]

In 1993 Russia made significant breakthroughs in arms sales to the Asian market. One sale, a deal to sell India cryogenic rockets, created a strain in relations with the United States, but was eventually resolved to the satisfaction of Washington. On the other hand, Russia negotiated one of its largest sales ever with the purchase by Malaysia of 18 MIG-29 fighters, an export made in competition with the American McDonnell Douglass Company. *Rossiiskaya Gazeta* commented at the time: "The time has come to acknowledge that where arms exports are concerned, we and the West—particularly the US—are not partners but competitors, both economically and politically."[20]

RUSSIA AND NATO

Another contentious issue was the question of Eastern Europe's potential membership in NATO. With the end of the Cold War, NATO soon found itself searching for a new mission and *raison d'etre*. Some NATO members believed that the alliance would survive only by expanding and becoming a security force for all of Europe. This view coincided with the desire of several Eastern European countries led by the so-called Visegrad states (Czech Republic, Poland, Hungary, and Slovakia) for security guarantees from the West, leading ultimately to full membership in the European Union and NATO. The movement for expansion was accelerated by NATO's decision in June 1992 to move "out of area" and place its military services at the disposal of the United Nations and the CSCE (now OSCE) for peacekeeping operations in the former Yugoslavia.

Russia's response to the proposed NATO expansion was negative. Although Yeltsin endorsed Poland's application to join NATO in a visit to Warsaw in the summer of 1993, he quickly reversed himself and joined those in his administration—particularly the military—in opposing NATO expansion. A report prepared by Russia's Foreign Intelligence Service (FIS) entitled "Prospects for the Expansion of NATO and Russia's Interests" summed up the government's objections. It acknowledged that part of the problem was psychological. Historically, NATO and the former Soviet Union viewed each other as enemies and that "this psychological mindset cannot be broken painlessly." Among the specific consequences of NATO expansion would be a fundamental rethinking of Russia's defensive posture and a restructuring of the Armed Forces; Romania as a member of NATO would be encouraged to absorb Moldova; the Baltic states would seek admission if the Visegrad states were embraced. In sum, "if the countries of Central and Eastern Europe join that organization [NATO], the objective result will be the emergence of a barrier between Russia and the rest of the continent."[21] As an alternative, Yeltsin proposed that NATO and Russia act as the joint guarantors of Eastern European security, an idea that appealed neither to NATO nor to its potential new members.

The Clinton administration's answer to the dilemma of Eastern Europe's quest for NATO membership and Russia's opposition was a plan known as the "Partnership for Peace" (PFP). First floated at a meeting of NATO defense ministers in late October 1993, the PFP idea was in part designed to keep Russia from being isolated and to avoid strengthening the hard-liners within Russia. At the same time, by holding out the promise of eventual membership for the former Warsaw Pact states, NATO sought to ameliorate Eastern European concerns. In the interim, the PFP provided for consultation in the event of an attack and joint exercises, planning and training between members of the partnership.[22]

The partnership offer was made to every member of the CSCE, including Russia. Concern over security in Eastern Europe was heightened by the Russian elections in December 1993 and the success of the aggressive nationalist, Vladimir Zhirinovsky. Notwithstanding their disappointment over the limited character of the PFP, the Visegrad states agreed to join. During January-February 1994, agreements to join the PFP were signed by Romania, Lithuania, Poland, Estonia, Hungary, Ukraine, Slovakia, the Czech Republic, Bulgaria, Latvia, Moldova, and Albania.

Moscow responded positively to the PFP plan, not only because it undermined Eastern-Central Europe's pressure to join NATO, but additionally because it gave Russia an opportunity to influence the structure of European security. Public sentiment in Russia, however, understood only too well that the PFP was based upon fear of Russian aggression and thus in its roots was "anti-Russian".[23] There was thus from the beginning an ambivalent attitude as to whether Russia itself should join the PFP and, if it joined, what conditions should be linked to its participation.

On the occasion of President Clinton's visit to Moscow in January 1994, Boris Yeltsin strongly endorsed the PFP initiative. Several months later, Prime Minister Viktor Chernomyrdin advised U.S. Defense Secretary William Perry that his country was prepared to join the PFP unconditionally. But there was strong opposition within the Federal Assembly, Russia's parliament. Sergei Yushkenkov, chairman of the Duma's Committee on Defense,

expressed the widely held view that Russia should join the PFP only if consideration was given to its special status, "the status of a nuclear power, the
status of a state with a mighty potential."[24] Doubts about the PFP were rekin-
dled by the military activity of NATO in Bosnia in the winter and spring of
1994 (see next section). NATO military strikes were made without consulting
Moscow, raising the deep-seated fear in Moscow that Russia was not accorded the equal status to which it felt entitled.

While the country debated whether or not to join the PFP, the Ministry of
Foreign Affairs was pressing for a security arrangement for Europe that
would downgrade NATO's primary role. Early in 1994, Foreign Minister
Kozyrev pressed for a new concept. He proposed

> *that the North Atlantic Cooperation Council (NACC) be transformed into*
> *an independent structure of military-political cooperation, but one that is*
> *closely linked to the CSCE. Under this proposal, the CSCE is assigned the*
> *role of coordinator of the efforts of NATO, the European Union, the Council*
> *of Europe, the Western European Union and the CIS in the areas of*
> *strengthening stability and security, peacekeeping and protecting the rights*
> *of national minorities in Europe.*[25]

In a word, NATO would be subordinated to the CSCE (now OSCE). NATO
would have none of it and Russia was forced to look again to the PFP for
whatever formal impact it might have on European security. On June 23,
Kozyrev signed the same basic framework document as the other states joining the PFP. No special consideration was given to the Russians, though a
protocol signed at the same time affirmed that "Russia and NATO have
agreed to prepare a wide-ranging individual program of partnership, in
keeping with Russia's size, importance and potential."[26] The protocol was a
victory of form over substance; it failed to dispel the gnawing concern of
NATO expansion.

The November 1994 elections in the United States brought Republican
control of Congress and with it a more critical stance toward Moscow. In particular, the Republican leadership was committed to NATO expansion, a
position supported by the Clinton administration. While the United States
had no timetable for expansion, it was determined that Russia would not be
in a position to veto the admission of new members. In December, Russia's
two foreign policy leaders shocked the West with an attack on NATO policy.
At a meeting in Brussels before the NATO Council, Andrei Kozyrev
unleashed a stunning demarche postponing Russian participation in the PFP.
He offered as the reason that a "hasty and unwarranted expansion of the
alliance [NATO] is not to Russia's liking."[27] This was followed by an equally
harsh speech by Boris Yeltsin at a Budapest summit meeting of the CSCE. He
again introduced his idea of using the CSCE rather than NATO as the foundation of a European security system. Pushing NATO up to Russia's borders,
he warned, risked plunging Europe into a "Cold Peace."[28] This hard-line

rhetoric was part of a general shift to the right in foreign policy. Within days of the Budapest speech, Yeltsin was to embark on the most controversial venture of his administration, the assault on the breakaway republic of Chechnya (see below).

THE YUGOSLAV CRISIS

The controversy over NATO's role in Eastern Europe was largely symbolic in that no Eastern European country was threatened by Russia or anyone else. It involved an issue for the future, not the present. The war in the former state of Yugoslavia was a different story. Here fierce fighting had already broken out and a major crisis confronted all of Europe. It exposed serious conflicts of interest between Russia and the West.

Yugoslavia fell apart approximately at the same time as the Soviet Union.[29] War broke out in Bosnia and Herzegovina in the spring of 1992 almost immediately after Europe and the United States recognized the republic's independence. The Serbs in Bosnia (31.3 percent of the population) and the Croats (17.3 percent) opposed a unified, independent Bosnia whose dominant population were Muslim Slavs (43.7 percent). The Serbs and Croats wanted a loose confederation in which they would be essentially self-governing communities or be free to unite with their brethren in Croatia and Serbia. The Bosnian War created for Yeltsin problems which were similar to the dilemma Iraqi aggression had posed for Mikhail Gorbachev in 1990-91.[30] In both cases a traditional ally of Russia (and the Soviet Union) committed aggression that was condemned by the West, thus compelling Moscow to choose between siding with a long-term friend or the West. Yeltsin's response vacillated over time, reflecting the changing pressures on his administration. Overall, however, he carefully avoided a rupture with the United States.

Initially Russia supported—albeit with some reservations—Western policy. At a Helsinki meeting of the CSCE in July, Russia joined the majority in voting to suspend Yugoslavia from that organization for giving aid to the Serbian aggression. In May the Russian delegation to the United Nations voted to impose sanctions against Yugoslavia notwithstanding Andrei Kozyrev's contention that negotiations were preferable to punishing Serbia. A factor in Russia's decision not to veto was the upcoming summit between Yeltsin and Bush scheduled for June. A memo from the Russian ambassador to the United Nations reportedly advised his government, "It is very important not to oppose on this point the Western countries and the United States, where public opinion is strongly against Milosevic."[31]

Conservative reaction to Russia's moves against Yugoslavia was swift and strident. The Supreme Soviet demanded a moratorium on UN sanctions against Yugoslavia (much as the U.S.S.R. Supreme Soviet in November 1990 condemned the U.S.S.R.'s decision to vote for a UN resolution to use force against Iraq). An article in the right-wing newspaper *Sovietskaya Rossia* claimed, "The consistent antinational policy pursued by the current Russian leadership has found its logical conclusion in the open and unconcealed betrayal of the fraternal people of the allied republic of Yugoslavia."[32]

During 1992 the Bosnian Serbs, abetted by Yugoslavia, embarked on a widespread campaign to expel Muslims from territories in Bosnia so as to link as many of the Serbian-dominated regions as possible. This policy of "ethnic cleansing" was carried out ruthlessly and led to Serbian control of approximately 70 percent of the entire country. Though sympathetic to the Serbs, the Russian government was unable to justify Serbian atrocities or Yugoslav support for Serbian aggression. In September the Forty-Seventh Session of the General Assembly debated the issue of Yugoslav membership in the United Nations. In late September, the Assembly and the Security Council voted to expel Yugoslavia from the organization. Andrei Kozyrev made no effort to use the Soviet veto in the Security Council to prevent Yugoslavia's expulsion.[33] In a similar vein, Russia supported Security Council resolutions in August authorizing the use of military force to guarantee the delivery of humanitarian aid in Bosnia.

Yeltsin was torn by his desire to support the Serbs and his wish to avoid drifting too far from the mainstream of international opinion. Parliament was less torn. A leading opponent of Russia's policy in the United Nations was Evgenii Ambartsumov, chairman of parliament's Committee on International Affairs and Foreign Economic Relations. Yeltsin's opponents in the Supreme Soviet used the issue to attack his administration for bowing to the United States. Serbia thus became an important issue in the debate between Atlanticists and Eurasians. To the anti-Western view of the Eurasians was added the idea of "Panslavism," whose roots date back to the eighteenth and nineteenth centuries. Modern Panslavism supports the idea of unity among the Slavic peoples of Europe, particularly between the Russians and the Balkan Slavs.

Russia's constitutional crisis dominated politics throughout 1993. Foreign affairs took a back seat to the domestic struggle between Yeltsin and his conservative opponents. Concerned lest nationalist forces use the war in Bosnia against him, Yeltsin shifted in 1993 toward a firmer position in support of the Serbs. In the face of growing Western pressure to relieve the Bosnian Muslims, Russia successfully blocked efforts to lift the arms embargo against the combatants in Bosnia and made clear its opposition to military intervention by the West.

On the other hand the Kremlin supported the political initiatives of Europe and the United Nations to negotiate a settlement of the war. The focus of Western diplomacy in 1993 was the Vance-Owen Plan to create a weak confederation in Bosnia Herzegovina organized around ten ethnically based cantons. Notwithstanding pressure from the West, Russia, and even Milosovic in Belgrade, Bosnia's Serbs rejected the plan in May. The decision by the United States not to press the Vance-Owen plan on the Serbs reflected its unwillingness to engage in military intervention and recognition at the time that the eventual settlement would involve acceptance of some Serbian territorial gains. These positions revealed a convergence between Russia's and Western policies.

That convergence was severely challenged early in 1994 as a result of an atrocity in Sarajevo. On February 5 a mortar attack on a public market, assumed to have been made by the Serbs, killed sixty-eight people and wounded at least two hundred. International public opinion expressed outrage, prompting renewed demands for air strikes against the perpetrators. Reflecting public sentiment NATO issued an ultimatum to the Bosnian Serbs demanding that they remove their heavy weapons 20 kilometers from Sarajevo or place them under UN control. A failure to comply would lead to air strikes against Bosnian Serb positions. Significantly the NATO threat was qualified by the condition that UN authorization would precede any use of military force.

Yeltsin converted a potentially damaging blow to Russian diplomacy to a diplomatic success. Opinion in Moscow strongly opposed Western use of force against the Serbs. This view, endorsed by nationalists, democrats and centrists, cut across the political spectrum. Kozyrev insisted that NATO military force could not be unleashed without a new Security Council resolution, which Russia could veto. First Deputy Minister of Foreign Affairs Anatoly Adamishin argued that if the West sided with the Muslim Bosnians the latter would have no incentive to negotiate an agreement. Many in Moscow were convinced that the mortar attack in the market place was in fact a Muslim provocation, though few denied the criminal nature of the attack. *Izvestiya* summed up Yeltsin's dilemma: "Having gone rather far in its support for the Serbs, the Kremlin is now forced to accomplish a very difficult task: preventing a rift with the West and saving face at the same time."[34]

Yeltsin's position was aided by the fact that of all the parties involved— the United Nations, Europe, the United States, the Serbs in Bosnia and Serbia and Russia—only the Muslims wanted NATO to unleash its big guns. After consulting Clinton, Helmut Kohl, and John Major, the Russian president came up with a winning solution. He appealed to the Serbs to withdraw their artillery from Sarajevo as demanded by NATO. To facilitate compliance he announced that four hundred Russian soldiers would join UN forces in the conflict zone. Slobodan Milosovic and Radovan Karadzic accepted the proposal and the crisis was diffused. A leading Russian newspaper described Yeltsin's success: "At first the West needed a very impressive dramatization, in which Russia was assigned the role of an extra . . . but it so happened that as the play proceeded Russia became the main character. In this production President Yeltsin collected quite a few foreign-policy dividends, both in the West and within our country."[35] One of the foreign policy dividends was Western acceptance of greater Russian involvement in the diplomatic efforts to find a solution to the Bosnian conflict.

When diplomatic efforts resumed in 1994, the initiators were a group of five nations—known as the Contact Group—which included Great Britain, France, Germany, the United States and Russia. For the first time, Russia was an active and equal partner in the search for a negotiated settlement. By the spring of 1994, Moscow was more amenable to putting pressure on the Serbs because of growing disillusionment with Bosnian Serb leadership. A new plan was presented to the parties in July that divided the country into two entities. Fifty-one percent of Bosnia would go to a federation of Bosnian Croats and Muslims and 49 percent would be under Serb control. For the Serbs that meant a reduction from the 70 percent they controlled at the time. The Croats eagerly accepted the plan, the Muslims reluctantly, and the Serbs not at all.

Notwithstanding the failure of its peace plan, the Contact Group continued to exert political pressure on the Serbs. Russia pursued a delicate balance between its efforts to find a diplomatic compromise and protection of Serb interests. It successfully resisted U.S. proposals to lift the arms embargo against the Muslim-led Bosnian government and the use of NATO forces against the Serbs, but it failed to get economic sanctions against Serbia lifted.[36] As the war moved into 1995 a new issue—the war in Chechnya—temporarily displaced the war in Bosnia as a source of contention between Russia and the West.[37]

RELATIONS WITH THE FORMER SOVIET REPUBLICS

We turn now to Russia's relations with the former Soviet republics. As important as were relations with the West relations with the fourteen other newly independent states—commonly referred to as the "near abroad" (*blizhneye zarubezhnye*)—were even more important. Indeed, for most Russians this issue is not so much a question of foreign policy as it is a question of the identity and nature of the Russian state itself. Russia viewed the Commonwealth of Independent States (CIS) as a mechanism for bringing together the former Soviet republics into some kind of a confederation. But after a few years it became apparent that at best the CIS could be a mechanism for cooperation among sovereign states. Even at that, cooperation was often extremely limited.

The boundaries established by the Russian state in 1992 had no precedent in history. The Russian state originated in the ninth century when Norsemen united several Slavic tribes into an independent polity identified as "Kievan

Russia".[38] The history of Russia was one of frequent wars and confrontations with neighboring tribes, nations and states, culminating in the Russian empire, which when displaced by the Soviet state, extended from the Baltic to the Pacific and the Arctic Ocean to the Black Sea, Persia, Afghanistan and China. The U.S.S.R. became the successor state to the Russian empire. Russia (or the Russian Federation) was one of the union's component parts; but the boundaries of that republic coincided neither with an historical Russian state nor with the population of those who considered themselves ethnic Russians. Post-Soviet Russia contained a population of 15 percent who were not Russian, but it did not encompass some 25 million Russians who lived in other republics, the "near abroad." Thus, inevitably there was confusion over its identity. Was Russia an empire or a nation? What were its legitimate boundaries? Toward what state goals ought Russia to aspire? The answers given by different members of Russian society contributed to the ongoing debate over Russian foreign policy. Some nationalists, represented most forcefully by Vladimir Zhirinovsky, wanted restoration of the Russian empire even beyond the Soviet boundaries.[39] Communists sought to restore the Soviet Union. More traditional nationalists such as Aleksandr Solzhenitsyn believed the Russian state should be composed of its historic Slavic core (Russia, Ukraine, and Belarus). For some the CIS offered the potential to create a new political configuration by a voluntary merging of sovereignty. Many Russians, on the other hand, were prepared to acknowledge a new post-imperial, post-Soviet order composed of fifteen completely independent, sovereign states.

During Yeltsin's first two years, foreign policy makers were unable to forge a consensus on these fundamental questions. Foreign policy focused initially on relations with the West. Internally the country was preoccupied with political and economic reform. In the aftermath of the adoption of a new constitution in 1993 and the stability that ensued for most of 1994, attention turned toward the states of the "near abroad" and a consensus that Russia should establish its hegemony over the states that had formerly been a part of the Soviet Union.

Andranik Migranyan, then a member of Yeltsin's Presidential Council, publicly argued the case for Russian hegemony early in 1994. He wrote that "the entire geopolitical space of the former Soviet Union is a sphere of Russia's vital interest."[40] His argument expressly compared Russian dominance to the Monroe Doctrine. He made reference to Russia's "special role" in the Dnestr region, Abhazia and Ossetia, the issue of Crimea and the Black Sea Fleet in Ukraine, economic links with Belarus, Kazakhstan, whose Russian population virtually equaled that of the native Kazakhs, and the Baltics where serious differences existed over the treatment of large Russian minorities in Latvia and Estonia. Toward the four Central Asian states of Uzbekistan, Kyrgystan, Tajikistan, and Turkmenistan, Migranyan rejected any kind of integration with Russia because of the "impossibility of integrating two ethnic groups—the Russian Christian group and the Turkic Islamic group . . ." Unlike his counsel for the rest of the "near abroad," he warned against Russian involvement in the internal squabbles of the Central Asian states, even though he put them within the sphere of Russia's vital interests. As to the Transcaucasus (Georgia, Armenia, and Azerbaidjan) he considered them vital because their economies "are totally linked to Russia." Migranyan concluded his essay with a warning to the West:

> Russia has clearly stated its special interests in the entire space of the former U.S.S.R., and attempts by third countries to block processes of the integration of this space around Russia or of the stabilization of the situation in this space with Russia's help will be regarded by Russia as unfriendly actions against it and could lead to difficulties in the Russian Federation's relations with those countries. Attempts by any countries to become guarantors of the borders that existed between the U.S.S.R. republics and to obstruct the natural and peaceful process of the integration of those countries into a single economic and military-political union . . . could seriously complicate the process of establishing a new world order and could raise doubts in Russia as to whether the US and Russia's other partners in the West are seriously prepared to take Russia's geopolitical interests into account.[41]

Migranyan's essay did not herald a radical shift in Russian foreign policy. It reflected more the culmination of trends whose origins go back to the beginnings of independent Russia. Even so, Yeltsin and Kozyrev were cautious in using rhetoric that suggested conflict with the United States. But there was a shift to the right as Yeltsin's administration moved into its later years, and the impetus to that shift may well have been the elections in 1993 and 1995 that revealed a powerful, latent nationalistic undertow in the electorate.

There are several concerns that motivate Russian involvement in the internal affairs of the near-abroad states. One issue that touches a particularly nationalist nerve is the fate of the approximately 25 million ethnic Russians living outside of Russia. Resentment toward Russians has been particularly strong in Latvia and Estonia, because these states never accepted Soviet absorption in 1940 and Baltic nationalists identify the Russians with their oppressors. The problem in the Baltics is further complicated because Russian immigration coupled with mass deportations of Balts in the 1940s severely diluted the indigenous peoples, particularly in Latvia and Estonia. The percentage of Russians in the total population in 1994 was 29.4 percent (Estonia), 33.5 percent (Latvia) and 8.5 percent (Lithuania).[42] Thus, many Balts are reluctant to accord full citizenship rights to the Russians living among them. This issue has strained Russo-Baltic relations.

In the early years of his administration, Yeltsin used the presence of Russian troops in the Baltic countries as a means of pressuring the republics to confer full citizenship rights on Russians. Lithuania was the first to accommodate Russia by signing an agreement guaranteeing minority rights for Russians and Lithuanians in both countries.[43] For its part, Russia withdrew its remaining troops in Lithuania in July 1993.

Problems arose with Estonia and Latvia because, unlike most of the Soviet successor states, these two were unwilling to grant automatic citizenship to its permanent residents when they became independent of Soviet rule. Restrictions on citizenship were placed on those (primarily Russians) who immigrated after June 1940 and on those who did not speak the native language. Yeltsin pressured Estonia and Latvia to confer full civil rights on their Russian residents and for a while delayed the withdrawal of Russian troops from their territory. However, even without full satisfaction of Russian demands, Yeltsin completed the withdrawal of troops in the summer of 1994. Resentment of Soviet rule was and remains stronger in the Baltic states than most of the other near-abroad states. That is why the Baltics are not members of the CIS and why they remain the most resistant to Russian aspirations toward the Near Abroad. Furthermore, the West never accepted Soviet annexation of the Baltic republics and has viewed their claim for independence as different from the other former Soviet republics.[44]

Ukraine was not only the most important of the near abroad but the country with the largest Russian population. According to the 1939 census, Russians numbered 11.4 million or 22 percent of Ukraine's total population. We have discussed previously the serious differences between Russia and Ukraine with regard to the Crimea, the Black Sea Fleet and nuclear weapons. Given the strong nationalist sentiment (particularly in the Western parts of the country), one might expect the Russian diaspora there to create additional problems, but in fact it did not. To date there has been no evidence of Ukrainian discrimination against Russians. While Leonid Kravchuk was president, Russo-Ukrainian relations were strained. Kravchuk was not so much anti-Russian as he was committed to asserting Ukrainian sovereignty and independence.

The election of the pro-Russian Leonid Kuchma as president in 1994 brought an improvement in relations with Russia. Yeltsin's overall strategy in dealing with this important neighbor has been to combine a mixture of pressure with compromise. He has carefully avoided involvement in the Ukraine's internal affairs, for example, by not supporting the Crimean struggle for independence. And on the whole he has ignored or rejected the more extreme demands of strident Russian nationalists. But until the Crimean issue and the disposition of the Black Sea Fleet are settled, the potential for discord remains.

Moldova (except for the Transdnestr region) shares with the Baltic republics the distinction of not having been a part of the Soviet Union before

1940. It was a part of Romania and its population is approximately two-thirds Romanian. Notwithstanding the generally liberal stance taken by Moldova towards its minorities, the Russian population (concentrated in the Transdnestr region) has struggled for independence since 1990. Russian separatism was stimulated in part by Moldova's law making Moldovan (Romanian) the official state language.[45] The claims of the Dnestr Republic have received strong political support from prominent nationalists in Russia. The region contains a major part of the country's industry and Transdnestr Russian leaders supported the coup attempt in August 1991.

Russian intervention lay in the fact that the Russian Fourteenth Army was headquartered in Tiraspol, the capital of the Transdnestr region. The Fourteenth Army was a remnant of the Soviet army that remained in place after Moldova's independence. Commanded by a Russian nationalist general, Alexander Lebed, the Fourteenth Army gave political and moral support to Russia's claims for independence. Although Yeltsin has chosen not to endorse the extreme demands of nationalists in Russia and the Transdnestr the fact is that he moved slowly to remove the Fourteenth Army from the area. In 1995, General Lebed resigned his command under pressure and Yeltsin has promised that in time the Fourteenth Army will be removed to Russia. Yeltsin has moved cautiously on this issue so as not to give his domestic opponents an issue to use against him. As of 1995, the Fourteenth Army remained as the last corps of soldiers under Russian command in any of the Near Abroad states.

Central Asia contained approximately 9.5 million Russians according to the 1989 census. Many came as agricultural colonizers, others to oversee the building of the railways and industry. Today they are disproportionately concentrated in urban areas. Culturally they form a distinct community from the Turkic and Persian peoples who constitute the majority. Among the five Central Asian republics, on average only 3 percent of the Russians know the titular language of the country. Only in Kazakhstan do the Russians come close to equalling the native people, the Kazakhs. Indeed, the combined Slavic populations (Russian, Ukrainian, Belarussian) outnumber the Kazakhs. None of the Central Asian states has denied Russians the rights of citizenship and Russia has not felt it necessary to intervene on behalf of its nationals. However, unlike the other former Soviet republics, there has been a substantial migration of Russians from Central Asia to Russia.

Transcaucasia has been the scene of major Russian intrusion, but not in order to protect the rights of Russians. The percentage of Russians in the population is very small: 1.6 percent in Armenia, 5.6 percent in Azerbaijan, and 6.3 percent in Georgia. In Belarus the Russian minority has posed no problem whatsoever. This is because Belarus and Russia have maintained such close ties that the prospects of uniting the two states is high. In a referendum on May 14, 1995 the people of Belarus voted by an overwhelming

83.3 percent to give the Russian language equal status with Belarussian, and by the same margin, agreed to integrate with Russia. Immediately following the referendum, the two countries abolished the customs checkpoints along their common border. "The border between Russia and Belarus no longer exists," proclaimed Yeltsin.[46]

In sum, Russians in the Near Abroad have been a significant, if limited, factor in Russia's relations with the states of the Near Abroad. Their influence could become much more important if Russia's neighbors were to suppress the rights of Russians. Russia's new military doctrine, approved by Yeltsin in 1993, affirms Russia's responsibility to intervene in the event of the suppression of the rights, freedoms and legitimate interests of Russian-speaking citizens in foreign states.[47] As of the mid-1990s, Russian involvement in the internal affairs of the Near Abroad has been motivated more by strategic interests than the need to protect ethnic Russians.

Of particular concern to Moscow has been instability in the Near Abroad along Russia's periphery. Fighting within and between several of the newly independent states poses two kinds of threats to Russia's security: One is that conflict might invite the intervention of outside powers; another is the threat the fighting on the periphery might spread to Russia itself and bring with it separatism within the Russian Federation. Even before Yeltsin's shift toward a more nationalist policy after the December 1993 election, he was determined to use military force to curb instability in the former Soviet republics. On February 28, 1993, he told a forum of the Civic Union that:

> *Stopping all armed conflicts on the territory of the former U.S.S.R. is Russia's vital interest. The world community sees more and more clearly Russia's special responsibility in this difficult undertaking. I believe the time has come for distinguished international organizations, including the UN, to grant Russia special powers as a guarantor of peace and stability in the former regions of the U.S.S.R.[48]*

That statement triggered a negative response from some of the CIS states, prompting Yeltsin to qualify his position by denying that he advocated unilateral Russian action, but rather Russian leadership in cooperation with regional international organizations. The CIS and the OSCE were suggested as examples of relevant regional organizations. However, it became increasingly evident after 1992 that Russia's central interest in regional organizations was to legitimize its interventions. Thus, Russia's peacekeeping operations during 1994 and 1995 in South Ossetia, Moldova, and Abkhazia were not true CIS operations but arrangements worked out bilaterally for Russian forces to maintain order. In the bitter struggle between Armenia and Azerbaijan over Nagorno-Karabakh, Moscow insisted that Russian—not OSCE—forces dominate peacekeeping activities in the region.[49] Another source of Russian pressure was the presence of Russian troops on CIS territories. On April 5, 1994,

Yeltsin issued a decree originating with the Ministry of Defense concerning the establishment of military bases on CIS territories. Arrangements were to be negotiated with each CIS member.[50]

Under Yeltsin, Russia's pursuit of hegemony over the Near Abroad was carried out flexibly and with responsiveness to changing conditions. Russia was particularly cautious toward its Slavic neighbors to the west. After the election of pro-Russian presidents (Leonid Kuchma in Ukraine and Stanislaw Lukashenka in Belarus), the Russian president carefully avoided involvement in their internal affairs. Specifically, Russia made no effort to support Crimea's struggle for independence from Ukraine. The Central Asian states were generally willing to accept closer economic and political ties than Moscow was prepared to permit. Undoubtedly the weak economies of these countries was a factor in Russia's avoiding a stronger link. Tajikistan was the Central Asian country with the strongest Russian military involvement, and here a major concern was keeping fundamentalist Islam from taking hold in a state along Russia's periphery.

If Russia moved cautiously in the European part of the CIS, it moved forcefully to bring the Caucasian states of Armenia, Georgia, and Azerbaijan under its wing. Russian peacekeeping forces in the Caucasus gave it a secure military presence there. Two factors motivated Russian policy. One was oil. Russia wanted to control the oil-rich resources in Azerbaijan. A second factor was Islamic fundamentalism. Russian intelligence reports often described fundamentalism as a bigger threat than NATO.[51] Although oil was by no means the only consideration in Moscow's decision to suppress Chechen separatism, it was an important one. The major pipelines from Azerbaijan to Russia and from there to Europe run through Chechnya.

CHECHNYA AND THE CRISIS WITH THE WEST

We have already observed the harmful consequences of the Russian assault on Chechnya that began in the waning days of 1994. That war was not the cause of the tense relations that developed in 1995 between the West and Russia, but in conjunction with a growing assertiveness on a range of issues it created widespread disillusionment with the Yeltsin administration in Europe and the United States. Just a week before the invasion, Yeltsin had taken a hard line at the Budapest meeting of the Conference on Security and Cooperation in Europe strongly opposing NATO expansion into Eastern Europe. Western leaders did not question Moscow's right to assert its authority over one of its provinces. But they objected strongly to the widespread killing of civilians and the indiscriminate bombing of Grozny, Chechnya's capital. Certainly the incompetent behavior of the armed forces in Chechnya seriously undermined the reputation of Russian troops and their leadership.

What particularly worried Western governments was the fear that the decision to invade—made three years after Chechnya futilely declared itself to be independent—was made by military leaders not fully responsible to Yeltsin's authority or, equally bad, that Yeltsin had himself moved sharply toward a more nationalist hard-line policy. In a manner reminiscent of Gorbachev in 1990, Yeltsin broke his political ties with his former democratic allies in favor of associates on the political right. Yeltsin seemed to ally himself with a so-called war party consisting of Defense Minister Pavel Grachev, Interior Minister Viktor Yerin, Chief of Federal Counterintelligence Agency Sergei Stepashin, Nationalities Minister Nikolai Yegorov, Security Council Chairman Oleg Lobov and his bodyguard, Aleksandr Korzhakov, all of whom played a role in the decision to invade Chechnya.

Chechen resistance prolonged the war into 1996, well beyond the expectations of the Kremlin leadership. The continued fighting complicated a scheduled summit in Moscow to celebrate on May 9, 1995, the fiftieth anniversary of the end of the European part of World War II. Yeltsin badly wanted Clinton to be present to acknowledge the Russian contribution to victory and symbolically to demonstrate the reality of the Russian-American partnership. President Clinton was concerned that his presence not appear to endorse Russia's continuing fighting in Chechnya, though he wanted a summit almost as much as the Russian president. During 1995, both governments were at loggerheads over several issues concerning military and nuclear policies. The most important involved a United States effort to stop a Russian-Iranian deal that had been under negotiation for more than two years. Russia had contracted to construct a light-water nuclear reactor at the Bushehr nuclear-power complex in southeastern Iran. Washington believed that Iran wanted the reactor for the purpose of acquiring nuclear weapons. Washington also wanted Russian acquiescence to the idea of NATO expansion and a commitment to move on ratification of the START II Treaty. The spring summit made marginal progress. Yeltsin did reaffirm support for START II but could not guarantee what his parliament would do. Yeltsin stood firm on the issue of the reactor sale to Iran, although he promised that the sale would not include a gas centrifuge that could be used to fabricate nuclear weapons.[52] He also remained adamant in opposition to NATO expansion.

These differences with the West were not incompatible with a cooperative relationship. Indeed, on most of these issues a case could be made that Russia was pursuing a legitimate national interest. Yeltsin's administration began with a liberal foreign policy committed to partnership with the Western world, and notwithstanding his nationalistic shift to the right, there was no reason why his original objectives could not be sustained. The problem was that domestic politics were so volatile that one could not be certain which forces would dominate policy making: democratic—military —nationalistic—bureaucratic—populist—communist—or what! As Yeltsin completed the fifth and last year of his administration, no clear picture emerged as to which forces would dominate parliament or who his successor would be. Indeed, in a more fundamental sense, the future of the Russian political system remained so problematic that one could not foresee what the general features of that system would be in a decade, let alone a generation. Thus, like domestic politics, foreign policy in the 1990s could move in one of many different directions.

ENDNOTES

1. Kenneth N. Waltz, *Man the State and War* (New York: Columbia University Press, 1965), p. 238. This concise statement of international political theory is commonly known as "realism." See Hans J. Morgenthau, *Politics Among Nations*, brief edition, revised by Kenneth W. Thompson (New York: McGraw-Hill, 1993). Also Kenneth N. Waltz, *Theory of International Politics* (Reading, Mass.: Addison Wesley Publishing Co., 1979). Many international relations scholars believe that realists place too much emphasis on the struggle for power and the use of force by states. See, e.g., Robert O. Keohane and Joseph S. Nye, *Power and Interdependence* rev. ed. (New York: Harper Collins, 1989).

la. Mikhail Gorbachev, *Perestroika: New Thinking for Our Country and the World*, New York: Harper and Row, 1988, p. 134.

2. *The New York Times*, June 18, 1992.

3. *Izvestiya*, January 2, 1992, p. 3.

4. *Nezavisimaya Gazeta*, March 28, 1992. See also Alexander Rahr, "'Atlanticists' versus 'Eurasians' in Russian Foreign Policy," *RFE/RL Research Report*, Vol. l, No. 22, May 29, 1992, pp. 17—22. For a description of the philosophical roots of the Atlanticist Eurasian Debate see Vera Tolz, "Russia's Westerners Continue to Challenge National Patriots," Ibid., Vol. l, No. 49, December 11, 1992.

5. Andrei Kozyrev, "Russia, A Chance for Survival," *Foreign Affairs*, Vol. 71, No. 2, spring 1992, p. 15.

6. *Current Digest of the Post-Soviet Press (CDPSP)*, Vol. XLIV, No. 13, April 29, 1992, p. 2.

7. Karen Dawisha and Bruce Parrott, *Russia and the New States of Eurasia: The Politics of Upheaval*. Cambridge: Cambridge University Press, 1994, p. 31. See also Mark Bassin, "Russia Between Europe and Asia, "*Slavic Review*, Vol. 50, No. 1, spring 1991.

8. *CDPSP*, Vol. XLIX, No. 32, September 9, 1992, p. 5.

9. Elizabeth Teague and Vera Tolz, "The Civic Union: The Birth of a New Opposition in Russia?," *RFE/RL Research Report*, Vol. l, No. 30, July, 24 1992, p. 9.

10. Stephen Foye, "Post-Soviet Russia: Politics in the New Russian Army," Ibid. Vol. 1, No. 33, August 21, 1992, p. 7.

11. Dawisha and Parrott, p. 65.

12. See Michael McGwire, *Perestroika and Soviet National Security*. Washington: The Brookings Institution, 1991, pp. 264–272, 371-379.

13. *RFE/RL Research Report*, Vol. 1, No. 33, August 21, 1992, p. 51. See also *The New York Times*, June 8, 1992.

14. *The New York Times*, January 30, 1992.

15. Thomas L. Friedman, "Reducing the Russian Arms Threat," Ibid., June 17, 1992.

16. John W. R. Leppingwell, "The Trilateral Agreement on Nuclear Weapons," *RFE/RL Research Report*, Vol. 3, No. 4, January 28, 1944, p. 14.

17. *The New York Times*, November 17, 1994.

18. The text of the CFE Treaty is in The United Nations, *Disarmament Yearbook*, New York: Department for Disarmament Affairs, 1991, pp. 373–379.

19. *Nezavisimaya Gazeta*, February 19, 1992, p. 2.

20. *Rossiiskaya Gazeta*, July 6, 1993, p. 5.

21.*Nezavisimaya Gazeta*, November 26, 1993, pp. 1, 2.

22. See Michael Mihalka, "Squaring the Circle: NATO's Offer to the East," Allen Lynch, "After Empire: Russia and Its Western Neighbors,"Alfred E. Reisach, "Central Europe's Disappointments and Hopes," and Kjell Engelbrekt, "Southeast European States Seek Equal Treatment" in *RFE/RL Research Report*, Vol. 3, No. 12, 25, March 25, 1994.

23. Vladislav Chernov, "Moscow Should Think Carefully," *CDPSP*, Vol. XLVI, No. 8, March 23, 1994, p. 11.

24. Ibid., Vol. XLVI, No. 11, April 13, 1994, p. 8.

25. Ibid., Vol. XLVI, No. 8, March 23, 1994, p. 13.

26. Michael Mihalka, "European-Russian Security and NATO's Partnership for Peace," *RFE/RL Research Report*, Vol. 3, No. 33, August 26,1994, p. 44.

27. *CDPSP*, Vol. XLVI, No. 48, December 28, 1994, p. 18.

28. Ibid., Vol. XLVI, No. 49, January 4, 1995, pp. 8-10.

29. A good description of Yugoslavia's disintegration is provided by Warren Zimmerman, the last American ambassador to Yugoslavia, in "Origins of a Catastrophe," *Foreign Affairs*, Vol. 74, No. 2, March/April 1995.

30. The difficult choices confronting Gorbachev as a consequence of the Iraqi invasion of Kuwait in 1990 are described in Joseph L. Nogee and Robert H. Donaldson, *Soviet Foreign Policy Since World War II*, 4th ed. New York: Macmillan, 1992, pp. 392-396. See also Graham E. Fuller, "Moscow and the Gulf War," *Foreign Affairs*, Vol. 70, No. 3, summer 1991.

31. Suzanne Crow, "Russia's Response to the Yugoslav Crisis, *RFE/RL Research Report* Vol. 1, No. 30, July 24, 1992, p. 32. See also *CDPSP*, Vol. XLIV, No. 21, June 24, 1992, pp. 19-21 and Ibid., Vol. XLIV, No. 22, July 1, 1992, pp. 1-6.

32. Ibid., pp. 3,5.

33. Ibid., Vol. XLIV, No. 38, October 21, 1992, pp. 20-21. See also Ibid., Vol. XLIV, No. 35, September 30, 1992, pp. 16-17.

34. *Izvestiya*, February 12, 1994, p. 8.

35. *Nezavisimaya Gazeta*, February 19, 1994, p. 3.

36. Steven Greenhouse, "Year's Effort by 5-Nation Group Accomplishes Little in Bosnia," *The New York Times*, March 22, 1995, p. A4.

37. On the impact of the war in Chechnya on United States-Russian relations see United States Congress, "Crisis in Chechnya," *Hearings before the Commission on Security and Cooperation in Europe*, One Hundred Fourth Congress, 1st session, January 19 and 27, 1995. See statement of James F. Collins, pp. 93–105.

38. On the origins of the Russian state and its development through the nineteenth century see George Vernadsky, *A History of Russia*, 3rd ed. New Haven: Yale University Press, 1951. Chapter 1 describes the origins of the Russian state. See pp. 14-30.

39. An irreverent collection of Zhirinovsky views is contained in Graham Frazer and George Lancelle, *Absolute Zhirinovsky*. New York: Penguin Books, 1994.

40. "Migranyan: Near Abroad Is Vital to Russia—I," *CDPSP*, Vol. XLVI, No. 7, March 6, 1994, p. 4.

41. Ibid., Vol. XLVI, No. 7, March 16, 1994, p. 11.

42. These figures, which are estimates, are from Martin Klatt, "Russians in the Near Abroad," *RFE/RL Research Report*, Vol. 3, No. 32, August 19, 1994, p. 35.

43. Richard Krickus, "Lithuania: Nationalism in the Modern Era," in Ian Bremmer and Ray Taras, eds. *Nations and Politics in the Soviet Successor States.* Cambridge: Cambridge University Press, 1993, p. 178.

44. Nils Muiznieks, "Latvia: Origins, Evolution and Triumph," in Ibid., p. 201. See also Walter C. Clemens, Jr., *Baltic Independence and Russian Empire.* New York: St. Martin's Press, 1991.

45. Daria Fane, "Moldova: Breaking Loose from Moscow,"in Bremmer and Taras, eds, *Nations and Politics in the Soviet Successor States,* p. 138.

46. *The Houston Chronicle,* May 27, 1995, p. 32a.

47. Fiona Hill and Pamela Jewett, *Back in the U.S.S.R.: Russia's Intervention in the Internal Affairs of the Former Soviet Republics and the Implications for the United States.* Cambridge: Harvard University Press, 1994, p. 7.

48. Quoted in John Lough, "Defining Russia's Relations with Neighboring States, "*RFE/RL Research Report,* Vol. 2, No. 20, May 14, 1993, p. 54.

49. "Moscow Feuds with CSCE Over Karabakh," *CDPSP,* Vol. XLVI, No. 46, December 14, 1994, pp. 10-12.

50. The decree created a furor because it included Latvia which protested the idea of military bases on its territory. Russia denied that it sought bases in Latvia. See "Yeltsin Order on Bases Abroad Raises Furor," *CDPSP,* Vol. XLVI, No. 14, May 4, 1994, pp. 1-4.

51. Alexander Rahr, "New Focus on Old Priorities," *Transition,* February 15, 1995, p. 11.

52. See *CDPSP,* Vol. XLVI, No. l9, June 7, 1995, "US-Russia Summit Focusses On Iran Nuclear Deal," pp. 1-4. It is not certain that the contract negotiated by the Russians originally included a gas centrifuge.

CHAPTER 8

The Prospects for Democracy

We conclude with an assessment of the prospects for democracy in Russia. To begin, we might consider the condition of democratic politics under the Yeltsin presidency. Is Russia in the mid-1990s a democracy? The answer is yes and no. We would be inclined to use the Freedom House label of "half free," or as John Lowenhardt put it, a "minimal democracy." President Yeltsin acknowledged as much when he addressed the first Federal Assembly on February 24, 1994: "[W]e must admit," he said "that Russia is . . . not yet a full-fledged, democratic state based on the rule of law."[1] A democratic system requires a constitutional order that provides for freely elected government representatives, a periodic rotation of elected leaders, legal restraints on the power of officials and a party system that permits diverse interests to mobilize the electorate during elections. Yeltsin's regime meets some of these constitutional requirements. On the positive (that is, democratic) side is the fact that Yeltsin was elected president in Russia's first popular election of a chief executive in its history. His mandate was reaffirmed in the April 1993 referendum, and the elections in 1993 and 1995 for new parliaments were free and reasonably fair. Undermining the integrity of the electoral process, however, were frequent rumors and proposals by responsible leaders (even within the "democratic" camp) that elections be postponed or deferred. So insistent were these demands that in 1994 Yeltsin had to organize a special agreement that all demands for early or deferred elections cease. To date all elections have been held on schedule, and the presidential election scheduled for June 1996 could very well force the retirement of the incumbent.

The issue of political parties is more complex. Political parties do exist in Russia—they number in the dozens—but to date, no party system has developed. There has yet to be established a group of parties with a national constituency, a cohesive organization, and a consistent program that could be expected to take power and form a government. Yeltsin chose not to build a political party to support his reform effort. He came to power with the aid of the umbrella group Democratic Russia, but that organization disintegrated into several factions and no longer dominates Russian politics. The biggest winner of the 1993 elections, the Liberal Democratic Party, was afflicted with many defections during the life of the first Duma. Only the Communist Party possesses a strong organizational base, but it is still a minority party. Two of the most promising reform parties, Russia's Choice and Yobloko, have yet to establish themselves as coherent national institutions. Most Russian parties to date have been organized around personalities and have been subject to the changing policies and whims of their leaders. Because there are so many small political parties, several have had to form electoral blocs to secure representation in the Duma. The evidence of the 1995 legislative campaign is that even these electoral blocs are unstable. So the requirement of political parties for democracy is more nascent than reality.

When we turn to the question of restraints on political power the issue become even more problematical. The question is: Who makes public policy and how is it done? To be more precise: How significant is the authoritarianism of the president? The most disturbing fact of Yeltsin's rule is that a large segment of the laws and policies under which Russians live emanated from his office as decrees. This is a result of Yeltsin's overruling the first post-Soviet Russian legislature, the Supreme Soviet, and then the adoption of a new constitution that was designed explicitly in favor of presidential over parliamentary power. The Congress of People's Deputies established parliamentary supremacy in theory, but in fact was often ignored by Yeltsin. The 1993 constitution reverses the distribution of power in favor of the president and in this case the facts conform to theory.

The argument that Yeltsin has ruled in an authoritarian manner is supported by several drastic measures taken by him that were clearly undemocratic. The most dramatic of these was his (illegal) suspension of parliament in 1993 followed by the bombardment of the "White House" to remove forcefully its occupants. Some have also pointed to his invasion of Chechnya as an example of authoritarianism notwithstanding the vindication of that action by the Constitutional Court in the summer of 1995. But it is clear that Yeltsin engaged the country in a war without consulting the parliament and without the support of the public.

A definitive assessment of Yeltsin is difficult because he is a person of contradictions ("In emergency situations, I'm strong. In ordinary situations, I'm sometimes too passive.")[1a] and has often made his political decisions behind closed doors. Since taking power, however, he has regularly demonstrated a willingness to compromise with his opponents. He made numerous concessions to his critics in the Congress of People's Deputies and the Federal Assembly that replaced it. It is our judgment that Yeltsin's commitment to democracy is genuine.[2] In this regard he stands in contrast to Mikhail Gorbachev who introduced limited democratic changes in the government of the U.S.S.R. essentially to preserve an authoritarian system. But Yeltsin's concept of democracy reflects the unique experiences of the Soviet past of which he was a part. As he explains it in his autobiography:

> We must finally admit that Russia comprehends democracy poorly—not merely for global, historical reasons but for rather prosaic ones: the new generation simply cannot break its way into power. The Socialist mode of thinking has left its imprint on all of us. I am not speaking of myself; I'm an obvious example. But the entire mid-level bureaucratic class in Russia came out of the party and government offices.[3]

Below we will consider what the Russians mean by democracy and how important it is to them.

Clearly any assessment of the future prospects for democracy cannot rely heavily on a particular leadership or constitutional order because the leadership will certainly change and so might the constitutional order. Political and other social scientists look at more fundamental elements of a social structure and its political culture. It is argued by some that democracy requires a strong middle class. India could be cited as an exception because it is a democracy with a large part of its population living in rural poverty. (But then many also feel that India's democracy is very precarious.) Russia has developed a large, educated, urban middle class that will probably increase with the transition to a market economy. But as Daniel Yergin and Thane Gustafson point out, this class owns little or no property and has only shallow traditions and structures. They consider Russia's middle class identity and status to be fragile.[4]

Before we turn to Russia's political culture we should mention the institution of a free press, which is a prime requirement for a democratic society. Throughout most of the Soviet period the press was completely state controlled except for the underground or *samizdat* "publications." All that changed under Gorbachev with his introduction of *glasnost*. We know that he used *glasnost* as a means to improve economic efficiency, not to bring about genuine democracy. The manipulative function of *glasnost* was clearly revealed by the way Soviet authorities initially concealed the nature of the tragedy of Chernobyl.[5] But Gorbachev learned from his mistakes in 1986 and moved steadily after the Chernobyl accident to eliminate censorship. Eventually the vigorous criticism of the print media played an important role in the collapse of the Soviet system. One of the most encouraging factors among those contributing to democracy in Russia is the relatively free press that flowered during the Yeltsin administration. Indeed, during the 1994-96 war in Chechnya it was the vigor of the Russian press that exposed the falseness of official reports about the war, mobilized opposition to the war and severely undermined Yeltsin's political authority.[6]

RUSSIA'S POLITICAL CULTURE

Of the many factors that are considered necessary for the development of democratic political institutions one that has been particularly stressed by political scientists in recent years is a political culture that is both congruent with and supportive of democratic political institutions. In a classic study Lucian W. Pye and Sidney Verba define political culture as "the system of empirical beliefs, expressive symbols and values which defines the situation in which political action takes place."[7] Put simply, political culture is the sum total of ideas and beliefs that a society has about government and politics. As Pye and Verba point out, a political culture is the product of both the collective history of a political system and the life histories of those individuals living in that system. There is a substantial literature defining and applying the concept to many different societies that we will not attempt even to summarize here. Suffice to note three important generalizations about the structure of political culture. One is that in no society is there a single, uniform political culture, and that in all political systems a distinction must be made between the political culture of those who hold power ("elite political culture") and that of the masses or public in general. Also, we note that, while public opinion on any subject may be volatile and frequently changing, political culture is more persistent and enduring, usually transmitted from generation to generation. Nevertheless, political culture is not static or unchanging.

The relationship between political culture and democracy is examined empirically in a ground-breaking study by Gabriel Almond and Sidney Verba in *The Civic Culture*.[8] Their definition of democracy is one widely shared by social scientists. It is a system in which there is control of government elites by nonelites and a government in which political elites must respond to the desires and demands of citizens. Furthermore, in a democracy the ordinary person must have the opportunity to take part in the political decision-making process. In addition, an electoral system must provide for the transfer of power from one group of rulers to another after a limited period of time. The formal institutions of a democracy include universal suffrage, political parties, an elected legislature, a rational bureaucracy, interest groups, and a media of communication. These institutions require a political culture consistent with the structure of government to function effectively and democratically.

Almond and Verba coined the term "civic culture" to describe the political culture of democracy. The concept of civic culture combines elements of the political culture with those of the larger culture of society, which together provide a "pattern of political attitudes and an underlying set of social attitudes that is supportive of a stable democratic process."[9] Briefly stated, the elements of the civic culture include the idea of participation, the belief that the ordinary person is politically relevant and has an obligation to participate in politics. Equally important is the nonpolitical attitude of trust in other people and social participation in general. This participation, however, is qualified by the fact that politics is only one of a citizen's concerns and usually not the most important one at that. The idea of political activism must be balanced by the necessity to accept government authority. As government must be responsive, so must it exercise power. "The maintenance of a proper balance between governmental power and governmental responsiveness represents one of the most important and difficult tasks of a democracy."[10] The informed, rational, active citizen must be tempered with some measure of passivity and noninvolvement. There is an affective or emotional commitment to politics in the civic culture, but again it is a qualified commitment. Too intense a commitment to a political issue can lead to a destabilizing level of fragmentation in the system. The differences that arise from conflicting interests in society must coexist with some form of consensus over the rules of the political game.

The scholarly community is generally agreed that a civic culture as just described did not exist in the Soviet Union, though among some strata of Soviet society (primarily the intelligentsia) there were aspirations toward a civic political culture.[11] Frederick C. Barghoorn, a foremost scholar of the Soviet political culture, argued in the 1960s that the development of a civic culture in the Soviet Union would require that "the political monopoly of a self-selecting political elite would have to be replaced by a conception of citizenship in which . . . political influence would be available to all citizens, who would be free to choose and even to create channels of access to government" and that "economic, professional, and other functional elites would have to achieve far more autonomy than they at present enjoy." He did not foresee either of these happening.[12]

Because of the closed character of much of Soviet society and the impossibility of outside observers to do survey research (or domestic researchers to obtain and analyze data objectively), it was very difficult to know with any reliability what the Soviet people thought about government and politics. Some analysts made a distinction between the "elite political culture"—the beliefs and attitudes of the political rulers as expressed in their speeches and writings—and "mass" political culture. While the data for the elite political culture were abundant (with its extensive commitment to Marxist-Leninist ideology) one could not be certain to what extent the leaders believed what they said.

During the later Soviet period, a substantial body of evidence was gathered by interviewing Soviet emigres. Two particularly important projects were the Harvard Refugee Interview Project of the 1950s and the Soviet Interview Project of the 1980s. Both projects produced important publications on the mass political culture of Soviet society. From the former came Alex Inkeles and Raymond Bauer's *The Soviet Citizen, Daily Life in a Totalitarian Society* and from the latter, James R. Millar, ed. *Politics, Work and Daily Life in the U.S.S.R.*[13] Drawing upon his own independent survey research and that of others Stephen White produced the first book length monograph on the subject of the Soviet political culture.[14]

Drawing primarily upon these sources we can summarize the Soviet political culture as follows: On the central issue of trust toward one's fellow citizens and feelings of efficacy toward influencing government policy, the findings were decidedly negative. There existed a widespread feeling of powerlessness in relation to political authorities.[15] Commonly citizens referred to political authorities as *vlasti* or "they," assuming a vast gulf between themselves and their rulers. Political trust in one's fellow citizens was severely undermined during the Stalin years when people were encouraged to inform on their neighbors. Emblematic of this distrust was the case of Pavlik Morozov in the 1930s. This fourteen-year-old boy informed on his parents who concealed grain and thereby he became a Soviet and Komsomol hero.[16] Conditions improved considerably in the post-Stalin period but the pervasiveness of the secret police produced widespread caution in expressing political views with strangers.

On the question of support for civil liberties the issue was complex. Consistently Soviet citizens supported civil liberties in the abstract, and if asked to rank personal freedom and economic security, chose the former. But when the issue was put in specific terms, respondents were willing to permit suppression of popular assembly or free speech if the government deemed these to be necessary.[17] In other words, Soviet citizens were prepared to let the government determine the boundaries within which freedom could legitimately be exercised.[18] Andrei Almarik, the dissident historian, was skeptical about the importance of personal freedom:

Whether because of its historical traditions or for some other reason, the idea of self-government, of equality before the law and of personal freedom— and the responsibility that goes with these—are almost completely incomprehensible to the Russian people. Even in the idea of pragmatic freedom, a Russian tends to see not so much the possibility of securing a good life for himself as the danger that some clever fellow will make good at his expense.

To the majority of the people the very word "freedom" is synonymous with "disorder" or the opportunity to indulge with impunity in some kind of antisocial or dangerous activity. As for respecting the rights of an individual as such, the idea simply arouses bewilderment.[19]

Fear and mistrust of government did not mean a lack of support for the Soviet regime. Indeed, the evidence supports the conclusion that public support for the government's policies was widespread. Particularly popular were the welfare features of the Soviet system: free education, medicine, and the guarantee of employment. The Harvard investigators concluded that the desire to live in a welfare state was "rooted in deep values of the Soviet citizen."[20] With some qualification, the public was in the majority satisfied with the material aspects of their lives.[21]

As to the general structure of the economy, there was widespread support for the Soviet economic system. Most respondents believed in public ownership of the economy, at least of heavy industry and communications. Nor was there opposition to state planning of the economy. The one feature of the economic system most strongly opposed by the populace was collectivization of agriculture. There was also a preference that handicrafts and services be in private hands.[22] Brian Silver concluded in his analysis of Soviet political beliefs:

This study provides empirical evidence for an interpretation of government-society relations in the Soviet Union based on an exchange from the government to the society, a supply of material goods to satisfy people's wants; from the society to the government, a store of political capital in the form of support for the established political order. These are not the only items in the exchange, but they are important ones.[23]

Among the other items in the exchange were national pride in the position of the Soviet Union in world affairs. Frederick Barghoorn and Thomas Remington argued that as of the early Gorbachev period, "Contemporary Soviet political culture derives much—perhaps most—of its emotional force from a broad spectrum of patriotic and nationalistic sentiments. . ."[24] The foreign policy accomplishments of the U.S.S.R., particularly victory in World War II, acquisition of nuclear weapons and space accomplishments and its status as a global superpower gave to the regime a legitimacy and popularity that compensated for much of the country's domestic inadequacies.

Two important questions have been raised about the Soviet political culture: 1) To what extent was it influenced by Marxist-Leninist ideology, and 2) how much of the Soviet political culture derived from traditional Russian political culture? Marxism-Leninism was the official creed of the Soviet regime and was a core part of the Soviet system of education, propaganda, and political socialization. From Lenin through Gorbachev every Soviet leader used the ideas and symbols of Marxism-Leninism in his speeches and slogans to justify and explain the government and Party policies. Much of this ideological invocation was made in a formal and ritualistic manner. While we cannot be certain how the leadership really viewed Marxist-Leninist ideas, we know that the ideology served as an important instrument of control over society and as a means to rationalize policy and legitimize its authority.[25] After all, without the ideology the Communist Party had no legitimate authority to control the Soviet system.

Implicit in Marxism-Leninism is a complex of attitudes which reinforced the authoritarian elements of the Soviet political culture. These attitudes addressed such questions as: What is the nature of politics? Are political relations essentially harmonious or conflicting? How should one view one's opponent? What are the best tactics for achieving victory? The answers to these questions were developed in what Nathan Leites and Alexander George called the "operational code" of communism. Briefly, this code emphasized the confrontational nature of politics as opposed to cooperation. Indeed, the writings of the Bolsheviks were replete with the language of war in describing politics. Words like "battle," "struggle," "front," "advance" and "retreat" were common in Party programs and slogans. In a world of differing social systems, war and conflict were viewed as the normal state of affairs; peace and cooperation were the exception.[26]

As to the mass public only a minority took Marxism-Leninism seriously. The public understood that there was a disconnect between the ostensibly democratic, egalitarian, and libertarian objectives proclaimed by Marx, and Engels and that disconnect only contributed to the apathy and cynicism that characterized Soviet society particularly in the years immediately before the Soviet collapse.[27]

The second question—What part of Russia's political culture has its roots in traditional Russian life?—is a more significant one. For if Marxism-Leninism can be abandoned by today's generation, the effects of the past cannot be so easily discarded. Many scholars believe that Russia's history and culture had a profound influence on the Soviet regime. For example, the argument is made that centuries of Russian autocracy have conditioned the Russian people to accept authoritarianism as a natural and inevitable way of government. The authoritarianism of Soviet Russia is seen as an extension of czarist autocracy. Stalin was a classic czar (perhaps a combination of Ivan the

Terrible and Peter the Great). The orthodoxy of the Russian Orthodox Church was reflected in the orthodoxy of Communist ideology (*sobornost* the equivalent of *partinost*). Even the institutions of Communism had their pre-Soviet counterparts: the *kolkhoz* in the *mir*; the KGB in the *okhrana* or even Ivan IV's *oprichnina*.[28]

Another argument has been made by anthropologists, philosophers and historians describing a Russian national character that predisposed Russians toward authoritarian rule. Many writers found in Russians a tendency toward temperamental extremes, making them incapable of moderation which is so vital in a democracy. To explain this so-called national character, a variety of causes— some rather strange—were introduced. They included the traditional Russian child-rearing practice of swaddling, the patriarchical structure of the Russian family, the conflicting influences of the Oriental and Western worlds, to mention a few. [29.] It needs to be stressed that this literature was often impressionistic and unsystematic. Almost all of these theories of national character have serious methodological problems and many contradict each other. Nevertheless, the common elements between the Russian and Soviet realities were too substantial not to be related in some way. Indeed, it is a truism that every society is to some degree a product of its history.

We turn now to the late Soviet and post-Soviet period when *glasnost* began to take hold, making it possible to investigate more rigorously what the Soviet public genuinely believed. In the waning months of the Soviet Union it became possible for the first time since the development of modern public-survey research to study public opinion in Russia in a systematic way. The opening began with Gorbachev's *glasnost* and has expanded under the even freer post-Soviet regime. Since the late 1990s there has developed a virtual cottage industry in polling in Russia.[29a] The results of this research are not yet conclusive and in some instances the findings are contradictory, but the research sheds important light on the contemporary Russian political culture.

Some of the most optimistic findings reported so far were based upon surveys done in the winter and spring of 1990 in the waning days of the Soviet Union. A research team of American and Russian scholars came to the conclusion that the Soviet political culture was evolving in a democratic direction. Looking for citizen attitudes toward democratic values, James Gibson, Raymond Duch, and Kent Tedin found that Russians did value political liberty, were committed (at least in the abstract) to democratic values, and were willing to assert their rights for themselves. The research findings concluded that "further efforts to democratize the Soviet Union will not meet resistance from Soviet political culture."[30] From the same data, Kent Tedin found among the citizens of greater Moscow and the European part of the

U.S.S.R. a solid commitment to competitive elections. Furthermore, this commitment was not based upon any expectation of personal gain as a result of free elections, but was of a diffuse nature, that is, the principle was supported for its own sake.[31] Focusing on perception, James Gibson concluded that "the Soviet people seem to be remarkably free."[32] This contention was based upon the degree to which respondents perceived themselves to be free, that is, it was a judgment about subjective sense of freedom. His study concluded:"This analysis has demonstrated that democratization permeated the mass political culture of the former Soviet Union, and that this democratization generated tangible benefits in terms of perceived political freedom."[33]

These same data, however, produced findings that were less sanguine for the prospects for democracy. Most political scientists believe that tolerance is absolutely vital to a functioning democracy and an essential element of a democratic political culture. Yet the 1990 surveys found that "By virtually any standard, there is simply not much political tolerance in the U.S.S.R." The authors concluded: "Soviet citizens seem to be more likely to claim rights and liberties for themselves than they are to extend the same rights and liberties to their political opponents. From this point of view, the democratization of Soviet political culture is far from complete." They acknowledged that their findings "do not bode well for the future of Soviet democratization."[34] Taken as a whole the analysis of the 1990 surveys supports the view that the Gorbachev period did witness a shift in Soviet thinking but not enough to be certain of the prospects for democracy in Russia.[35]

Donna Bahry, however, has shown that analysts of changing social values in Russia differ on which values have shifted, by how much, and why. Modernization, which we usually associate with a shift toward more liberal and democratic values, could in her view have led to support for the core values of the Soviet system or undermined support depending on the data one selected She notes the findings of Arthur M. Miller to the effect that in 1990 more people in Russia and Ukraine supported an authoritarian regime than a democratic one.[36] A popular text on public opinion cautions that "support for democratic values is mostly determined by how the question is framed."[37] Then there is the phenomenon dubbed "chameleonism" by James R. Millar (who initiated and directed the Soviet Interview Project) or "the ability of Soviet citizens . . . to change sides on issues 180 degrees without blinking or feeling intellectually guilty."[38]

So it should not be surprising that there are varied conclusions about not only Soviet, but post-Soviet political values. A study by the Cambridge Energy Research Associates was conducted on change in the space of the former Soviet Union and published as *Russia 2010*. Its authors assessed the situation in Yeltsin's Russia as follows:

> *When all is said and done, the prospects for democracy will depend on the quality of the human material, the civic values of the community, the attitudes of individuals. In the long run, there can be no democracy without democrats, without a democratic culture.*
>
> *Many of the traits Russians show in political dealings with one another are not especially democratic. Leaders usually feel superior to ordinary citizens, and citizens typically relate to leaders as clients to patrons. . . Feelings of mutual trust and tolerance are low, not only among different nationalities but even among neighbors and colleagues.*[39]

Their assessment of public opinion was equally bleak:

> *Public opinion is still a very weak force in Russian politics. Since a brief peak in 1989 and 1990, interest and participation in politics have dropped off sharply. Most citizens are simply apathetic; fewer than 10 percent express any interest in politics and almost none belong to parties or are otherwise politically active.*[40]

This could change as a result of the 1995 and 1996 elections because of the intense controversy generated by Boris Yeltsin's policies.

An important issue in the debate over what kind of political system the Russians will seek is regime performance with the economy, that is, what effect economic reform will have on the lives of people. Some have described the relationship between elites and nonelites as a contract or "deal" in which the standard of living is an important part. [41] This contention is supported by evidence that links economic well-being in the minds of Russians with democracy. That link appears to be rather constant as shown by the table be on page 192.[42]

And yet, James R. Millar concluded that the same public that regards economic well-being as essential for democracy to work lacks "any stable convictions about how the economy ought to be ordered."[43] In the first large-scale, personal-interview survey ever conducted in the Soviet Union, Ada Finifter and Ellen Mickiewicz found an equal division between those who looked to the state and those who looked to the individual for individual well-being. "Since this is a central aspect of what change in the economic systems of the former republics is all about," they concluded, "the lack of consensus on this item suggests the potential for serious divisions in the former Soviet states."[44] Their survey found support for democratic change (and change in the scope of state control) to be tentative. They argued that there would have to be "timely outputs—both economic and political—that alleviate the serious material problems . . . for institutional development to move foward."[45] Raymond Duch, on the other hand, analyzing a 1990 survey was more sanguine about the prospects for both democracy and free-market reforms. In the late Soviet period he detected a "nascent free-market culture"

What Is the Single Most Important Characteristic of a Democracy? (in %)

	June 1992 N=1,800	January 1993 N=1,804	September 1993 N=1,837
Economic prosperity in the country	29	32	29
A judicial system that treats everyone equally	23	25	21
A government that provides for citizens' basic needs	15	14	21
At least two strong political parties competing in elections	6	8	2
A free-market economy	6	5	2
Freedom to criticize the government	3	1	1
Protection of the rights of minorities	2	1	1
Opportunity to chose the government through free elections	NA	NA	13
Don't know/no answer	17	14	9
Total	100	100	99

James R. Millar, "From Utopian Socialism to Utopian Capitalism," *Problems of Post-Communism,* May-June, 1995. Reprinted by permission.

(although very underdeveloped). This free-market culture and democratic values he found to be mutually reinforcing.[46] The Swedish economist, Anders Aslund, who contends that by 1995 Russia had become a market economy, believes that during the Yeltsin years, "An entire culture had been transformed." [46a]

Many scholars agree that there is a strong institutional link between democracy and a free market economy.[47] Certainly the developed democracies of the West operate with free markets (although not all free-market economies are democratic). But the novelty of the Russian (and Eastern European) experience is that democracy preceded free markets. It remains to be seen whether a nascent democracy can survive the harsh conditions—declining wages, unemployment, inflation—that are the short-term effects of the transition from a command to a market economy.

In the spring of 1995, the newspaper *Sevodnya (Today)* published the results of a survey conducted in the fall of 1994 by the All-Russian Center for the Study of Public Opinion which asked about 1,600 respondents: "Do you agree that the principles of Western democracy are incompatible with Russian traditions? 48 percent reponded either complete or more-or-less agreement to 27 percent who completely or more-or-less disagreed. [48]

It should not surprise us that there is ambivalence in Russia regarding democracy. Economic and social conditions deteriorated from 1992 through 1995. Furthermore, it is useful to keep in mind that the "revolution of l991" that destroyed the Soviet Union was not carried out in the name of democracy or liberty but on behalf of the national cause. Sometimes thought of as the Second Russian Revolution, it was no French Revolution made in the name of liberté, fraternité and egalité. Still it is undeniable that the drive for democracy and liberty were part of it. Certainly by implication a struggle to destroy the Soviet Union—the antithesis of democracy—carried with it democratic strivings. So we conclude with the observation that while nothing is certain, the prospects for democracy in Russia are greater today than they have ever been before. A people who have produced a Dostoevsky, a Tolstoy, and a Tchaikovsky certainly deserve a better polity than history has given them to date.

ENDNOTES

1. *Current Digest of the Post-Soviet Press (CDPSP)*, Vol. XLVI, March 23, 1994, p. 6. Close observer Anders Aslund claims that regardless of important flaws, Russia has become a democratic society. *How Russia Became a Market Economy*. Washington, D.C.: The Brookings Institution, p. 273.

la. Boris Yeltsin, *The Struggle for Russia*. Translated by Catherine A. Fitzpatrick. New York: Belka Publishing Company, 1994, p. 205.

2. We agree with the assessment of Daniel Yergin and Thane Gustafson that Yeltsin's "policies on the whole have been democratic." *Russia 2010 and What It Means for the World*. New York: Vintage Books, 1995, p. 78.

3. Yeltsin, pp. 290–291.

4. Yergin and Gustafson, p. 123.

5. See David R. Marples, *Chernobyl and Nuclear Power in the U.S.S.R.* New York: St. Martin's Press, 1986, chapter one. See also Marshall Goldman, *Gorbachev's Challenge, Economic Reform in the Age of High Technology*. New York: W.W. Norton, 1987, p. 233.

6. See Ellen Mickiewicz, *Split Signals: Television and Politics in the Soviet Union*. New York: Oxford University Press, 1988. For some examples of the press taking Yeltsin to task see *The Current Digest of the Post-Soviet Press (CDPSP)*, "Russians Bomb Grozny; Signs of Dissent in Army," Vol. XLVI, No. 51, January 18, 1995, pp. 1–9; "Russian Forces in Chechnya Find the Going Heavy," Vol. XLVI, No. 52, January 25, 1995, pp. 1–15; "Grozy: Ill-Trained, Ill-Led Russians Chopped Up," Vol. XLVII, No. 1, February 1, 1995, pp. 1–12; "War In Chechnya Bares Sad State of Russian Army," Vol. XLVII, No. 2, February 8, 1995, pp. 1–17.

7. Lucian W. Pye and Sidney Verba, eds. *Political Culture and Political Development*. Princeton: Princeton University Press, 1965, pp. 7–8.

8. Gabriel A. Almond and Sidney Verba, *The Civic Culture, Attitudes and Democracy in Five Nations*. Princeton: Princeton University Press, 1963. See particularly chapters 1 and 15.

9. Almond and Verba, p. vii.

10. Ibid., p. 476.

11. Frederick C. Barghoorn, "Soviet Russia: Orthodoxy and Adaptiveness," in Pye and Verba, p. 453.

12. Ibid., p. 508.

13. Alex Inkeles and Raymond Bauer, *The Soviet Citizen: Daily Life in a Totalitarian Country.* Cambridge: Harvard University Press, 1959. James R. Millar, ed. *Politics, Work and Daily Life in the U.S.S.R., A Survey of Former Soviet Citizens.* Cambridge: Cambridge University Press, 1987.

14. Stephen White, *Political Culture in Soviet Politics.* New York: St. Martins Press, 1979.

15. White, p. 110.

16. For his treachery Morozov was garroted by a group of peasants led by his uncle. Adam Ulam, *Stalin, The Man and His Era.* New York: The Viking Press, 1973, p. 345.

17. White, pp. 101–102. Also Donna Bahry, "Rethinking the Social Roots of Perestroika," *Slavic Review,* Vol. 52, No. 3, fall 1993, pp. 537–538.

18. White, p. 107. Also Raymond A. Bauer, Alex Inkeles, and Clyde Kluckholm, *How the Soviet System Works.* New York: Vintage Books, 1960, pp. 142–143.

19. Andrei Almarik, *Will the Soviet Union Survive Until 1984?* New York: Harper and Row, 1970, pp. 33–34.

20. Inkeles and Bauer, *The Soviet Citizen,* pp. 236–242. See also Brian Silver, "Political Beliefs of the Soviet Citizen: Sources of Support for Regime Norms," in Millar, pp. 105, 111–113.

21. Silver, p. 105.

22. White, pp. 98–100; Bauer, Inkeles and Kluckholm, pp. 133–143; Silver, pp. 108–114. Bahry, pp. 514-519.

23. White, p. 132.

24. Frederick C. Barghoorn and Thomas F. Remington, *Politics U.S.S.R.* Boston: Little Brown, 1986, p. 38.

25. Ibid., pp. 54–60.

26. The term "operational code" was developed by Nathan Leites in a classic work, *A Study of Bolshevism.* Subsequently he published a portion of the larger study as *The Operational Code of the Politburo.* See also Alexander L. George, "The 'Operational Code': A Neglected Approach to the Study of Political Leaders and Decision-Making," in *The Conduct of Soviet Foreign Policy,* Erik p. Hoffmann and Frederic J. Fleron, Jr., eds. Chicago: Aldine-Atherton, 1971, pp. 165–190.

27. This cynicism and apathy is described in many journalistic (and scholarly) accounts of life in the Soviet Union. See for example, Hedrick Smith, *The Russians.* New York: The New York Times Book Co., 1976, and David K. Shipler, *Russia, Broken Idols, Solemn Dreams.* New York: Penguin Books, 1983.

28. This argument is made by Edward Crankshaw in his *Cracks in the Kremlin Wall.* See White, chapter two, "The Impact of Autocracy" for the argument linking czarist and Soviet political culture.

29. These theories are discussed by John S. Reshetar, Jr. in *Problems of Analyzing and Predicting Soviet Behavior.* Garden City: Doubleday and Company, 1955, pp. 14-30.

29a. According to Anders Aslund, the widely preferred polls are carried out by the Russian Center for the study of Public Opinion. *How Russia Became a Market Economy.* Washington: The Brookings Institution, 1995, p. 24.

30. James L. Gibson, Raymond M. Duch, and Kent L. Tedin, "Values and the Transformation of the Soviet Union," *The Journal of Politics,* Vol. 54, No. 2, May 1992, pp. 329, 335, 341, 352. Robert J. Brym argues that these findings are overly optimistic. See Robert J. Brym, "Voters Quietly Reveal Greater Communist Leanings," *Transition,* Vol. I, No. 16, September 1995, p. 33.

31. Kent L. Tedin, "Popular Support for Competitive Elections in the Soviet Union." *Comparative Political Studies,*Vol. 27, No. 2, July 1994, pp. 241–265. See also Ada W. Finifter and Ellen Mickiewicz, "Redefining the Political System of the U.S.S.R.: Mass Support for Political Change," *American Political Science Review,* Vol. 86, No. 4, December 1992, p. 860.

32. James L.Gibson, "Perceived Political Freedom in the Soviet Union." *The Journal of Politics,* Vol. 55, No. 4, November 1993, p. 936.

33. Ibid., p. 964.

34. James L. Gibson and Raymond M. Duch, "Political Intolerance in the U.S.S.R., The Distribution and Etiology of Mass Opinion," *Comparative Political Studies,*Vol. 26, No. 3, October 1993, pp. 300, 309. Gibson and Duch define tolerance as "putting up with one's political enemies." p. 289.

35. Further analyses of the 1990 surveys relevant to Soviet politics in the latter Soviet period are Raymond M. Duch, "Tolerating Economic Reform: Popular Support for Transition to Free Market in the Former Soviet Union, "*American Political Science Review,* Vol. 87, No. 3, September 1993; Kent L. Tedin and Oi-Kuan Fiona Yap, "The Gender Factor in Soviet Mass Politics: Survey Evidence from Greater Moscow," *Political Research Quarterly,* Vol. 46, No. 1, March 1993; James L. Gibson, "Understanding of Anti-Semitism in Russia: An Analysis of the Politics of Anti-Jewish Attitudes," *Slavic Review,*Vol. 53, No. 3, fall 1994; James L. Gibson, "Survey Research in the Past and Future U.S.S.R.: Reflections on the Methodology of Mass Opinion Surveys," *Research in Micropolitics.* Vol. 4, 1994; James L. Gibson and Raymond M. Duch, "Postmaterialism and the Emerging Soviet Democracy." *Political Research Quarterly,* Vol. 47, No. 1, March 1994.

36. Donna Bahry, "Society Transformed? Rethinking the Social Roots of Perestroika," *Slavic Review,* Vol. 52, No. 3, fall 1993, pp. 512–513, 518–519.

37. Robert Erikson and Kent Tedin, *American Public Opinion,* 5th ed., Boston: Allyn and Bacon, p. 155

38. James R. Millar, "From Utopian Socialism to Utopian Capitalism, the Failure of Revolution and Reform in Post-Soviet Russia," *Problems of Post-Communism,* May-June 1995, p. 12. For a discussion of the problems of survey research in the U.S.S.R. see James L. Gibson, "Survey Research in the Post and Future U.S.S.R.: Reflections on the Methodology of Mass Opinion Surveys," *Research on Micropolitics,* Vol. 4, 1994, pp. 87–114.

39. Daniel Yergin and Thane Gustafson, *Russia 2010 and What It Means for the World,* New York: Vintage Books, 1995, p. 108.

40. Ibid., p. 93.

41. See Bahry, pp. 516-517.

42. Millar, p. 13. John Lowenhardt makes the same observation in *The Reincarnation of Russia, Struggling with the Legacy of Communism, 1990–1994.* Durham: Duke University Press, 1995, p. 146.

43. Ibid.

44. Ada W. Finifter and Ellen Mickiewicz, "Redefining the Political System of the U.S.S.R.: Mass Support for Political Change," *American Political Science Review*, Vol. 86, No. 4, December 1992, p. 860.

45. Ibid., p. 870.

46. Raymond M. Duch, "Tolerating Economic Reform: Popular Support for Transition to a Free Market in the Former Soviet Union," *American Political Science Review*, Vol. 87, No. 3, September 1993, p. 590.

46a. Anders Aslund, p. 312.

47. See Robert Dahl, *Democracy and Its Critics.* New Haven: Yale University Press, 1989.

48. "Pollster Levada Finds Many Obstacles to Real Democracy," *CDPSP*, Vol. XLVII, No. 14, May 3, 1995, pp. 4–5.

INDEX